SHADOWS OF THE SUPERNATURAL

Contributors

John Allan, Senior Youth Worker, Belmont Chapel, Exeter: *'Cross my Heart and Hope to Die'; Written in the Stars; The Occult*

The Rev. Colin Chapman, Principal, Crowther Hall, Selly Oak, Birmingham, England and formerly Lecturer in Mission and Religion, Trinity College, Bristol: *Religion Past and Present; Let's Have a Festival! Myths and Legends; What is Popular Religion? The Substance*

The Rev. Dr John Fenwick, Archbishop of Canterbury's Assistant Secretary for Ecumenical Affairs: *Rites of Passage; Saints; Churches*

Iain McKillop, Head of Art, Sir William Perkins's School, Chertsey: *Visions of Glory*

Dr Berj Topalian, director of music at Christ Church, Clifton, Bristol: *Heavenly Music*

Additional research on the history of religion was carried out by the Rev. Richard Cook

SHADOWS
of the
SUPERNATURAL

COLIN CHAPMAN

A LION BOOK

Oxford · Batavia · Sydney

Text copyright © 1990 Colin Chapman
This edition copyright © 1990 Lion Publishing

Published by
Lion Publishing plc
Sandy Lane West, Oxford, England
ISBN 0 7459 1274 5
Lion Publishing Corporation
1705 Hubbard Avenue, Batavia, Illinois 60510, USA
ISBN 0 7459 1274 5
Albatross Books Pty Ltd
PO Box 320, Sutherland, NSW 2232, Australia
ISBN 0 7324 0270 0

First edition 1990
All rights reserved

Printed and bound in Yugoslavia

Contents

Introduction

What are people to make of festivals such as Hallowe'en and Christmas, or rituals like weddings and funerals? What are they to think of St Christopher and St George, and all the myths and legends which are part of our culture? Why is so much art and music mixed up with religion? And what of all the interest in superstition, in astrology and the occult?

If these are some of the things in the 'popular religion' or 'folk religion' of the Western world that are worth exploring, the first need is for basic information. Where do all these things come from? What do they mean? And how do they work? So for example:

What's the origin of May Day and Easter? What is a baptism or 'Christening' all about? What's the meaning of gargoyles, lych gates and yew trees? Why the statues of the Virgin Mary? Who was St Nicholas and how is he connected with Father Christmas? What's the meaning of a Greek icon or a Dali painting of the crucifixion? What's special about Handel's *Messiah* or negro spirituals? Why do people 'touch wood' and think it bad luck to walk under a ladder? Why do they read horoscopes and follow their stars? And why the current fascination with the occult?

But it isn't enough simply to describe these different things and explain their origin and their function. At some stage further questions need to be asked. What's at the heart of this popular religion? How does it relate to Christianity, which has been the 'official' religion in the Western world for so many centuries? How does it relate to the other great world religions?

And what are the implications of seeing all these manifestations of popular religion as 'shadows of the supernatural'? Although a shadow has no substance in itself, it gives some idea of the object that's casting the shadow. Is it the same when dealing with religion? Can the 'shadows' reveal anything about the 'supernatural'...?

This enquiry begins by looking into history and exploring the development of religion in the Western world (Part One).

Where does it all come from? Is it possible to work out the different stages through which our civilization, religion and culture have developed in the Western world? How much derives from Greek and Roman religion? Where do the Druids and the Vikings come in?

The main body of the book is Part Two, It deals with the faces of popular religion and provides basic information on these ten subjects:

Festivals
Rites of passage
Saints
Churches
Art
Music
Myths and legends
Superstitions
Astrology
The occult

In each case the aim is to try to understand the *role and function* that they play in the life of an individual or a community, and to find out the *origin* of the different customs and ideas. Each chapter ends with some basic conclusions and questions which are taken up in the final chapters.

Part Three explores further questions about popular religion:

▶ *What is popular religion?* How should it be described and defined? How does it differ from the more traditional forms of religion? Do all people have religious instincts, and is religion as much a part of human make-up as sex?

▶ *What's the substance behind the shadows?* At the end of the day is there anything more than a catalogue of beliefs, customs and traditions? Is religion a grand free-for-all in which people 'do their own thing'? If it's entirely a matter of personal choice and preference, and if everything depends on each individual's ideas of the supernatural, then it's obvious that everybody has to decide what they want to believe and how (if at all) they want to relate to the supernatural world. But what if it *doesn't* all depend on each individual's ideas? What if it *is* possible to know something about the supernatural world?

Part One

Introducing Popular Religion

Religion Past and Present

1 Past and Present

Humanity does not pass through phases as a train passes through stations: being alive, it has the privilege of always moving yet never leaving anything behind. Whatever we have been, in some sort we still are... We shall understand our present, and perhaps even our future, the better if we can succeed by an effort of the historical imagination, in reconstructing that long-lost state of mind...

C.S. Lewis

If, as C.S. Lewis says, 'whatever we have been, in some sort we still are', looking back into our past ought to help us to understand our present.

Is it possible, therefore, to get a kind of 'bird's eye view' of our history, to see at a glance the various stages by which religion has developed in the Western world? While it is not possible to take note of the particular history and culture of every individual country, what are the main developments which have affected both the popular and official religion of the whole Western world? How, for example, does European history move from the cave paintings in France, from Stonehenge and the Druids to the creation of Christian Europe? And how does the old Christendom develop into today's society in which there are so many different religions?

This chapter looks at the religions of the past that have had the most impact on Western Christianity—Egyptian, Greek, Roman, Celtic and Scandinavian—and some of the philosophies which have influenced religion in the past and continue to do so in the present.

In looking at these religions and philosophies, some key questions must be asked:

▶ *What kind of society did people live in, and how did the social context affect the religion of the people?*

▶ *What were their ideas of the gods, and how did they worship them?*

▶ *How did they think about the world, and what did it feel like to see the world in this way?*

▶ *How did they decide between right and wrong?*

▶ *Are there elements of the religions and philosophies of the past which have become part of the religion and culture of the Western world?*

▶ *Is it possible to describe the process by which Europe was converted to Christianity?*

▶ *Why was Christianity accepted?*

▶ *How have Christians thought about the beliefs and practices of other religions?*

▶ *Why does popular religion seem to have survived the challenges of the modern world?*

▶ *What happens when the majority of people in a community reject Christian beliefs?*

Egyptian Religion

The earliest written evidence of any kind of religion comes from Egypt. Although the Egyptians worshipped many gods, they tended to think there was one High God, who was generally known as Re, the sun god. Most of the gods and goddesses were originally represented in the form of different animals, and associated with one particular city-state. When cities joined together or one city overcame another, the gods of the two cities became merged with each other, and the priests elaborated stories to show the power of their gods.

One particular king, Akhenaten, tried to get people to worship Aten as the one and only god, the creator of everything, and to deny the existence of other gods. But this attempt to impose monotheism on the people was a failure, and his successor, the famous Tutankhamon, restored the worship of Re as the High God.

Egyptian religion was interested in the mystery, how does the world beyond influence our world? And so tombs were of great importance, where people were prepared for their journey between two worlds. Many Egyptian statues and paintings have been found in tombs.

Is there a spiritual wisdom greater than human knowledge? At the Temple of Apollo at Delphi, Greece, the ancient Greeks would 'consult the oracle', as a priestess with special gifts of wisdom gave them words from the god.

The pharaoh, the king of Egypt, was seen as the agent or representative of the sun god Re and as the vital point of contact between heaven and earth. The stability of society and the fertility of the soil therefore depended on him. To ensure that he would continue to be a means of divine blessing after his death, his body was mummified and placed in a pyramid. Mummification was at first an expensive business, and was only for kings and their immediate family; but gradually it was also made available to others. The Book of the Dead (about 1000BC) explained the judgment that takes place after death and described the correct rituals for honouring the dead. Carrying them out carefully gave individuals an opportunity of gaining immortality themselves.

Alongside these official religious ceremonies which were conducted by the priests in the temples, there were many other popular cults among the ordinary people, many of which involved different forms of magic. '-Mystery religions', which were like secret societies of people who re-enacted stories about gods such as Isis and Osiris, spread to many countries outside Egypt.

According to tradition, Christianity was brought to Egypt by Mark and before long was widely accepted throughout the country. There were times when Christians were persecuted by the Roman authorities, but in AD391 all the temples in Egypt were closed on the orders of the emperor Theodosius.

Greek Religion

The religion of the ancient Greeks developed in the many city states, especially from around the eighth century BC onwards. It had no prophets or messiah, no specialized clergy, no sacred books or fixed creed. Rather it was a loose system of beliefs and practice which allowed considerable freedom of thought and feeling. Mythology was fundamental, because it meant that stories learned in childhood shaped the imagination, while public recitals of poetry helped adults to see how the whole of life depended on the supernatural world of the immortal gods. Ritual sacrifices were intended to bring worshippers into direct contact with divine beings. The visual arts, including beautiful sculpture, provided another mode of religious experience and expression.

The Greeks believed in many different gods and goddesses who were all related to each other in the 'pantheon', which developed in time and varied from one city or shrine to another. Zeus was the sky god, who ruled the world of gods and people and enabled justice to prevail; he and his wife Hera stood for marriage. He presided over a whole company of deities—such as Poseidon the god of the sea, and Hades who ruled the underworld, the world of the dead. Ares was the god of war, Dionysus the god of wine, and Aphrodite the goddess of love. These were all superhuman beings who were immortal and powerful, but not omnipotent. They had very human passions, could often misbehave or be immoral, and could interfere in the lives of humans.

Every city state or *polis* had its own patron god or gods, whom the people worshipped at the official temples. Alongside these gods the Greeks recognized 'the divine race of heroes', whom they called 'demi-gods', and looked back to a Golden Age in the past when people like Achilles and Hercules were taller, stronger, more beautiful, and closer to the gods. Local heroes, such as the anonymous hero of Marathon, were also very much a part of life, and had a power over the imagination which made them more than mere mortals.

Sacred sites included temples, groves, springs, mountain peaks, enclosures, crossroads, trees, stones and obelisks. Blood sacrifices were offered on an outside stone altar in daylight: a domestic animal, crowned and decked with ribbons, would be led forward to have its throat cut. The entrails (especially the liver) were then examined for evidence of divine favour, and the fatty bones, with herbs and spices added, were burned to produce a sweet-smelling smoke, while the meat was boiled and either eaten immediately or taken home. Offering sacrifices in this way established contact with the gods by pleasing them.

All this official state religion, however, didn't seem to meet the spiritual needs of ordinary people, and life beyond death was thought of as a dismal existence. Many people therefore turned to the mystery religions. After being initiated into one of these secret groups, they would take part in certain rituals associated with one of the gods which gave them an assurance of salvation and happiness in this life and of life after death.

Greek Philosophy

Philosophy began in Ionia (now the west coast of Turkey) when thinkers started asking questions such as these:

How does the universe work? If, as the astronomer Thales was suggesting, the sun and moon were not gods, but circles of fire, what role did the gods have in controlling the universe? And what were the basic elements out of which the universe was made?

What of all the stories about the gods? Protagoras wrote that Homer and Hesiod, the famous poets, had 'attributed to the gods acts that are a disgrace and reproach among men—stealing, committing adultery, and deceiving one another'.

What is the origin of religion? They put forward theories like these to explain how religion had started:

▶ People took stories about the gods literally, instead of taking them as poetry.

▶ Religion had its origin in fear, such as fear of thunder and storm.

▶ Religion was invented by statesmen as a way of putting moral pressure on their people to make them conform.

▶ People have made God or gods in their own image. Xenophanes said, 'If horses and cows had hands to carve and paint, they would represent their gods as horses and cows.'

If the Greeks ever took their religion at all seriously, the questioning of these philosophers must have undermined many of their beliefs. The famous poets and playwrights of Athens wanted to preserve the spirit of reverence which was part of religion, and therefore didn't openly attack the gods. The Sophists, however, who were travelling teachers of philosophy, questioned everything to do with religion and morality.

One of the most famous philosophers of Athens was Socrates (469–399BC), whose questioning attitude was summed up in the famous saying, 'An unexamined life is not worth living.' Although he himself worshipped the gods, he upset the rulers in Athens and was condemned to death, on the charge of 'corrupting the youth of Athens and introducing new gods'.

It was one of his students, Plato (427–347BC), who recorded Socrates' teaching and himself became an outstanding philosopher, writing many books in the form of dialogues. He was concerned about the irreverent and irreligious spirit that had developed in Athens, and argued against the materialists (who reduced everything to matter) and the sceptics (who doubted everything). He tried to discover the inner meaning of the old myths, and came very close to believing in one God.

The third great Greek philosopher was Aristotle (384–322BC), who wrote about a wide range of subjects, including philosophy, ethics, biology, art and music. The god he believed in wasn't a very personal god, and seemed to be little more than 'the Prime Mover', the force that set the whole universe in motion and keeps it in motion. He said that everything in religion over and above this basic belief was 'mythical addition for the persuasion of the multitudes'.

Apart from these great philosophers, there were two

schools of philosophy which were popular for several centuries. The Epicureans (followers of Epicurus, 341–270BC), denied the existence of the gods and had a strong hatred of superstition. They wanted to free people from false religion and taught that if the world had been formed by chance and there is no afterlife, people should pursue happiness and pleasure as their goal in life. The Stoics, on the other hand, seemed more religious, because they believed in what they called '-natural religion', and thought of God as a kind of 'World-Soul'. They also had a strong emphasis on morality, stressing the importance of reason, self-sacrifice and endurance.

Greek philosophy is significant for this study of religion because it raised many basic questions which need to be asked about any kind of religion, and because the Greek philosophers (especially Plato and Aristotle) had a profound influence on Christian, Jewish and Muslim thinkers for many centuries.

Roman Religion

The religion of the ancient Romans was originally an agricultural religion in which people worshipped the mysterious and impersonal forces of nature, but it changed and developed considerably up to the time of the emperors. It was essentially practical and concerned with physical needs and prosperity for the family and the state. The aims of all its rituals were to avoid the anger of the gods and win their favour, since without their approval nothing could ever succeed. Cicero called the Roman people 'the most religious in the world'. Our English word 'religion' comes from the Latin word *religio*, which meant 'bonds', referring to the tie or link between the gods and human beings.

Roman gods were thought of as personal, heavenly beings; but originally there were no myths about the gods in human form, and no statues to represent them. The best known were: Jupiter (the direct equivalent of the Greek Zeus), the god of thunder, lightning and rain, and god of the state; Mars (Ares), the god of war; Juno (Hera); Minerva; Venus (Aphrodite), the goddess of love and beauty; Neptune (Poseidon), the god of the sea and rivers; Mercury (Hermes), the god of merchants and thieves, the messenger of the gods; Ceres (Demeter), the goddess of cereals; and Janus, the god of beginnings.

Later emperors took the title 'Augustus', implying that they had the approval of the gods. After their death they were declared to be gods by the senate, provided they had not misbehaved (as Caligula and Nero had). This whole cult of the emperor made distant provinces feel that they were part of the Empire, and helped to strengthen the *Pax Romana*, the peace and security established by the Empire.

These Roman household gods were found in the remains of a house at Pompeii, Italy. The state religion of Rome went on alongside the popular religion of the home.

Private worship centred round the household gods in the home. At every meal, for example, the head of the family (*pater familias*), would make an offering to the gods. Correct observation of burial ceremonies was essential, and gifts were brought to the family tomb every February to calm the souls of the dead and prevent them from becoming evil spirits. In making any decisions it was considered very important to know the will of the gods. Elaborate methods of augury therefore developed, such as observing the flight of birds and studying the entrails of dead animals, to interpret the signs sent by Jupiter.

As with the Greeks, the official state religion wasn't really concerned with the spiritual needs of individuals. Alongside it, therefore, were popular religions with their own rituals. Tavern keepers, for example, worshipped their own wine god. There was great interest in magic, astrology and dreams. In the later period ordinary people began to experiment by introducing new, private cults and philosophies, especially from the East; and through the influence of Judaism and Christianity there was a growing interest in monotheism. Roman religion was already in decline by the third century AD, and its temples and sanctuaries were officially closed or destroyed in AD399.

Celtic Religion

Current knowledge of Celtic religion comes from archaeological remains and from Greek, Roman and Christian writers. There were over 300 gods and goddesses, each with different functions or associated with different tribes. The tribal goddess was particularly important because she was 'the divine epitome of all that ideal womankind stands for—sexuality, maternity, the conveyor of delight, the healer of all sorrow'. Ancestors had to be respected, because they could still help the tribe in war and bring peace and fertility. Animals and birds had a significant role, because it was thought that the gods could take on the form of an animal or a bird. Boars were regarded as the most sacred animals, and birds could provide omens for the future.

Celtic places of worship consisted of a sacrificial platform surrounded by banks of earth or ditches, with pits nearby filled with sacrificial bones and other offerings. The priests who carried out the rituals in the open air were the Druids. Most of the ritual consisted of offering sacrifices, usually of animals, but sometimes of humans. Prominent natural features, such as hills, pools, wells, sources of rivers and clumps of trees, as well as man-made features such as burial mounds or standing stones, were regarded with special reverence as places where the gods and other spirits were active and where mortals could communicate with them.

The Celtic people were very conscious of the spiritual world and had their own ideas of how they could gain access to it—such as by helping the gods to defeat their enemies in battle, or by imitating the gods in showing cleverness and cunning. Reaching the other world had nothing to do with good behaviour, since 'ethics did not enter into Celtic religion'. Their two main feasts were Beltane at the beginning of summer (1 May), and Samhain at the end of summer (1 November). This feast was a time when the division between the two worlds became very thin, when hostile supernatural forces were active and ghosts and spirits were free to wander as they wished.

The Druid stronghold of Anglesey was destroyed by the Roman legions in AD61, and the historian Tacitus described the scene in this way:

'On the beach stood the enemy army, a solid mass of arms and men, with women running to and fro. Like Furies in black robes and with wild hair they waved torches, while a circle of druids raised their hands to heaven and showered down curses. The soldiers were struck with such fear and awe at this strange sight, that they stood paralysed, until their general reassured them.'

The Druidic religion persisted in various forms for many centuries after the Roman conquest, elements surviving into the Middle Ages and beyond.

Scandinavian or Norse Religion

This was the religion of northern Europe, and especially Scandinavia, for many centuries until the coming of Christianity. One of the best-known features of this religion was the triad of Nordic gods called Odin, Thor and Frey:

Great standing stones or stone structures, such as Trevethy Quoit on Bodmin Moor, Cornwall, England, are common in Celtic lands such as Brittany, Ireland, Wales, Cornwall... These were sacred sites, centres of the religion of the Druids.

▶Odin was the High God, the supreme authority in the universe. He was known as the Father of All, the king of the gods, and was thought to be powerful and terrible, and a master of magic. His wife was Frigg, the Earth Mother, and their son was Balder, the most beautiful and wisest of the gods. His brother, Loki, represented the forces of evil and was thought to be dangerous. His most treacherous act was the murder of his brother Balder.

▶Thor (from whom derives the name *Thursday*, meaning Thor's Day) was a god of power, who controlled the thunder, and a warrior god, portrayed with an axe or a hammer, who was the ideal for all warriors.

▶Frey (from whom comes *Friday*, meaning Frey's Day)

was the god of fertility, the god of the whole world, who controlled the sun and the rain. His sister was Freya, the most important of the goddesses, who had relations with all the gods.

The Norse people had their own distinctive world-view which was reflected in their rich mythology. They believed that in the centre of the world stood a tree, known as the cosmic or world tree, the tree of knowledge. They had a strong belief in life after death, and believed that most of the dead go to an underworld called Hel. Warriors, however, were specially fortunate and could look forward to their own special paradise in Valhalla, where they would eat, drink and engage in combat. Entry to Valhalla was a reward for courage

The great ash tree, Yggdrasil, of Norse mythology. Yggdrasil was believed to hold all creation together, its roots reaching to all the elements under the world

rather than for goodness. It was thought that at the end of the world there would be a severe winter, followed by a Last Great Battle. After this everything would be destroyed by fire in a universal cataclysm, and a new heaven and a new earth would then emerge.

The supernatural world was always intensely real for ordinary people, who believed that supernatural beings controlled every aspect of their daily lives. Many tales were therefore told of fairies and elves, trolls and giants, of spirits who lived in the woods, the streams, the forests or the mountains. People lived in fear of all these beings and offered sacrifices to placate them, because any of them could be dangerous and cause trouble or suffering. They sacrificed animals (horses, pigs and dogs) and also occasionally humans, and sprinkled the blood on those who were taking part in the sacrifice. They worshipped the sun and practised many fertility rites. One of their main festivals was Yule, when offerings were made to the spirits of ancestors. There was a strong belief in fate, to which even the gods were thought to be subject. This meant that there was little idea of human free-will, and many techniques of augury and divination were developed to predict the future. The moral code was largely the code of the family unit and depended largely on a sense of personal honour. Losing one's honour meant exclusion from society, and any attack on one's honour had to be avenged.

The Conversion of Europe

The conversion of Europe was a gradual process. There must have been Christians in Rome very soon after the death of Jesus in AD30. But there is no clear evidence that the gospel came to Britain before about AD200, and it wasn't until AD563 that Columba landed in Iona and AD596 that Augustine landed in Kent. Boniface of Devon took the gospel to the Low Countries and parts of Germany in the mid eighth century, but Scandinavia didn't accept Christianity until the eleventh century.

Even when Christianity was accepted by a tribe or a kingdom in a particular place, the process of conversion was gradual. It took years for the ordinary people to accept the new religion which their leaders had adopted, and there was often considerable opposition from those who wanted to hold on to their former religion.

Bede, the famous English historian, gives many examples of how Christian missionaries approached the people in different parts of Britain. In one passage he describes how Augustine and his monks first met the king of Kent and settled in Canterbury. The king's response to the gospel was cautious, but he at least gave the missionaries freedom to preach and make converts.

Although some people seem to think that the Anglo-Saxons readily embraced Christianity, this is far from being true. This is how David Edwards, an English church historian and writer, explains the process of gradual conversion:

'In spite of there being good political and cultural reasons for the conversion of kings to Christianity, in spite of an extraordinary galaxy of able and saintly missionaries, it took nearly ninety years to convert just the kings and a greater part of their aristocracy, not to speak of the countryside which was a question of centuries. In the course of that near-ninety years hardly a court was converted which did not suffer at least one subsequent relapse into paganism before being reconverted. The old religious instincts died hard.'

A study of this period of history suggests that the Christian faith was accepted in different parts of Europe for a variety of reasons.

Christianity was seen as offering good news for this life. It offered hope in this world and seemed to make life more bearable. It also offered a new dimension of human kindness to a warlike people who lived in a harsh environment.

Christianity was seen as good news about life after death. Bede recounts that Edwin, the king of the Angles, asked his advisers and friends whether or not to accept the Christian faith which had been preached to them by Paulinus. One of the king's chief men described how human life was like the flight of a sparrow through a hall during the winter—offering a few moments of light and warmth as respite from the darkness outside. He urged the king to accept the new faith if it could 'reveal any more certain knowledge' about life after death.

People were attracted by the lifestyle of the missionaries. Bede describes the impression that the Christians made on the people of Kent. They prayed a great deal, fasted, and kept vigils. They were eager to preach the gospel, and did so whenever they could. At the same time, they lived simply and accepted only food from the people they taught. Their exemplary way of life won them the admiration of the people they had come to convert, who took their message all the more seriously as a result.

Leaders could see that the adoption of Christianity would have benefits for the life of their nations. Bede gives the text of a letter sent by Pope Gregory to King Ethelbert, who is described as 'King of the English'. In this letter the pope urges the king to 'raise the moral standards of his subjects' and refers to the positive results of the acceptance of Christianity in the Roman Empire.

Christian Attitudes to Popular Religion

Christians have had differing attitudes to other religions. What did Christians think when they first came in contact, for example, with Celtic or Scandinavian religions? If they had accepted everything they found, there would have been no difference between the Christian faith and the other religions. If on the other hand they simply rejected the previous customs and put nothing new in their place, they would have created a dangerous vacuum which would have been filled by something else. In practice, therefore, there were only two approaches which Christians could adopt:

Reject and replace. One approach was to call on people to reject certain beliefs and practices in their religion which were definitely not consistent with Christianity, and find different ones to take their place.

This is basically what Paul urged the people of Lystra to do. After they had witnessed a miracle of healing, they thought Paul and Barnabas must be gods and wanted to offer sacrifices to them. But Paul urged them to turn away from these ideas and rituals, which he described as 'worthless things', and to trust in the one Creator God:

'*In Lystra there sat a man crippled in his feet, who was lame from birth and had never walked. He listened to Paul as he was speaking. Paul looked directly at him, saw that he had faith to be healed and called out, "Stand up on your feet!" At that, the man jumped up and began to walk.*

'*When the crowd saw what Paul had done, they shouted in the Lycaonian language, "The gods have come down to us in human form!" Barnabas they called Zeus, and Paul they called Hermes, because he was the chief speaker. The priest of Zeus, whose temple was just outside the city, brought bulls and wreaths to the city gates because he and the crowd wanted to offer sacrifices to them.*

'*But when the apostles Barnabas and Paul heard of this, they tore their clothes and rushed into the crowd, shouting: "Men, why are you doing this? We are only men, human beings like you. We are bringing you good news, telling you to turn from these worthless things to the living God, who made heaven and earth and sea and everything in them. In the past, he let all nations go their own way. Yet he has not left himself without testimony: He has shown kindness by giving you rain from heaven and crops in their seasons; He provides you with plenty of food and fills your hearts with joy."*'
(Acts 14:8–18)

When Paul went to Ephesus, the centre of the worship of the great goddess Artemis (Diana), he found himself among people who were very much aware of the supernatural. When some of them believed his message, they demonstrated their renunciation of their occult practices in a very dramatic way:

'*God did extraordinary miracles through Paul... Some Jews who went round driving out evil spirits tried to invoke the name of the Lord Jesus over those who were demon possessed. They would say, "In the name of Jesus whom Paul preaches, I command you to come out." Seven sons of Sceva, a Jewish chief priest, were doing this. The evil spirit answered them, "Jesus I know and Paul I know about, but who are you?" Then the man who had the evil spirit jumped on them and overpowered them all. He gave them such a beating that they ran out of the house naked and bleeding.*

'*When this became known to the Jews and Greeks living in Ephesus, they were all seized with fear, and the name of the Lord Jesus was held in high honour. Many of those who believed now came and openly confessed their evil deeds. A number who had practised sorcery brought their scrolls together and burned them publicly. When they calculated the value of the scrolls, the total came to fifty thousand drachmas. In this way the word of the Lord spread widely and grew in power.*' (Acts 19:11–20)

Bede gives an account of how the high priest of a pagan temple near York in the north of England set out to destroy the temple in which he had previously led the worship, in order to show that he had accepted the Christian faith.

An early biography of Boniface of Devon describes an occasion when he felt he had to destroy a sacred oak tree which was associated with pagan worship. The tree had been struck by lightning, and was thought to be a place where Thor, the god of thunder, dwelt. In front of an angry crowd, Boniface took an axe and made a single notch on the tree. Immediately a strong wind sprang up, and it blew the tree over. This amazing event so impressed the crowd that they began to take Christianity seriously.

Change and adapt. Instead of calling people to reject the practices of their own religion, another approach would be to find ways of giving previous practices a new, Christian meaning.

When Paul visited Athens, he was profoundly disturbed by the statues of different deities which he saw all round the city. When he spoke at a meeting of the Areopagus, however, he didn't begin by attacking their religion, but by finding common ground. Later in his address he strongly challenged some of their beliefs and practices, and called on them to recognize the meaning of what God had done through Jesus, and to change their minds. But he was prepared to start where they were and lead them on from there. This is Luke's account of what Paul was able to say before he was interrupted:

'*Men of Athens! I see that in every way you are very religious. For as I walked round and observed your objects of worship, I even found an altar with this inscription: TO AN*

UNKNOWN GOD. *Now what you worship as something unknown I am going to proclaim to you.*

'The God who made the world and everything in it is the Lord of heaven and earth and does not live in temples built by human hands. And he is not served by human hands, as if he needed anything, because he himself gives all men life and breath and everything else. From one man he made every nation of men, that they should inhabit the whole earth; and he determined the times set for them and the exact places where they should live. God did this so that men would seek him and perhaps reach out for him and find him, though he is not far from each one of us. ''For in him we live and move and have our being.'' As some of your own poets have said, ''We are his offspring.''

'Therefore since we are God's offspring, we should not think that the divine being is like gold or silver or stone—an image made by man's design and skill. In the past God overlooked such ignorance, but now he commands all people everywhere to repent. For he has set a day when he will judge the world with justice by the man he has appointed. He has given proof of this to all men by raising him from the dead.' (Acts 17:22–31)

It was this kind of policy which was followed by most of the missionaries who brought Christianity to Britain. The clearest statement of this approach is recorded by Bede in a letter in which the pope explained the policy which Augustine was to adopt in his work among the English, and the reasons for it.

He was to purify the old pagan temples with holy water, but leave the buildings intact. Moreover, instead of simply trying to abolish old practices which were associated with devil-worship, he said that Augustine was to find new, Christian rituals which could take their place. The sacrifice of oxen, for example, was to be replaced with a day of dedication that would involve feasting. His thinking ran as follows:

'If the people are allowed some worldly pleasures in this way, they will more readily come to desire the joys of the spirit. For it is certainly impossible to eradicate all errors from obstinate minds at one stroke, and whoever wishes to climb to a mountain top climbs gradually step by step, and not in one leap.'

He goes on to explain that this is the approach that God himself adopted in his dealings with the people of Israel in the Old Testament.

Aidan, the person who brought the gospel to the north-east of England, is another example of someone who followed this general approach. According to Bede, it was because of his more gentle and accommodating approach that he was chosen to take over where another missionary had failed.

This policy of adapting previous practices and giving them a Christian meaning sometimes proved reasonably successful. So, for example, the celebration of Christmas for many centuries must have been a genuine celebration of the birth of Christ as well as being a mid-winter festival.

In other cases, however, the policy of trying to 'christianize' previous practices was far less effective. Many people today, for example, are hardly aware that the church turned 1 November into the feast of All Hallows (All Saints), and 31 October to the Eve of All Hallows (Hallowe'en) in an attempt to suppress the pagan practices associated with the old Celtic Samhain and the Eve of Samhain which fell on these dates. The popularity of Hallowe'en and the ignorance about its history suggest that the attempt was hardly successful!

Throughout the history of Christianity, therefore, there has been a tension between these two attitudes to the beliefs and practices of other religions. Since the time of the Reformation Roman Catholics have tended to adopt the more tolerant and accommodating approach, while Protestants have generally been less tolerant towards other religions. The Puritans adopted a very strict policy towards everything associated with popular religion, and even went so far as to try to abolish the celebration of Christmas. These different attitudes are still to be found among Christians today.

The Modern Mind

In the past four hundred years, various philosophies have emerged in the Western world, and some of them challenge traditional religion.

The Scientific Revolution

One of the less expected effects of the Reformation was the rise of scientific thinking in Europe as a whole and England in particular. Protestantism was hostile to magic and ritual, it emphasized experience above authority, and it replaced the complex theological system of the Middle Ages with one that was simple and could be grasped easily. So in the seventeenth century educated people increasingly began to look at the world around them with new eyes. Scientists such as Galileo in Italy and Isaac Newton in England began to draw a new picture of a universe. In 1687 Newton published his *Mathematical Principles of Natural Philosophy*, which for the first time described the world under a single set of laws. Alexander Pope summed up the dramatic effect of Newton's system when he wrote:

'Nature and nature's laws lay hid in night;
God said, ''Let Newton be!'' and all was light.'

In the new intellectual climate popular beliefs in magic

continued, but by the 1670s prosecutions of witches had almost ceased, because sceptical judges and jurors would rarely convict. Supernatural explanations became less and less necessary, but soon people began asking how there could be a theory of the universe which accommodated both God and the new science. Newton's answer was to see God as a great clockmaker, who wound up the mechanism of the world at the creation and then left it to run on its own. This idea gained ground during the 1700s, and as it did so traditional Christianity, in which God intervened directly in the world, supremely in Jesus who was both God and man, fell out of favour with educated people. Newton himself was in private not so convinced that he had explained the universe. Shortly before his death in 1727 he made this comment:

'I do not know what I may appear to the world, but to myself I seem to have been only like a boy playing on the sea-shore,

Seventeenth-century scientists such as Galileo, seen in this statue, came to understand that the universe was different from how it had traditionally been pictured. Such scientists were people of faith, who sought to fit their discoveries into a Christian framework.

and diverting myself in now and then finding a smoother pebble or a prettier shell than ordinary, whilst the great ocean of truth lay all undiscovered before me.'

The Enlightenment

The principles of reason and observation which had been applied in the 1600s to the physical world began to be applied in the 1700s to human behaviour. Just as natural laws had been found to govern the natural process, so it was hoped that natural laws governing morality, government and the social order would be found by reason and observation. It is this attempt to find the natural laws, or self-evident truths, of human behaviour and apply them to knowledge, government and religious belief which is called the Enlightenment. Immanuel Kant summed it up in this way in 1784:

'We do not lack reason, but we lack the resolution to use it without direction from someone else. ''Have courage to use your own reason!''—that is the motto of enlightenment.'

Jean-Jacques Rousseau's *Social Contract* (1762) developed an ideal of popular sovereignty and equality of all before the law, ideas taken up by others in the French Revolution of 1789. Tom Paine's writings such as *The Rights of Man* and *The Age of Reason* brought these radical political ideas to England.

The Romantics

The Romantic movement flourished in England from the late eighteenth century and through the nineteenth, led by the poets Wordsworth, Coleridge, Blake, Keats, Shelley and Byron. In many ways it was a reaction to the classical forms of the Enlightenment. Imagination and emotion rather than naked reason and poetry rather than philosophy were its modes of expression, and there was a return to interest in the weird, mysterious and grotesque. In architecture the change of mood is seen with the transition from the cool and measured rhythms of the classical style to the excitement and restless movement of the gothic. The Romantics reacted to the wild and unspoilt scenery of the English Lakes, and found God in their awe before nature. Although the great poets had either died or ceased to write poetry by 1820 their influence gradually spread. Romanticism had been described as 'spilt religion', and its tendency to sentimentality and a rose-coloured view of the past greatly affected Victorian religion, especially its hymns. The Oxford Movement in particular, with its love of colour and medievalism, and its gothic-style churches, shows the Romantic spirit, as does the adoption of customs such as the use of Christmas trees and maypoles, looking back to the ritual of the past and '- merrie England'. The rejection of reason in favour of feelings meant that although there was a greater sense of the spiritual, there was dangerously little analysis of this sense. A Birmingham preacher in the 1850s said, 'I love religion and flowers; but I hate botany and theology.' This neglect of the intellectual foundations of belief caused trouble when challenges such as Darwin's theory of evolution emerged.

The High Tide of Atheism

'Men have left GOD not for other gods, they say, but for no god; and this has never happened before.'

T.S. Eliot's comment from *The Rock* (1934) shows the change in English society in the 1920s. Amongst intellectuals atheism, or at least agnosticism, had become the only defensible way of understanding the world. Many felt themselves to be 'tone-deaf' to religion,

and the rising stars of the 1920s were almost without exception atheists: Bertrand Russell, the philosopher, and the novelists Virginia Woolf, D.H. Lawrence and E.M. Forster, for example. The influence of Darwin had indirectly destroyed a belief in the reliability of the Bible, while Marx had suggested that religion was the 'opium of the people', invented in order to help them forget the agony of everyday life and cynically used by the governing classes as a means of social control. Freud wrote of religion as 'the universal obsessional neurosis of humanity', something which a well-adjusted person had to grow out of. Yet there were signs that the cold and inhospitable prospect of a world without religious belief was beginning to be rejected. T.S. Eliot was one of the 'bright young things' of the early 1920s, who in 1922 had written *The Waste Land*, a poem expressing the desolation of contemporary life. In 1927 he was baptized and confirmed in the Church of England, having found that the non-religion of his friends did not satisfy him.

Two of England's most famous Romantic poets, William Wordsworth and Samuel Taylor Coleridge, lived in the **English Lake District and loved its scenery. They wrote about nature as if God were really there in the trees and the hills.**

Virginia Woolf wrote that

'dear Tom Eliot…may be called dead to us all from this day forward. He has become an Anglo-Catholic believer in God and immortality and goes to church. I was shocked…there's something obscene in a living person sitting by the fire and believing in God.'

Eliot stood against the tide of atheism, but in doing so showed that it was perhaps about to turn.

It took a while for this turning of the tide to become apparent. Communist governments in Russia and China were confident for many years that, after the older generation of religious people died out, everyone would cease to believe in the supernatural and accept the atheism on which Marxism is based. If it's so clear that our expanding knowledge is exploding all the old myths and legends of the past, there isn't room any longer for the supernatural.

But everyone knows that it hasn't worked out like this! The so-called 'modern man/woman' who is totally secular, rational, scientific, atheistic and non-religious isn't as common as one might expect. The evidence which proves that popular religion is alive and well is staring us in the face from every direction:

▶ The interest in astrology, the occult, the paranormal

▶ The fascination with festivals such as those held at Stonehenge

▶ The success of the cults

▶ The number of books and magazines dealing with different aspects of the supernatural

▶ Children's fascination with witches and poltergeists

▶ The popularity of the New Age movement

The list could be extended. But, according to all the theory, popular religion should have died out in the modern world long ago. Since it hasn't, perhaps it means that human beings are 'incurably religious' after all.

We are now witnessing a resurgence of pre-Christian popular religion. A great deal of popular religion disappeared as a result of the coming of Christianity to Europe. Some of its more acceptable forms, however, like the holly and the ivy at Christmas, continued to exist *alongside* and *within* formal Christianity in the churches. The less acceptable forms, like astrology, magic and the occult, simply went *underground*. This state of affairs existed for the best part of a thousand years, when people felt they belonged to 'Christendom'.

But what happened when more and more people rejected the Christian faith and when the Christian assumptions on which society was based were questioned and rejected? At an intellectual level, there were new philosophies and ideologies expressed by writers, philosophers, scientists and artists, which came in to fill the vacuum left by Christianity. For ordinary people, however, popular religion continued to meet 'the hunger of the heart'. And what we are witnessing today is a resurgence of several aspects of popular religion which have been practised almost in secret. Now they are being practised more openly, by larger numbers of people, and without any sense of shame.

W. A. Visser t'Hooft speaks of what he calls the 'neo-pagans' of Europe:

'The masses outside the churches are considered lapsed Christians who need to be 're-called' to an active participation in church life… But there are today in Europe even more millions who are not adequately described as lapsed Christians, because they have in fact turned to another religion. But is it really possible for men and women who are the products of an old Christian civilization to return to paganism? … Paganism is far more deeply rooted in European history than is generally realized.'

He reminds us that Goethe, the German poet, called himself 'pagan' and 'a determined non-Christian'. He also points out that Hitler's Nazism was 'an attempt to restore paganism', and comments:

'What is striking about the Hitler period in Germany is precisely that it was possible for an essentially neo-pagan ideology to reduce to submission a nation of thinkers, scientists, poets and technicians. Its defeat had to come from outside. All our Western nations should consider this as a tremendous warning.'

He ends by quoting a French writer's comment that 'the gods only go away to make place for other gods'.

Our subject is popular religion rather than paganism. But where does one begin and the other end?

Our task now is to look as closely as we can at the many different faces of popular religion—the ones that come closest to formal or official religion and those which are furthest removed from it, the more acceptable and the less acceptable. Only then will we be in a position to define more carefully what we mean by 'popular religion' and how much of it can fairly be called 'paganism'.

Part Two

The Faces of Popular Religion

Let's Have a Festival!
Rites of Passage
Saints
Churches
Visions of Glory
Heavenly Music
Myths and Legends
'Cross My Heart and Hope to Die'
Written in the Stars
The Occult

2 Let's Have a Festival!

These things…are deeply ingrained in people's lives, loved, enjoyed, but not taken too much for granted. They are not museum pieces; they are as much a part of our lives as summer holidays and Sunday lunch.

Brian Shuel, Guide to Traditional Customs of Britain

Our ancestors had a sure instinct for holding on to anything that served a practical purpose.

Ralph Whitlock, A Calendar of Country Customs

Perhaps this is why we have festivals. With actions, music, singing, playing and dancing we can say more than words can ever tell.

Norma Fairbairn and Jack Priestly, Holy Week

Many of the customs practised on Hallowe'en find little or no authority in the Church, and at no other time of the year are pagan and Christian observances so confused.

Victor J. Green, Festivals and Saints Days

The *Concise Oxford Dictionary* sums up what festivals are all about with this simple definition: 'Feast day, celebration, merry-making'.

The Function of Festivals

Before trying to find out the origin of particular festivals and explain the customs associated with them, it's worth asking some basic questions about festivals in general. What function do they perform for a community? What do they do for any society? What needs do they meet? Here are four obvious needs that are met by having festivals.

Marking the seasons of the year. People long ago were much more aware of the changing seasons than people are today. They understood the rhythm of nature, and were fully aware of all the tasks that had to be done at particular times of the year, such as ploughing, sowing, mating animals and pruning fruit trees. It is understandable, therefore, that times like the beginning of spring and the mid-winter solstice should have been marked by special festivals. They provided a valuable way

of keeping in time with nature. However, since they could never be sure that nature was utterly reliable, there were certain rituals they had to perform in order to influence the working of nature to their advantage.

Meeting other basic human needs. If people think of themselves as members of a community rather than as individuals, they can recognize certain needs that are felt by societies all over the world, even though their cultures are totally different from each other.

Reminding people of their nation's history and holding their society together. People need opportunities to express their loyalty and devotion to the nation to which they belong, and to remember crucial events in their history.

Interpreting the meaning of the world. Many festivals also express important aspects of a community's world-view—that is to say, what they believe about the universe and the meaning of life. In many cases this dimension is added on or grafted on to festivals which originally met other basic needs. Easter, for example, was originally a spring festival celebrating new life in the natural world;

but for Christians it was also an opportunity to celebrate the resurrection of Jesus and his victory over death.

The Origin of Festivals

In order to understand all the customs and traditions associated with a particular festival, such as Christmas trees and Easter eggs, it is necessary to find out the origin of the festival and trace its development over many centuries. Each of the following stages through which Western culture has passed has left its mark on the traditions in one way or another:

Pre-Christian Europe

Most people today know little or nothing about the religion of their ancestors, yet many of their customs and traditions are still part of Western culture. The use of mistletoe goes back to the Druids. And 'hot cross buns' have been unearthed which were made in pre-Christian Britain.

The Christianization of Europe

When Christianity spread all over Europe the old agricultural calendar was taken over and Christianized. Rather than force people to give up all of their old customs, the leaders of the church decided to transform the old pagan festivals into Christian ones.

Degeneration, Protest and Revival

The problem with the Christianization process was that Christianity in Europe came to include a large number of customs associated with a pagan world-view. The vast majority of people probably didn't make a clean break with their pagan past, but rejected only some of their traditional beliefs and practices. Their Christian faith was therefore a mixture containing elements of the new and of the old.

During the Middle Ages there were several attempts to get the church to recognize what had happened and to root out some of the more obviously pagan elements which remained. But the most significant and far-reaching protest came at the time of the Reformation in the sixteenth century. This was a genuine attempt to persuade the church to get rid of teaching and practices which had developed over the centuries but which had little to do with the teaching of the Bible. When Luther protested against the sale of indulgences, for example, he was trying to reject the essentially pagan idea of winning approval from God by buying something or doing something good.

Another example of this same kind of protest can be seen in the Puritans in the seventeenth century. They were very critical of what they regarded as unchristian superstitions, not only in the Roman Catholic Church but also in the Church of England, and when they were able to gain political power under Oliver Cromwell, they went so far as to persuade the British parliament to abolish Christmas and May Day.

Needless to say, this negative attitude wasn't popular with most people, and after Cromwell's death most of the old customs were revived. For this reason Samuel Pepys was able to write in his Diary that May Day in 1661 was 'the happiest May Day that hath been many a year in England'. The fact that these customs were revived with such enthusiasm at the Restoration of the monarchy in 1660 shows how much they had become part of the culture of the nation.

Developments in Modern Times

The eighteenth century saw the beginnings of the Industrial Revolution. People were drawn from the country into the towns and cities and lost contact with the customs and practices of the farmers. It wasn't so easy for them to go into the woods on May Day to bring back branches of hawthorn and sycamore, and when it came to Christmas they had to decorate their homes with coloured streamers instead of holly and ivy.

New opportunities for travel brought new ideas. For example, it was Dutch sailors who brought the original stories about St Nicholas from Asia Minor (Turkey) to Holland, where he became 'Sinta Klaas'.

In recent years, new patterns of immigration have influenced the festivals that are celebrated in different parts of the world. For example, although the festivals of the Eastern religions were being practised in the East centuries before the coming of Christianity to Europe, it is only recently that people in the West have become aware of them, through the presence of people of Asian origin.

Festivals from Pre-Christian Times

Several festivals that are commonly celebrated go back to very old traditions indeed.

New Year's Day

The Druids seem to have celebrated certain rituals using mistletoe at this time of the year, although little is known about them.

The Romans celebrated New Year, and it is known that they used the greeting 'A Happy New Year!' Those who could afford it gave each other dates and figs decorated with gold. Originally the new year was celebrated at the beginning of March, no doubt because of its association with spring. This explains why September, which comes from the Latin *septem* meaning seven, was originally thought of as the seventh month. October, November and December are names of Latin origin referring to the eighth, ninth and tenth months respectively.

The New Year was later moved to January, the month named after the god Janus, who had two faces—one looking back to the past, the other looking forward to the future. The Romans brought their New Year customs to Britain, where they were eventually combined with the old Celtic customs.

Various different customs are practised at New Year:

Hogmanay. The word probably comes from the Old French '*au gui l'an neuf*', which means 'to the mistletoe, the New Year', or from '*au gui menez*', meaning 'to the mistletoe go!' According to a seventeenth-century writer, this was the greeting used by the Druids as they came out of the woods carrying mistletoe. In Roman tradition it was mistletoe that Aeneas picked from the oak tree at the gate of the underworld, because it would ensure that he would pass safely from the underworld to the real world. It was therefore no doubt thought that it could guarantee a safe passage from one year to the next.

First footing. This custom used to be carried out as follows: as soon as possible after midnight had struck, a man—preferably one who was young, good-looking and dark, and was a stranger to the house—knocked at the door of the house where people had gathered to welcome the New Year. If there was no stranger who could visit, then someone from the group dressed up as a stranger in order to carry out the first footing.

When the door was opened he came in, carrying a branch and a piece of mistletoe. He put the branch on the fire and, after kissing all the ladies under his piece of mistletoe, put it on the mantelpiece. He might also bring bread, salt, coal or money. The owner of the house then greeted him, gave him wine and cake, and all who were present greeted each other with the words 'Happy New Year!' After this ceremony people went out visiting other families and wishing them a Happy New Year.

The symbolism of this ceremony seems to have been that the stranger stood for the new year, which comes without invitation and must be welcomed in. He brought with him gifts that represented some of the basic necessities of life which would be needed during the coming year. If he came without the right gifts, it was a bad omen which meant that the family would experience bad fortune and poverty during the coming year.

Church bells. These are often rung to toll the death of the old year and greet the new year. No doubt it used to be thought that the noise of the bells would frighten away evil spirits.

Watch Night services. These services were first started by the Methodists in the eighteenth century. They are still popular in churches which want an alternative to thoroughly 'secular' parties.

May Day

The Romans had a festival on 1 May and offered sacrifices in honour of Maia, the mother of Mercury, since the month was named after her.

In the Celtic year there was a fire festival on 1 May, named Beltane, when fires, called Beltane Fires, were lit to mark the end of winter and the beginning of summer. People would dance energetically round the fire in a clockwise direction, believing that by imitating the direction in which the sun moved it would help it to grow stronger. Because they were herders more than farmers, animals were very important for them. So in order to protect their flocks from harm during the summer months they offered sacrifices on the fire, sometimes even human sacrifices.

At some stage customs associated with the Roman festival must have been grafted on to the old Celtic fire festival. In this way the festival retained what was important for the Celtic herders (like the fire and the animals) and for the Roman farmers.

When Christianity spread throughout Europe, it is significant that May Day (unlike the mid-winter and spring festivals) was not given a Christian meaning but remained more pagan than any of the other festivals. People would spend the night in the woods, often having a riotous time together. In the morning they picked flowers and cut down branches bursting into leaf from the trees, especially the hawthorn (which was thought to be sacred to the goddess Maia, and is still known as 'may' or 'whitethorn'), and sycamore. They would run through the fields and streets, making loud noises, with the aim of driving out the spirits of winter and of evil.

After these rituals, which were intended to cleanse the town, they had to do something to ensure good fortune for the coming summer. To do this they felled a tall, straight tree, cutting off all its branches except the boughs at the very top, which were left to represent life at the beginning of spring. Green leaves were wound round the trunk, and it was decorated with flowers and ribbons. In Scandinavia they still bring in the May tree every year. The tree was set up in an open space in the village, and people would join in dances round the maypole.

Customs of this kind continued throughout the Middle Ages, and the whole exercise was called 'a-maying', which meant going out and having a good time on May Day. Characters dressed in green leaves and boughs and representing symbols of growth, with names like 'The Green Man', 'Jack in the Green' and '- Robin Hood', took part in the celebrations.

The church tended to be very critical of some of the superstition, the revelling and other excesses involved in the celebration of May Day. The Puritans were especially critical of this festival, and under their influence the Long Parliament in 1644 made it illegal to celebrate May Day (as well as Christmas), and maypoles were cut down.

After the Restoration in 1660, however, the celebrations were allowed once again, much to the delight of most people. For the occasion a huge maypole more than 134 feet (41 metres) high was erected in the Strand, and remained there for 50 years. Some maypoles were very tall, sometimes even as tall as church towers; often they were left standing all year round, painted with spiral bands of colour, and decorated again each year.

In the eighteenth century May Day was almost forgotten, and it was only at the end of the nineteenth century that men like Tennyson, William Morris and Ruskin revived May Day and made it largely a festival for children.

It was also at the end of the nineteenth century that May Day was given a new significance. The Industrial Revolution had brought many people from the country to the towns and cities. People of all ages worked very long hours, often in appalling conditions in factories, and they had little opportunity to go to the woods to gather branches on May Day.

In 1883 Robert Owen, a Scottish mill-owner who was concerned to improve working conditions in factories, decided to make 1 May a Festival of Labour. He wanted it to be the first day of a new millennium in which there would be no poverty or injustice. The trades unions in the United States and Canada called for a strike on 1 May and demanded that the working day should be reduced to eight hours.

Then in 1889 the International Socialist Congress, which brought together in Paris leaders of the Labour movement all over Europe, asked for 1 May to be a day of demonstrations to force governments to limit the working day to eight hours. Labour Day has remained a tradition in most industrialized countries since then, although in the United States and Canada it is held in September.

The maypole. In traditional May Day celebrations in England in the past the focal point in the celebrations was the maypole, a young tree, 12 to 15 feet (3 to 4 metres) high, decorated with flowers and ribbons.

The maypole dances, with their intricate patterns by which ribbons are wound round the pole, are part of spring in countless English towns and villages.

Maypole dancing. The tradition of dancing around the maypole while holding the ribbons attached to the top came from southern Europe, and was first introduced into England in the nineteenth century by the writer John Ruskin. It soon became very popular. Elaborate dances were developed, with children holding the coloured ribbons attached to the maypole and weaving intricate movements.

Crowning the May Queen. This custom probably goes back to ancient rituals involving the May Queen, who represented the goddess of summer growth. In some ancient rituals there was a Queen of May and a Queen of Winter (who was a man dressed as a woman). At the beginning of summer every year a battle had to be fought between these two, who represented summer and life on one hand, and winter and death on the other. Naturally the Queen of May and summer were always victorious. In crowning ceremonies today the girl chosen to be queen has to be unmarried, and is chosen for her beauty.

May singing. At 6 a.m. on May Day the choir of Magdalen College in Oxford, England, sings from the top of the college tower, and Morris dancers perform in the streets below. Similar gatherings for singing are held in other places.

Morris dancing. This is specially popular at this time of the year, and is found all over Europe. Some believe that that it has its origins in some kind of ancient fertility rites depicting a battle between opposing forces in nature. It is also suggested that the name 'Morris' comes from 'Moorish', and that Crusaders may have brought the dances back with them from North Africa and the Muslim world. Even if there is some truth in these explanations, most of those who take part in or watch Morris dancing today are probably blissfully unaware of these associations.

Harvest

Harvest festivals have their origin in the desire to give thanks to whatever being or power is thought to be responsible for the harvest, and the need to ensure that crops will grow again the following spring.

The main harvest festival among the Celts was the feast of Samhain on 1 November, which marked the end of summer and the beginning of winter. Many of the customs associated with this festival have been continued in one form or another in the festivities of Hallowe'en.

Some time after the coming of Christianity to Britain, a festival of first-fruits was developed, known as Lammas (from the Anglo-Saxon word 'Llaf-maesse' or loaf mass) and held on 1 August. Loaves were made from the first ripe corn, in accordance with the custom described in

Harvest festival in Britain is above all the festival of rural communities. In the United States, 'thanksgiving' also gives a chance to bring the products of farm and garden into church.

Deuteronomy 26:1–11, and presented to the priest as an offering.

It seems that in pre-Christian times there used to be a popular belief that spirits lived in the crops; cutting the crops therefore meant killing the spirit which lived in them. This is probably the belief which underlies the custom of 'crying the neck' which has survived in some parts of England: several people together cut the last sheaf of the harvest, to make sure that no single reaper is responsible for cutting it (and thereby killing the spirit that lives in the crop). This last sheaf is then carried to the farmhouse, where it is made into a 'corn baby' or 'corn dolly' and kept over the fireplace until Plough Monday (the first Monday in January after the twelfth day of Christmas) in order to ensure that the corn spirit will continue to live and give the next harvest.

It used to be the custom to hold a Harvest Supper on the last evening of harvest for all who had helped to bring the harvest in. They would eat roast beef, plum pudding and apple pies and drink ale and cider. This was followed by toasts, singing and dancing.

The modern Harvest Thanksgivings, which have become so popular, can be traced back to the year 1843, when Robert Hawker, vicar of the village of Morwenstow in Cornwall, invited his congregation to a Communion service using bread made out of the new corn from that year's harvest. Since then the custom has spread rapidly, and harvest festivals are held during September or October. Churches and schools are decorated and everyone is encouraged to bring gifts of flowers, fruit, vegetables or any other produce, which are then distributed to needy people in the area. In many rural communities the Harvest Festival is regarded as one of the most important festivals of the year.

Hallowe'en, All Saints and All Souls

Among the ancient Celtic peoples who lived in Wales, Ireland, Scotland and the north of England, the year was divided into two seasons: winter from November to April, and summer from May to October. New Year's Day was 1 November and it was celebrated as the Feast of Samhain. The day before, 31 October, was therefore the Eve of Samhain, or New Year's Eve, and was kept as a kind of harvest festival marking the end of summer.

During the festival, fires would be lit which would burn all through the winter. Surplus animals which couldn't be fed during the winter were slaughtered and everyone joined in a great feast. Sacrifices would be offered to the gods on the fires. But this was also a special time of the year when the supernatural world broke into the natural world in special ways, which meant that the spirits of the dead could return to wander on earth. People would therefore take brands out of the fire and carry them round the village to chase away the spirits of the dead and any evil spirits. To find out what the future held in store, spells would be cast and various rituals performed.

These customs would have met three important needs: the need to ensure survival during the winter; the need to remember and honour the dead, and in some cases to pray for them, and the need to acknowledge and show respect for all spiritual forces, to obtain protection from evil spirits and to ensure good fortune. One writer says that 'Samhain acknowledged the entire spectrum of non-human forces that roamed the earth during that period'.

The Romans had similar festivals at this time of the year: the Feralia, a feast for honouring the dead; and Pomonia, a feast in honour of the goddess of fruit, in which nuts and apples were used in games. At some stage features of these Roman festivals must have been combined with those of the Celtic festival of Samhain.

What happened when Christianity spread to these parts of Europe? It seems that, instead of trying to abolish these pagan customs and ideas, people tried after a time to introduce ideas which reflected a more Christian world-view. Someone must have thought that if people were afraid of being visited by the spirits of the dead, then it would be helpful to make this festival an opportunity for remembering before God all the saints who had died and all the dead in the Christian community.

It was no doubt for reasons of this kind that All Saints' Day was moved from 13 May to 1 November in 834. This meant that 31 October came to be known as All Hallows' Eve. As 'hallow' means 'saint', it could also be called All Saints' Eve, the Eve of All Saints' Day. Later, in 988, 2 November was made All Souls' Day, a feast for honouring all the dead, not only those regarded by the church as saints. All these measures together must have been part of an attempt to Christianize the old Eve of Samhain and to wean people away from the old pagan ideas and customs. They might then remember and pray *with* and *for* the dead rather than praying *to* them, and focus their attention on the lives of saints of the past rather than on spirits, whether good or bad.

At the time of the Reformation there was a serious attempt to cut out some of the ideas, particularly concerning prayer for the dead. It was pointed out that there is nothing in the Bible which encourages us to pray for the dead; they are in the hands of God and their eternal destiny has been determined by their response to God in *this* life; so praying for them cannot alter their condition. As a result All Souls' Day was removed from the church's calendar, and wasn't restored until 1928.

Bonfires. These were an important part of the old Celtic Eve of Samhain celebrations, and had several different functions: burning rubbish and dead vegetation which had accumulated over the summer; burning sacrifices of animals, crops, and sometimes even human beings (or at a later stage an effigy) to placate the gods; ensuring that the sun would return after the winter; and frightening away evil spirits and witches.

Fireworks. Invented in China and later introduced to the West, these may have replaced the old custom of throwing nuts on the fire so that they would explode. The old custom was intended to drive away evil spirits.

Lanterns. The traditional Jack O'Lantern is made by carving out the inside of a turnip, mangold or pumpkin, cutting holes in the side and putting a candle inside. This would originally have been intended to frighten away evil spirits, and would have been carried round the village boundaries.

Food. Today either soup and sausages or hamburgers are served at bonfire parties. The old Samhain was an

Jack O'Lantern would scare anyone on a dark night. Would he scare evil spirits away? Today such a lantern is part of the fun of Hallowe'en, especially in the United States. He is made by hollowing out a pumpkin, making a face from the skin and putting a candle inside.

opportunity for feasting, since all the cattle which couldn't be fed through the winter had to be killed off and the meat either eaten or salted. Special food was put out for the dead who might visit their relatives. There used to be a custom of leaving the best food at an empty place at the table in case any of the spirits of the dead returned. The traditional 'soul cakes' developed out of the early custom of begging for cakes for the dead. These soul cakes were given to the poor, and later fruit, beer, sweets or money were given instead.

Guizing. The word comes from 'disguise' and refers to the practice of dressing up and going round the village entertaining people. Wearing masks and other disguises and blackening the face with soot would originally have been ways of hiding oneself from the spirits of the dead who might be roaming round during Hallowe'en night and of driving away evil spirits. Another explanation suggests that the masks and disguises may have been a way of imitating supernatural beings, who, when they visited people in their homes, would be offered gifts of food and drink.

In many parts of Britain and Ireland this night used to be known as 'Mischief Night', which meant that people were free to go round the village playing pranks and getting up to any kind of mischief without fear of being punished. Many of the different customs were taken to the United States by Irish and Scottish immigrants in the nineteenth century, and they developed into 'trick or treat'. Nowadays in the United States, the vast majority of children under the age of ten or twelve go in costume from house to house after dark on 31 October. When someone comes to the door the children say 'Trick or treat' and are given a treat—usually a small piece of candy. Children usually do this in groups, with parents accompanying them from a safe distance.

Witches. At one time people accused of being witches were burned on the Hallowe'en bonfire. This practice was stopped around 1600, and an effigy of a witch was sometimes burned instead. They continue to be an important part of the traditions surrounding Hallowe'en, and are prominent in decorations in schools and at Hallowe'en parties.

Many people today think of witches not as real people who practise magic, but simply as imaginary figures who represent the supernatural world and everything that is 'spooky'. Others are concerned by this fascination with witches, partly because some children are genuinely frightened by all they see and hear about witches, and partly because some children develop a fascination with the supernatural which leads them later into more sinister occult practices.

Decorations. In addition to witches, bats and owls are particularly popular. Originally this would have been because people used to be afraid of bats and owls and other nocturnal animals, believing that these creatures could communicate with the spirits of the dead. The main colours associated with Hallowe'en are orange and black.

Hallowe'en Games. The various activities traditional to Hallowe'en are mostly associated with the idea of obtaining good fortune and foretelling the future:

▶ Ducking, dooking or bobbing for apples is the game of trying to take a bite from an apple floating in the water or hanging from a string. The idea behind it seems to have been that snatching a bite from the apple enables the person to grasp good fortune. In the countries where this custom developed, apples are plentiful at this time of the year.

▶ There used to be a custom of placing a stone in the hot ashes of the bonfire. If in the morning a person found that the stone had been removed or had cracked, it was a sign of bad fortune.

▶ Peeling an apple and throwing the peel over one's shoulder was supposed to reveal the initial of one's future spouse.

▶ Nuts have been used for divination: whether they burned quietly or exploded indicated good or bad luck.

▶ One way of looking for omens of death was for people to visit churchyards, because the spirits of those who were going to die during the coming year were thought to walk around the churchyard during this night.

Major Festivals of the Christian Year

Many festivals in countries with a Christian culture are the festivals of the church. They celebrate the most important events in the story of Christ.

Christmas

The word 'Christmas' comes from the old English *Cristes masse*, meaning 'the festival mass of Christ'.

Christmas as people know it today is an incredible mixture of customs and traditions from many different times and places. Some come from the Romans and others from different parts of Europe. Some come from pre-Christian times, some from the time when Europe was gradually being converted to Christianity, while others have been added during the nineteenth and twentieth centuries.

There are at least six different stages by which the festival has developed:

The Roman Saturnalia and the Day of the Unconquered Sun. The mid-winter festival in Rome began with the Saturnalia during 17–24 December, which was named after Saturn, the god of everything that grows. It was celebrated with a week's holiday, when schools and courts were closed, houses were decorated with evergreens, lamps, torches and candles were lit, and presents were exchanged. There was plenty of eating and drinking; there were games, charades and singing, and differences between masters and slaves were forgotten, with masters often waiting on their slaves at table.

The next significant development came in AD272 when the emperor Aurelian made 25 December, the day following the end of the Saturnalia, a special festival in honour of the sun god, making it a public holiday and giving it the name *dies natalis invicti solis*, 'the Day (or Birthday) of the Unconquered Sun'. The worship of the sun had been popular in Rome for a long time, and as part of the feast people used to light bonfires to help the sun on its way. By creating a feast on 25 December, the emperor was no doubt trying to encourage these ideas and practices, and may have been trying to promote the old religion of sun worship as an alternative to Christianity, which was becoming more popular.

The mid-winter festival. All over northern Europe, and especially in Britain, Germany and Scandinavia, people celebrated a Yule feast in the middle of winter around the period of the winter solstice. The word 'Yule' comes either from the old German 'jol' meaning 'turning wheel', and thus referring to the increase of sunlight after the mid-winter solstice, or from the Anglo-Saxon 'goel', meaning 'feast'.

The feast took different forms in different countries, but everywhere it seemed to meet two basic needs: the need to enjoy festivities and cheer everyone up in the middle of winter, when the weather was at its worst and the working day at its shortest; and the need to ensure that everything would grow again in the spring. Christmas traditions which have their origin in this pre-Christian period include decorating homes with holly, ivy and mistletoe, burning the yule log, lighting candles and feasting.

Some time during the second century a group of Christians in Alexandria in Egypt, who were followers of a heretical Christian teacher called Basilides, began to celebrate the baptism of Jesus on 6 January, and called it the 'Epiphany', from the Greek word for 'appearing'. They may have chosen this day because it was already used for different pagan festivals such as the feast of Dionysus, which was associated with the idea of the lengthening of the days at this time of the year, the feast of the goddess Aeon (Time), and a feast of Osiris, the Egyptian god of the dead. It was also believed that during the night before 6 January the water of the Nile had special magical powers. By choosing this day, these Christians wanted to express their belief that the one true God had appeared on earth in the person of Jesus, and that his baptism in the River Jordan was the beginning of his 'appearing'.

It seems likely that other Christians took over the festival of 6 January from them, and by about AD300 many Christians were celebrating the *birth* of Jesus during the night of 5 January and his *baptism* on 6 January. Part of an Egyptian papyrus has survived which includes the liturgy used for the celebration of the birth of Jesus, and there is other evidence which shows that by 300 the Epiphany had become an important and popular feast throughout the East.

Speculation about the dates of the birth and death of Jesus. We know from several writers from the third century onwards (including Hippolytus and Augustine) that arguments like these were being put forward in an attempt to decide on the dates of the birth and death of Jesus:

'*The spring equinox is 25 March, and it must also have been the first day of creation.*'

'*The first Good Friday, the day when Jesus died, was on 25 March, the fourteenth day of the Jewish month of Nisan.*'

'*Jesus must have been conceived on the same date as his death.*'

'*If 25 March was the date of the conception of Jesus, he must have been born on 25 December. He was therefore conceived at the time of the spring equinox and born on the winter solstice.*'

Although this kind of speculation seems unconvincing to people today, it's very possible that it was convincing to many in the third century, when this style of argumentation was widely accepted.

The celebration of Christmas in the West. Many have argued that Christians deliberately chose 25 December as the date for celebrating the birth of Jesus because they wanted to displace the pagan celebration of the birthday of the sun on this day. What better day could there be for celebrating the birth of Jesus than the day on which the people of Rome had for fifty years been celebrating the birth of the sun—25 December?

Others have suggested that it wasn't quite as simple as this, and that the association of 25 December with a thoroughly pagan feast could have created many problems for new Christians. Wouldn't they be confused between the ideas of worshipping the sun and worshipping Christ? It has therefore been suggested that Christians must have been influenced by the other arguments which pointed to 25 December.

It could be, however, that both ideas came together and suggested the same day. Whichever reason seems more appealing, it remains clear that the choice of the date must have been related in one way or another to the cycles of the sun.

It can't merely be coincidence that these developments took place during the time that the emperor Constantine was trying to establish Christianity as the official religion of the Roman Empire. When in 312 he adopted the Christian faith, he didn't immediately reject all his old pagan beliefs and practices. In fact he seems to have wanted to combine the worship of the sun with the worship of Christ. He probably believed that Christianity would be a better religion for uniting the empire than the old religions with their many gods and goddesses.

He called the Council of Nicaea in 325, and on that occasion bishops representing most of the churches in the Mediterranean area confirmed the orthodox Christian belief that Jesus was fully human and fully divine. They also rejected as heretical other beliefs which cast doubt either on his divinity (for instance, by suggesting that he was a created being from heaven), or on his humanity (by saying that he only appeared to be human). It's very probable, therefore, that soon after the Council of Nicaea the leaders of the church thought that one way of affirming the church's belief in the divinity of Christ and in his true incarnation 'in the flesh' would be to have an annual festival commemorating his birth.

Already in 321 the emperor Constantine had made the first day of the week—traditionally regarded as dedicated to the sun god and kept by Christians as 'the Lord's Day'—the official weekly day of rest for the whole Roman Empire. So, since the resurrection of Jesus was already being celebrated on the weekly day of the sun, it must have seemed natural to link the birth of Jesus with the annual festival of the birth of the sun on 25 December.

There is therefore no need to think of the new Western Christmas on 25 December simply as a deliberate attempt to stamp out a pagan festival. By this time the old pagan religions had probably already lost much of their attraction, and many people were coming to appreciate the universal appeal of the Christian faith. They thought of Christ as the fulfilment of the prophet Malachi's words that 'the sun of righteousness will arise with healing in its wings' (Malachi 4:2). And they spoke of him as 'the light of the world' (John 8:12) and 'a light to lighten the Gentiles' (Luke 2:32). It was very natural, therefore, that Bishop Ambrose of Milan in one of his sermons in about 380 could point out the contrast between Christmas and the old pagan festival by saying, 'Christ is *our* new sun!'

Other written records confirm that by 336 Pope Julian had fixed 25 December as Christmas Day for the Western church. This date soon came to be accepted by Christians in many different countries in the West and the East—except the Armenians and the Coptic Orthodox Christians in Egypt, who still celebrate Christmas on 6 January.

Later developments. During the time of Pope Gregory the Great (AD540–604), the period of Advent was developed as a time of preparation for Christmas. The idea probably came from the six-week period of preparation for Easter, known as Lent. Like Lent, it also became a period for preparing those who wanted to be baptized.

Every element of the children's 'christingle' has a meaning. The candle, for example, stands for the light of Jesus, and the orange for the world.

In the early sixth century Christmas was made a public holiday by the emperor Justinian.

When Christians took their faith to the northern parts of Europe, they found the Yule festival which the Norsemen and others celebrated at the winter solstice. They must therefore have absorbed many of the customs associated with the winter festival.

The Christmas festival developed its own set of traditions (discussed later in this section). In the seventeenth century, the Puritans in England did their best to discourage its observance, because they disapproved of the many traditions and superstitions that surrounded it. In 1652 Christmas was actually abolished by act of Parliament! But when Parliament met on Christmas Day, public reaction was so strong that there were riots in several cities. One Puritan writer, Hezekiah Woodward, wrote a tract in 1656 in which he described Christmas in these terms:

'The old Heathens' Feasting Day, in honour of Saturn, their Idol-God, the Papists' Massing Day, the Profane Man's Ranting Day, the Superstitious Man's Idol Day, the Multitude's Idle Day, Satan's—that Adversary's—Working Day, the True Christian Man's Fasting Day...'

The spirit of the Puritans was kept alive in America, where, for example, in 1659 the General Court in Massachusetts passed this law:

'Anybody who is found observing, by abstinence from labour, feasting, or in any other way, any such days as Christmas Day, shall for every such offence five shillings.'

Christmas Day remained an ordinary working day in America until the middle of the nineteenth century, and in Scotland it wasn't until the early 1950s that it became a public holiday.

Nevertheless, after the Restoration of Charles II in 1660 the celebration of Christmas was revived in England. In the nineteenth and twentieth centuries many more traditions became part of the festival.

The list of customs and traditions that are current today is a very long one.

Advent. The period of four weeks leading up to Christmas marks the beginning of the Christian year. The first Sunday in Advent falls on the Sunday nearest to St Andrew's Day (30 November), and is known as 'Stir Up Sunday' because of the words of the special prayer or Collect for that day which begins, 'Stir up, we beseech Thee, O Lord, the wills of Thy faithful people...' This is traditionally the day for mixing the ingredients of Christmas cakes and puddings, and for all the family to make a special wish as they take their turn in stirring the mixture.

The Advent wreath originated in America. This circular wreath, made out of evergreens, carries four candles,

The Christmas crib scene always has Mary, Joseph and their baby at the centre. Often they are joined by shepherds, the wise men, farm animals. Here children have a place.

with a fifth in the centre. One is lit on each of the four Sundays of Advent, and the fifth on Christmas Eve or Christmas Day.

Bells. It is traditional to ring church bells on Christmas Day to greet the birth of Jesus, and at midnight before New Year's Day to ring out the old year and ring in the new.

Boxing Day. This name was first given to 26 December in England in 1849. One explanation is that it was the day when the poor boxes or alms boxes were opened in church and the money in them was given to the poor. Another explanation is that it was on this day that servants received their 'Christmas Box', a special gift for Christmas. For many years until recently the various tradespeople who made deliveries throughout the year would call to receive a tip for their services.

Candles. People originally lit candles during the mid-winter festival to represent the light and heat of the sun. Later they were given a Christian meaning, and were regarded as symbolic of Jesus, the Light of the World.

Carols. These originated in the Middle Ages as singing dances with a strong rhythm and refrain. They came to be popular songs sung at church festivals, especially at Easter and Christmas, but were not confined to religious subjects.

Christingle. This custom started in the Moravian Church in Germany. On Christmas Eve 1747 the bishop gave each child a candle with a red ribbon as a reminder of Jesus, the light of the world. The custom spread and changed in the process. A candle is inserted into the top of an orange; cocktail sticks with nuts and raisins are stuck all round, and a red ribbon is tied round the middle.

The orange represents the world, and the candle represents Jesus as the Light of the World. The nuts and raisins represent the fruit of the earth, and the red ribbon represents the blood of Jesus shed on the cross. Children are encouraged to bring their orange to a special service in church before Christmas, and all the candles are lit together.

Christmas cards. These date back to the time when the Penny Post was started in England in 1840. Cards were first produced in larger numbers in 1860, and they soon took the place of the traditional New Year cards. They became even more popular when, from 1870 onwards, cards could be sent in an unsealed envelope for a halfpenny. Soon after this the custom spread to other countries.

Crackers. The tradition of having crackers comes from France, where a bag of sweets used to be wrapped in paper and then pulled apart by two children. They were first produced commercially in England in 1860, with a cracker to make the noise when they were pulled apart.

Crib. As far back as the eighth century there had been a permanent crib in the Church of St Maria Maggiore in Rome, where the pope would celebrate Mass at Christmas, using the manger as an altar. From the eleventh century a nativity drama was performed in many churches. But it was St Francis and his followers who made the idea of the crib so popular. He set it up in a cave on a hillside outside the town of Grecchio in Italy on 24 December 1224, using an ordinary manger filled with hay, and real people and animals.

Epiphany. The feast of Epiphany is celebrated on 6 January. It commemorates the revealing of Christ to the world, the word 'Epiphany' meaning 'appearing' or 'revealing'. It focuses in particular on the story of the visit of the Wise Men.

Father Christmas or Santa Claus. The traditions associated with this character provide an excellent example of how these develop over a long period of time, gathering new elements and sometimes being changed radically as they travel from one country to another. These are the main stages in that development:

▶ In Britain during the later Middle Ages there was a figure known as 'Father Christmas' who represented the spirit of Christmas but was not connected in any way with St Nicholas. He was known in the fifteenth century, and is mentioned in a carol from the period which begins, 'Hail, Father Christmas, hail to thee!' He also appeared in versions of the Mummers' plays.

▶ The original St Nicholas was the Bishop of Myra in Asia Minor (now Turkey) during the fourth century. He came from a wealthy family and is said to have used the fortune left to him by his parents to help the poor—but only in secret ways. The story is told that when he heard of a man who was so poor that he was being forced to sell his three daughters as slaves, he threw three purses full of gold through their door as dowries, so that each of them could be married.

When, after his death, the secret of his generosity was revealed, it became a custom to give presents secretly on St Nicholas' Day (6 December), pretending that they had been given by St Nicholas himself. He later became the patron saint of all children, and especially of orphans. He was also considered the patron saint of pawnbrokers: the three golden balls of their trade sign are a reminder of his three bags of gold. Merchants and sailors also came under his patronage.

▶ Dutch sailors heard the story of St Nicholas in Turkey and brought it back to Holland, where the bishop came to be called Sinta Klaas, and portrayed as a bearded man on a white horse. At this stage he probably also took over some of the characteristics of the Teutonic Santa Klaus, who earlier had represented the god Odin riding through the skies. It was said that on St Nicholas' Day he used to bring presents secretly to good children, but a bunch of birch rods to naughty children.

▶ The figure of Sinta Klaas/Santa Klaus was taken during the nineteenth century by Dutch settlers to the United States where his name became Santa Claus. He was now said to come from the North Pole, and was given a sledge pulled by reindeer instead of a white horse. Clement Clarke Moore's poem 'A Visit from St Nicholas' written in 1823 popularized the idea of the sledge drawn by reindeer, and even gave names to each of the eight reindeer. The portrayal of Santa with a white beard, wearing a red coat trimmed with fur and carrying a sack of toys can be traced back to a drawing by the American Thomas Nash, which appeared in Harper's Magazine in the 1860s. The song 'Rudolph the Red-nosed Reindeer' was composed in 1939. All these elements have helped to create the figure of Father Christmas/Santa Claus which has travelled all over the world.

Festival of Nine Lessons and Carols. The first service of this kind was held in Truro in 1880 by Bishop Benson. When he later became Archbishop of Canterbury, the tradition was adopted at King's College Chapel in Cambridge, where the first such festival was held on Christmas Eve in 1918.

Gifts. The custom of giving gifts at Christmas goes back to the Roman custom of exchanging gifts during the Saturnalia feast, when the rich used to give money and clothes to their poor neighbours, and receive in return garlands, tapers or some grains of incense. Alternatively, it may go back to the exchange of gifts within the family on 1 January, New Year's Day, when gifts were intended to bring good luck and prosperity. In some countries, such as France, gifts are still exchanged on New Year's Day.

During the early years of Christianity in the Roman Empire the Christians probably did not exchange gifts at New Year, because the practice was associated with a pagan feast.

In many parts of Europe St Nicholas is thought of as the one who brings gifts when he visits, either on 5 December or Christmas Eve.

Holly and ivy. Evergreens of all kinds, and especially holly and ivy, used to be regarded throughout Europe in pre-Christian days as symbols of survival and perpetual life. They were used to decorate sacred buildings and

Santa Claus is derived from St Nicholas. In Holland this generous saint gives presents on St Nicholas Day, 5 December. His companion is Black Peter.

homes during the mid-winter festival. The prickly holly was seen as a symbol of the male principle (and therefore lucky to men), and engaged in a constant battle with the female principle, which was represented by the ivy, eventually overpowering it.

The church at first discouraged these customs, because they were seen as essentially pagan. Tertullian, for example, wrote to Christians, 'If you have renounced temples, do not turn the door of your house into a temple!' Eventually, however, Christians overcame their misgivings and began to use evergreens to decorate their houses and their churches.

Midnight Mass. The custom of celebrating Mass at midnight on Christmas Eve began in Rome in the fifth century, probably on the model of the celebration of Easter beginning on the evening of Easter Eve and continuing through the night. It was celebrated in Rome in the Church of St Maria Maggiore in a shrine which was designed as a replica of the crib at Bethlehem.

Mistletoe. This plant was thought to have magic power to ward off evil. It was therefore popular with the Druids, especially if it grew on an oak tree, and branches were hung over doorways to keep out evil spirits. In Scandinavia mistletoe was for a long time regarded as a protection against fire and lightning, and as containing power to heal and ensure fertility. The practice of kissing anyone caught under the mistletoe no doubt goes back to this custom and to ancient fertility rites. Unlike other evergreens, mistletoe has not generally been used for decorations in church, because of its associations with pagan rites. In many churches it is completely banned.

There is an old Norse myth which tries to explain the popularity of mistletoe. The story is that Balder, the sun god, was killed by a sharp arrow made from a branch of mistletoe and shot by Loki, the god of evil. The other gods, however, brought Balder to life again, and the mistletoe tree promised never to harm anyone again. This is said to explain how mistletoe became a symbol of love.

Stockings. The custom of putting out stockings on Christmas Eve is connected with a story told about St Nicholas. Once when he was out at midnight he threw some gold coins down a chimney, and they landed in a stocking which was drying on the hearth.

Tree. The fir tree was called the 'Tree of the Christ-Child' by Boniface, an English missionary working in Germany in the eighth century. The story is told that once on Christmas Eve he came across a child who was about to be sacrificed beneath an oak tree to the god Odin. He rescued the child and ordered the oak tree to be cut down. When this was done, he found a small fir tree growing beside the stump of the oak tree, and from that time called the fir tree the 'Tree of the Christ-Child'. The fir tree thus became a symbol of the Christian faith taking the place of the old pagan religion represented by the oak tree.

According to tradition it was Martin Luther in Germany in the sixteenth century who popularized the custom of decorating the tree with real candles. It is said that when he was walking in the woods one night and saw the winter stars twinkling through the branches, he had the idea of putting a fir tree in his house and putting candles on it to give his children the idea of the starry sky.

From there it was taken to America by Hessian soldiers fighting in the English army of George III during the American War of Independence. It was first brought to England by Germans in the 1820s, and quickly became popular after Prince Albert from Germany married Queen Victoria in 1840 and introduced the tree to the royal family at Windsor Castle in 1841. Charles Dickens in 1850 called it 'the new German toy'. But by 1870 trees were being put up all over the country. As they became popular they took the place of the older Kissing-Bough, a garland of evergreens decorated with candles, coloured paper and mistletoe, which hung from the middle of the ceiling in the main living room and provided a focus for the Christmas celebrations.

Other ornaments on the tree, such as glass balls, were introduced to take the place of apples, which used to be painted and hung on evergreens in houses in honour of the god Woden.

Mounted at the top of the tree there is often a doll. Originally a doll representing the baby Jesus or the angel Gabriel was chosen, but a frequent choice today is a fairy, a princess, or a star.

Tinsel on the Christmas tree is explained by a legend about a poor woman and her tree. When spiders spun webs on the tree one night, the Christ-Child turned the spiders' webs into silver as a reward.

Wreath. The custom of hanging wreaths of evergreen on doors and inside windows comes from the United States.

Yule log. The lighting of the yule log used to be one of the most important items in the Christmas festivities. A large log was cut from an oak, ash or apple tree, and brought ceremonially into the house at dusk on Christmas Eve. When one end of it was placed on the fire, a glass of wine was poured over it, and the fire was then lit using the remains of the previous year's log. The fire would burn for at least twelve hours, and in some cases for the whole of the twelve days of Christmas. The purpose of the log was

A 'Chrismon tree' stands in an American church. It is an ordinary Christmas tree decorated with Christian symbols that span the centuries.

to bring prosperity to all in the house and ensure that the sun would return and the days grow longer. Sometimes ashes from the log were used as charms for healing or protection against harm.

Lent and Holy Week

Lent is the period of five-and-a-half weeks which leads up to Easter. Since for many centuries Easter was a special day for baptizing new Christians, the weeks of Lent were the time they were taught the basics of the Christian faith and prepared for baptism. It was also a reminder to all Christians of the forty days which Jesus spent in the wilderness at the beginning of his public ministry. Evidence shows that Lent was being celebrated in the church at Rome by about 340. When Easter ceased to be a special time for baptisms, Lent came to be regarded as a period of penitence during which people could examine themselves and prepare to celebrate Easter.

The word 'Lent' is a shortened form of the old English 'lenten', meaning 'length' or 'lengthen', and hence the season of spring, since this is the time of year in the northern hemisphere when the days begin to lengthen. It begins on Ash Wednesday and continues for six weeks until Easter Eve. This makes a total of forty-five days; but since Sundays are not counted as fast days, Lent lasts for forty days.

Many Christians use the Lenten period as a time of self-examination and self-denial in preparation for Holy Week and Easter. Some follow the tradition of not eating meat on Wednesdays and Fridays, while others simply deny themselves something in their usual diet, such as sugar or sweets, or they deny themselves some luxury. Fasting in general was relaxed on Sundays, and especially on Refreshment Sunday in the middle of Lent, which is otherwise known as Mothering Sunday.

Shrove Tuesday

The day before the beginning of Lent gets its name from the word 'shrove', which is the past tense of the Anglo-Saxon word 'to shrive', meaning 'to impose a penance'. When people had been to church on this day to confess their sins in preparation for Lent, they were said to be 'shriven', meaning forgiven or absolved from sin.

Shrove Tuesday is a kind of 'final fling' before the fasting of Lent. Because certain foods were not supposed to be eaten during Lent, it was the custom on the Monday of this week (Shrove Monday) to eat up all the meat left in the house which could not be eaten during Lent. Then on Shrove Tuesday all eggs, fats, milk, cream and flour were finished up by making them into pancakes. The months of February and March, coming at the end of the winter, must have been lean days with

less food in the larder. Writer and folklorist Ralph Whitlock suggests that the 'ecclesiastical injunction to fast during Lent merely made a virtue out of what was usually a necessity'.

Mardi gras

This is the French name for Shrove Tuesday and it means 'Fat Tuesday', because of the fat which had to be used up on this day before the fast of Lent. The day is also associated with the ancient custom (probably pre-Christian) of leading a fattened cow through the streets, which was probably part of an ancient spring festival. It may be that this old custom was Christianized by suggesting that the cow represented all the good things which should be given up during Lent. The procession is often still led through the town by a cow.

These customs were taken to America in the eighteenth and nineteenth centuries and soon the festival became an important carnival with processions and fancy dress, especially in the South in places like New Orleans. It was in this context that the black

descendants of the slaves developed jazz. The customs were also taken by the French to the West Indies and developed in their own way, with particular emphasis on dressing up as slaves and slave masters.

Mardi gras processions have become very important carnivals in the West Indies and elsewhere. The festivities now cover both Monday and Tuesday, and people are dressed in elaborate costumes representing witches, ghosts, clowns, cowboys, and characters such as St George and the Dragon. Months of advance preparation are devoted to the festival. There is much singing and dancing, and there are fireworks and picnics.

Ash Wednesday

This day marks the beginning of Lent, and gets its name from the ancient ceremony in which people who had committed serious sins had to come back to church on this day. The crosses from the previous year's Palm Sunday were burned, and the priest put some of the ashes on the forehead of each person, making the sign of the cross. The penitents were given a hair shirt which they

had to wear until the Tuesday of Holy Week, and they also had to perform some penance. After a time it wasn't only people who had committed serious sins who came for this ceremony; others joined voluntarily, asking to receive the mark of the ashes and to do some penance. By about AD1120 the custom had become common throughout Europe.

In some churches the old custom has been revived of burning the palm crosses from Palm Sunday the previous year. When the ashes are blessed and sprinkled with holy water, the priest dips his thumb into the ashes and makes the sign of the cross on the forehead of each person, saying the words, 'Remember...that thou art dust and unto dust shalt thou return'.

Holy Week

This is the week before Easter, in which Christians remember the events leading up to the crucifixion of Jesus on Good Friday. Since Jesus died during the feast of Passover, it is very probable that Christians celebrated

Palm Sunday is the Sunday before Easter. It commemorates Jesus' entering Jerusalem for the last week of his life. He was welcomed as a king. This dramatization took place in 1970 during the ten-yearly passion play at Oberammergau in Bavaria, Germany.

his death right from the beginning at this time of the year. It has been called Holy Week since about 300. Before that it was known as 'Great Week', because of the 'great deeds' that were done by Jesus.

Palm Sunday

The Sunday before Easter commemorates the triumphal entry of Jesus into Jerusalem five days before he died. We know that as early as 390 it was celebrated in Jerusalem with a procession starting outside the city. The people held palm or olive branches in their hands, and after a reading of the story from the Gospel they entered the city singing.

In villages in Europe in the past Palm Sunday used to be celebrated with special processions in the church or around the village. Since palms don't grow in these regions, villagers used to cut branches of willow (-especially the 'pussy willow', which is one of the first trees to bud and therefore a sign of spring) or hazel, box or yew, and carry them in procession. They would keep the branches in their homes to protect themselves from evil during the following months. Sometimes they were made into crosses and hung on the walls in the house. This may be an example of a pagan, pre-Christian custom which was originally associated with fertility rites being adopted and given a Christian meaning.

Since it has been possible to import palms from overseas, palm branches have been used, and everyone in the church is given a cross made out of a strip of palm, which they keep in their home throughout the year.

Maundy Thursday

The word 'Maundy' has its origin in the Latin word '*mandatum*', meaning 'commandment', and comes from the words of Jesus spoken at the Last Supper: 'A new commandment I give unto you.' In Latin the text is '-*mandatum novum do vobis*'.

In some churches a foot-washing ceremony is held, in which the priest washes the feet of some or all of those present, as a reminder of the way Jesus washed the feet of his disciples at the Last Supper on the evening before his death. It probably began with monks in monasteries washing one another's feet, and was known in Britain as early as AD600. Later the custom of giving food, money or clothes to the poor was added to the foot-washing ceremony, with poor people being invited into the monastery to receive money and have their feet washed.

The pope still holds a special service in the Vatican in which he himself does the foot washing. He washes the feet of thirteen priests; twelve of them are elderly and represent the apostles while the thirteenth is a young priest representing the angel who, according to

On Good Friday in Jerusalem a procession of pilgrims carry a cross. Their route takes in the traditional places Jesus may have passed as he went to his execution.

tradition, came to the table when Gregory the Great was serving on Maundy Thursday.

Good Friday

The day which commemorates the crucifixion of Jesus was probably originally called 'God's Friday', and later became 'Good Friday' (in the same way that 'God's Heavens' became 'Good Heavens' and 'God be with you' became 'Good-bye').

Good Friday services. These include readings, meditations and hymns, and commemorate the last three hours that Jesus was on the cross. In some churches the people move in procession to all the fourteen 'stations of the cross' which recall different events recorded in the Gospels.

Processions. Good Friday processions are held in many countries in Europe and round the Mediterranean which are predominantly Catholic or Orthodox. A cross is carried, and in some places other symbols such as a coffin or a crown of thorns.

Passion plays. Dramatic performances of the crucifixion events used to take place more often in the past. The famous passion play at Oberammergau was first performed in 1634. When the people of this village in southern Germany survived the Black Death which killed millions of people all over Europe in 1633, they decided to perform the play every ten years as a way of expressing their gratitude to God.

Easter

Easter is the oldest and most important festival of the Christian year. Both of the two possible explanations of the name connect the word 'Easter' with 'spring'. The Venerable Bede, the famous English church historian writing in the eighth century, suggested that it comes from 'Eastre' or 'Eostre', the old Anglo-Saxon goddess of spring. According to the second explanation, which is favoured today, the word is derived from '*Eostur*', the Norse word for 'spring'.

How did a word associated with spring become the name for the festival commemorating the resurrection of Jesus? The Gospels say that Jesus was crucified during the feast of the Jewish Passover, which was always in the spring. It was therefore natural that the first Christians (most of whom were Jewish) would have celebrated the death and resurrection of Jesus at Passover time each year, and more specifically on the fourteenth day of the Jewish month Nisan. The only changes they made were to celebrate it on a Sunday, because the first day of the week was the day of Jesus' resurrection, and also to extend the festival from Sunday to the following Sunday, no doubt because one of the appearances of the risen Jesus to his disciples took place a week after the resurrection. (John 20:26–29)

When Christians came to northern Europe, bringing their traditions with them, they couldn't help being aware of all the different ways in which people celebrated the arrival of spring around the time of the spring equinox. It must have seemed utterly natural for them, therefore, to continue to celebrate the resurrection at this time of the year, and to combine it with the celebration of spring. The celebration of new life in Christ must have seemed to fit in well with the celebration of new life in nature. As this tradition continued and developed, it would have affirmed those beliefs and practices which were consistent with belief in a Creator God, while gradually easing out those which were inconsistent with a Christian world-view, such as fertility rites and magic.

Like Christmas, therefore, Easter is a Christian festival grafted on to a pre-Christian festival. But, unlike Christmas, it has been observed from very early times—and certainly long before Christmas was thought of. It is very likely that Easter has been celebrated in Britain since Christianity first came to the country.

The date of Easter, which was fixed for the Western churches at the Council of Nicaea in 325, has to be after the equinox of 21 March. Around the same time also the emperor Constantine made Easter a public holiday, when slaves were given their freedom and alms were given to the poor. When Dionysius Exiguus' new calendar was adopted in Rome in 525, it meant that Easter could be celebrated between 22 March and 25 April. In order to calculate the date in any year one must find out when is the next full moon after the equinox. Easter falls on the *first* Sunday after the full moon.

The Eastern churches have a different way of fixing the date of Easter, and it can therefore fall anything up to three weeks before or after the Western Easter. Attempts have been made to get Eastern and Western churches to agree on a single fixed date for Easter, such as the first or second Sunday in April, but little significant progress has been made.

Easter services. In the Eastern churches services begin on the Saturday evening and continue until early on the Sunday morning. The church is in complete darkness until midnight, when the priest comes from the sanctuary into the main part of the church, holding a lighted candle. With the words 'Come ye, come and partake of the never-setting light and glorify Christ, who is risen from the dead,' he begins to light the candles held by those standing around him, and they in turn light their neighbours' candles, until the whole church is lit up by candle-light. The priest and the congregation then go outside the church, where the priest reads the Easter story from the Gospel. He then proclaims the resurrection with the words 'Christ is risen!' and the people reply 'He is risen indeed!'

In some churches people stay all through the night, waiting for the dawn and the Easter services. Sometimes the discovery of the empty tomb is acted out in drama.

Easter or Paschal candle. A special tall, fat candle is lit at the midnight service before Easter Day, and remains alight at all services for forty days until the ascension. This practice was started in the fifth century, representing Christ, the Light of the World, and his resurrection. The popularity of candles may also reflect the pre-Christian custom in northern Europe of lighting bonfires on hilltops to celebrate the arrival of spring.

Dawn services. Popular all over the world, these no doubt reflect the ancient custom of gathering at some prominent place like the top of a hill before sunrise in order to greet the sun. In some countries in northern Europe bonfires are still lit during Saturday night, and people gather round them for singing and dancing. Dawn services are particularly appropriate in view of the fact that the first disciples of Jesus discovered the empty tomb 'early on the first day of the week, while it was still dark' (John 20:1).

Easter eggs. Nowadays Easter eggs are generally made of chocolate, but the custom of giving them probably goes back to the pre-Christian custom of giving eggs as gifts at this time of the year, and it is easy to see how they could be regarded as symbols of the new life of spring. They were usually hard-boiled and coloured with dye, especially with red, which is another symbol of life. The custom was known in China as early as 900BC, where they were painted red to symbolize life, and also in Egypt, Greece and Rome.

In some countries of Eastern Europe decorating eggs with paint, wax or dye has become a form of art. According to an old Polish legend, Mary the mother of Jesus painted eggs red, blue and green to entertain her child, and all Polish mothers have done the same since then. A Romanian legend says that eggs are painted red because Mary placed some eggs at the foot of the cross, which were then covered by the blood of Jesus.

It isn't hard to work out how the pagan and the Christian symbolism of the egg come together. The shell of the egg is hard and curved and reminds people of the shape of the tomb of Jesus, which was carved out of rock. Jesus didn't need anyone to let him out of the tomb any more than a chick needs anyone to break the shell to let it out.

Easter bunny. This character is a later development of an earlier pagan tradition. The animal that was considered sacred to the goddess Eastre, and probably offered as a sacrifice to her in pre-Christian times, was the hare, not the rabbit. The reason for the choice may have been that it was known as a very fertile animal, and so came to be seen as a symbol of the coming of spring. So, for example, tales were told of hares running to Rome to fetch eggs. And games were played in which children were let loose in the house to find eggs which the goddess Eastre had hidden around the house. At some stage the hare was transformed into a rabbit, since the two have

At Easter services round the world, a large 'paschal candle' stays lit in church. Worshippers often light their own candles from the church candle, and carry the 'light of Christ' in procession into the neighbourhood.

often been confused in folk belief.

Ascension and Whitsunday (Pentecost)

The name 'Whitsunday' comes from the Old English '-Hwita Sunnandaeg', meaning 'White Sunday'. This was because this used to be a special day for baptisms, and those who were being baptized used to wear white clothes. The name 'Pentecost' comes from the Greek word meaning fifty, because the Jewish feast of Pentecost falls exactly fifty days after Passover.

Ascension Day falls on the sixth Thursday after Easter and commemorates the final appearances of the risen Jesus to his disciples before he returned to heaven. There is evidence to show that it was being celebrated by some Christians around 400. Whitsunday always falls seven weeks after Easter, and is the time when Christians remember the coming of the Holy Spirit to the disciples of Jesus. For many years Easter and Pentecost used to be the only annual festivals of the Christian year, and their date was fixed by the Jewish Passover.

Although Whitsunday used to be a public holiday in some countries, it has to some extent been overshadowed in recent years by May Day and public holidays at that time of year.

Other Festivals, Saints' Days and Special Days

There are a variety of other festivals celebrated in countries that have a Western culture. The emphasis that is given to each varies from one country to another, and most countries have some festivals that are unique to them.

St Valentine

Spring is the time of the year that people associate not only with new life in the natural world, but also with the stirring of love. In the lore of the countryside mid-February is the time when birds choose their mates. In spring 'a young man's fancy turns to love'. These two ideas may have been connected in ancient societies which practised special rites at this time of the year to ensure that everything would grow, and that young people would find their marriage partners.

The Romans had a feast to mark the beginning of spring on 15 February, called Lupercalia. The derivation of the name was based on the word *luper*, meaning wolf, so this was 'the Feast of the Wolf'. The choice was no doubt because a young man chasing a girl was called a wolf, an idea that survives in the English expression 'a wolf whistle'. Young people would draw lots to choose their partners for the coming year.

No doubt the church was unhappy with some of these pagan ideas about spring and the debasing of sex that went with it, and wanted to have a more Christian feast which would celebrate the meaning of true love. They probably therefore decided to hold their festival the day *before* the Lupercalia. But what were they to call it? Someone must have come up with the happy suggestion of using the name of a saint who seemed to represent the spirit of true love—St Valentine—who had died on 14 February.

One problem with the traditions, however, is that there appear to have been *two* Valentines. One of them was the Bishop of Terni in Italy, who was martyred in 270. The story is told that when the Roman emperor ordered that soldiers in the army should not marry, Valentine refused to obey and went on performing secret weddings for soldiers. While he was in prison, he and the daughter of the jailor fell in love with each other. And when Valentine was taken from his cell to be beaten with clubs and then beheaded, he left a note addressed to her which was signed 'Your Valentine'. Because of this story Valentine was seen to represent the spirit of true love, and he was made a saint. According to tradition, he died on 14 February, which happened to be the feast of Pulercalia, the Roman spring festival, when birds were thought to choose their mates.

In the Middle Ages it would seem that the custom continued of young men and women receiving by lot one of the opposite sex as his or her 'Valentine' for the coming year. The custom is mentioned in Chaucer and Shakespeare. In some cases the choice of a partner by lot could be a serious business, eventually leading to marriage, while in most cases it was simply treated as a game. There was a popular belief that the first man to be seen by a woman on 14 February had to be her Valentine, whatever she thought of him. People would sometimes give expensive gifts to their Valentine.

Valentine cards. The custom of sending cards was started during the eighteenth century, taking the place of the earlier expensive gifts. They were at first hand-made and included original verses. Cards were later produced commercially and became very popular during the Victorian period. Earlier in the twentieth century, however, they went out of fashion for a time, partly because many of them were vulgar and sometimes cruel. Then in the 1930s romantic Valentines came back into fashion.

In North America Valentines are sent to all and sundry—brothers, sisters, parents—the lot. (It sells far more cards than romantic love would pay for.) Elementary schools spend hours with their scissors and paste making class sets of cards, from all to all. Giving flowers (especially red ones) and/or candy is especially popular.

A nineteenth-century Valentine card. Is the Valentine festival based in history, in our need for love, in commerce?

Mothering Sunday/Mother's Day

Mothering Sunday and Mother's Day were originally two quite distinct festivals on different days of the year. In Britain the two festivals have been combined into one, celebrated on the fourth Sunday in Lent. In the United States Mother's Day is still held in May.

Mothering Sunday comes from the ancient custom of the priest and his congregation visiting the central church in their area, called the Mother Church. The Sunday for this visit was generally the fourth Sunday in Lent, and it came to be known as Refreshment Sunday, perhaps because it was felt that there should be some break in the fasting during Lent, and partly also because the Gospel reading of the day tells the story of the feeding of the five thousand. The festival therefore began as a *church* custom, but gradually developed into a *family* gathering, with children visiting their mothers.

It remained as an ordinary family occasion with no additional Christian meaning being added until the middle of this century. In England it became a custom that household servants and apprentices were given a holiday on Mothering Sunday to enable them to visit their mothers. In the seventeenth and eighteenth centuries this might have been the *only* time in the year when they were reunited with their families. The custom was called 'Going-a-Mothering'.

Mother's Day had its origins in America about eighty years ago. The idea came from a Miss Anna Jarvis of Philadelphia, who asked a friend to visit her on 9 May 1907, exactly a year after her own mother's death. She also arranged for a service to be held in a local church on the same day, and asked everyone who came to wear a white carnation. Within a year she had persuaded the people of Philadelphia to recognize the second Sunday in May as 'Mother's Day'. And in 1914 the US Congress officially dedicated the day 'to the memory of the best mother in the world—*your* mother'.

It is still widely celebrated in the United States today by giving gifts to mothers and wearing red or white carnations—red for living mothers, and white in memory of mothers who have died. Mother is relieved of kitchen duties, and families go out for their main meal. This is the busiest day of the year for American restaurants.

The custom was brought to England during the Second World War by American servicemen. On this Sunday in May they treated the mothers in the homes where they were living as if they were their own mothers, giving them gifts, flowers and cards as they had done at home in America. The custom soon caught on in Britain, but was transferred to the traditional Mothering Sunday.

Father's Day has been introduced in recent years, and it is celebrated with gifts and cards for dad on the third Sunday in June.

American Independence Day

The first colony to be founded in America was Virginia, in 1608. The Pilgrim Fathers landed in New England in 1620, and by the time of George III there were thirteen colonies established on the east coast of America.

Although they had their own governors, they were still subject to the king and Parliament in England, and paid taxes. As time went on the people became more and more resentful at having to pay taxes and not being allowed to have representatives in the British parliament.

After the Boston Tea Party in 1773, when 340 chests of tea were emptied into the harbour at Boston as a protest against the tax levied by the British authorities, the colonists united to resist the government. They produced a Declaration of Rights in which they set out their demands.

The War of Independence began in 1775, and on 4 July 1776 the Declaration of Independence, which had been drafted by Thomas Jefferson, was adopted by the Congress in Philadelphia. The war didn't end until 1782, when Britain and America signed the Treaty of Paris recognizing American independence.

The Fourth of July is a public holiday, when parades are held in many places. Flags of the United States are displayed prominently, and there is an opportunity for speeches.

Later in the day there are barbecues and picnics, at which almost everyone eats hot dogs and hamburgers. In the evening there are always firework displays. Every American youth, when thinking of 4 July, thinks of fireworks, since every American city and even many small towns have a large public firework display. Most states prohibit the sale of almost all fireworks to the public, so that it is only official displays that have big fireworks.

Special prayers are said for the nation in churches on the Sunday before 4 July.

Thanksgiving Day

In July 1620 a group of English and Dutch Puritans, men, women and children, set sail from Holland in the ship called the *Mayflower*. They put in to Plymouth and sailed from there on 6 September, landing in December on the east coast of America. There they established a settlement named Plymouth in the area that is now Massachusetts in New England.

The Pilgrim Fathers were not the first Europeans to settle in America—the colony of Virginia had been founded in 1608 by John Smith. The Puritans' aim was to establish a community based on Christian principles, where they could practise their Christian faith without interference from the government and without the discrimination they had experienced in England and Holland.

Nearly half of them died during the first winter. But after sowing crops in the spring and reaping the harvest in the autumn of 1621 with the cooperation of the American Indians, they held a special feast of Thanksgiving at the end of November. It soon became an established tradition, and is celebrated by all Americans on the fourth Thursday in November every year.

Thanksgiving therefore has many of the features of a harvest festival. But it also reminds Americans of crucial events early in their history as a *nation*. And it has become a major *family* gathering.

Many Americans today, however, pay little or no attention to the origin of the holiday, or even to the real meaning of its name. They know it has something to do with being thankful, but hardly realize that originally it was an occasion for being thankful *to God*.

Family reunions. Thanksgiving is generally regarded as a major family event, although Christmas is still the main family reunion of the year.

Church services. Special church services are held on the Sunday before Thanksgiving, and sometimes on the day itself, where the Christian element in the festival is strongly emphasized.

Parade. The Macy's Thanksgiving Day parade held on the morning of Thanksgiving Day in New York City is a major TV event for the whole nation.

Meal. The afternoon or evening meal is the main event of Thanksgiving Day. It usually consists of turkey and stuffing, cranberry sauce, mashed potatoes, sweet potatoes or yams and vegetables, followed by a dessert of pumpkin pie or apple pie.

Decorations. Homes are decorated with autumn colours and/or harvest displays, including Indian corn cobs or the Horn of Plenty.

Pageants. Pageants depicting the story of the Pilgrims are often performed in schools.

Sport. Thanksgiving is a special day for sport. There are always a couple of major professional football games on TV, as well as college playoff games. It is a day for spectator sport only, and football is the main sport which Americans associate with Thanksgiving.

Festivals of Other Religions

In most countries in the West people are gradually becoming aware of the festivals of the other world religions, such as the Jewish New Year and the Hindu festival of Diwali. It is important to be aware of the main festivals of some of the religions, because they help people from one religious tradition to understand what it's like to belong to another. It is also important to notice how much these festivals have in common with the traditional festivals, both religious and secular, of the Western world. Each religion has its own way of marking the changing seasons, and of remembering the most significant events, stories or ideas on which it is based.

Conclusions

Festivals meet real human needs. People have to have festivals! All the festivals described are related to one or more of the basic needs noted at the beginning of this chapter.

Seasons. May Day marks the beginning of summer; Harvest and Hallowe'en come at the end of summer and beginning of winter; and Christmas is a mid-winter festival.

Personal needs. St Valentine's Day is about the need to choose a mate or a lover, and Mother's Day is for honouring mothers. Thanksgiving is partly a family reunion.

Nation and society. The special days for patron saints give an opportunity for people to express their pride in their nation. Other civic festivals, such as the American Independence Day, have a similar function.

Meaning. Every religion has its stories which are retold and re-enacted at different times of the year. The birth, death and resurrection of Jesus are important for Christians. Many festivals therefore celebrate the events or the ideas which provide the vital clues to the meaning of the universe.

There is much in Western culture which is a mixture of pagan and Christian elements. The names of several days of the week, for example, come from the gods of pre-Christian Europe. Customs such as giving gifts at the mid-winter festival have come down from the Romans, and folklore is full of characters like fairies and giants which come from the Celts or the Norsemen.

'Commercialism' is playing a more and more significant role in the celebration of festivals. There's money to be made out of the celebration of festivals, and preparations for them appear in the shops long before the festival date. Cards, presents and knick-knacks will all find purchasers. It's impossible to ignore the financial factor which keeps festivals going!

Questions

▶ Is it *Christianity or is it paganism that is winning the battle for the soul of the Western world*? Looking at festivals and understanding their origins and development over the years shows that a struggle has been going on for centuries between Christianity and the older and newer forms of paganism. It is intriguing to speculate about how this conflict will develop. Which will capture the minds and hearts of the majority?

▶ What *do people have to celebrate*? People celebrate the changing seasons of the year and national festivals. But is there anything more to celebrate? What if these words from the book of Ecclesiastes in the Bible express the feeling of the modern person? 'Utterly meaningless! Everything is meaningless.'

Facing: **Every American town enjoys a firework display on the Fourth of July, to celebrate American Independence.**

3 Rites of Passage and Other Rituals

There are three important days in a person's life: the day of birth, the day of marriage, and the day of death. We are not old enough to celebrate the first and not around for the last, so we make the most of our marriages.

A South Indian villager

Men and women are not simply born, nor do they merely procreate and die; they are made what they are through ceremonies.

Encyclopedia of Religion

As a social animal, man is a ritual animal… Social rituals create a reality which would be nothing without them. It is not too much to say that ritual is more to society than words are to thought. For it is possible to know something and then find words for it. But it is impossible to have social relations without symbolic acts.

Mary Douglas

Man's chief end is to glorify God and enjoy him for ever.
Westminster Shorter Catechism

'Rites of passage' is a term which refers to *rites*, or rituals, which mark the *passage* of a person from one stage of life to another, or from one role to another. The term was first coined by the anthropologist Arnold van Gennep in 1909, and has been used widely since then in studying the customs of different cultures all over the world.

One could say that life is one long succession of ritual actions—like shaking hands when meeting someone for the first time, saying good morning, kissing, saying goodbye, saluting the flag, giving prizes at school or at a sports day, or capping students with a hood or giving them a certificate when they graduate from college or university. It's hard to imagine what life would be like if people didn't have rituals of this kind! Many of the rites that we are concerned with here, however, are related to birth, marriage and death, the three most significant events in a life.

These rites of passage combine one or more simple ritual actions with words that interpret the action. It is through this combination of actions and words in these ceremonies in every culture that people say something about the meaning of life, and are 'made what they are'.

These are the kind of questions being asked in this chapter:

▶ *What are the main rites of passage which have developed within the Christian tradition in the Western world?*

▶ *What is the ritual in each case and how does it express what is happening?*

▶ *What are the words which interpret the ritual and explain what is happening?*

Major Rites of Passage

The variety of lifestyles in modern Western culture has made even the three major rites of passage something that people can choose not to follow. Nevertheless, many people still do seek to have a formal ceremony at major transitional stages in their lives.

Baptism

People generally think of baptism as something that happens to babies. However, baptism differs from most other rites performed on young children, which are specifically designed as *birth* rites. Baptism, by contrast, is essentially a rite for *adults*, though it is now used for children as well. In the New Testament all the people whose baptisms are described are adults. In fact there are no descriptions of babies or children being baptized at all, though many Christians believe that when the baptism of a whole household or family is mentioned, it must have included the children as well.

The origins of Christian baptism can be traced back to John the Baptist (or John the Baptizer as he should be called). John was a relation of Jesus and only a few months older than him. The Gospels describe him as the last of the prophets foretold by God, whose task was to prepare the people of Israel for the coming of God's Chosen One—the Messiah—Jesus Christ. When he came to manhood, John began teaching near the banks of the River Jordan, telling people to give up their old wrong ways of living and prepare themselves for the coming of the Messiah. And the way that they were to show their sorrow for their sins and the fact that they were awaiting the Messiah was by being baptized in the Jordan. This probably meant wading out into the river and being immersed in the water, or else having water poured over them by John. The Gospels tell us that many people took seriously what John said and were baptized.

No one knows how John came to use immersion in water as the mark of those who wanted to prepare themselves for the Messiah's coming, though it may have been linked to a rite used when non-Jews wished to become Jews.

Some time later when Jesus began his teaching and healing, the first thing that he did was to go to John to be baptized by him. It was a very special occasion, for it showed that he identified himself with sinners. Jesus heard a voice from heaven saying, 'This is my beloved Son: listen to him,' and the Holy Spirit, the power and presence of God, entered him.

After Jesus rose from the dead, he commanded his disciples to baptize anyone who came to believe in him. From that time on, baptism has been the distinctive mark of a disciple of Jesus Christ—a Christian.

In the first few centuries after Christ, to be baptized could cost a person their life, as it still can today in a few countries. To accept baptism meant to be clearly identified as a Christian, and hence liable to persecution when the state turned hostile. So people who wanted to become Christians usually underwent a preparation course lasting up to three years and were then baptized secretly at dawn, often on Easter day. Couples with children would have their children, even tiny babies, baptized with them. If a child was too young to speak and make the promises, a parent or close friend made them on his or her behalf.

Once the emperors became Christian in the fourth century, however, it became an advantage to be baptized. Gradually more and more people were baptized in Europe until, over several centuries, the entire population (with a few exceptions, for example Jews) became at least nominally Christian. All parents had their children baptized automatically when they were a few days old, especially when it began to be thought that those who were not baptized would not go to heaven when they died. Many churches still baptize infants but others, in the Baptist tradition which is particularly strong in the United States, only baptize adults.

At baptism, right from the early Christian centuries, those being baptized have been asked important questions. When infants are baptized their parents and godparents answer for them, as those who will bring them up in Christian faith. One set of questions is about their decision to follow Christ:

▶ Do you turn to Christ?

▶ Do you repent of your sins?

▶ Do you renounce evil?

The other set is about central beliefs:

▶ Do you believe and trust in God the Father, who made the world?

▶ Do you believe and trust in his Son Jesus Christ, who redeemed mankind?

▶ Do you believe and trust in his Holy Spirit, who gives life to the people of God?

The person is then baptized with water in the name of God the Father, Son and Holy Spirit. The water pictures the promises of God to believers in Jesus Christ: having your sins cleansed and forgiven; dying to sin and coming alive to Christ; receiving the life-giving Holy Spirit...

Confirmation

Most people think of confirmation as the service in which teenagers who have been baptized as babies make in their own name the promises that their parents and godparents made on their behalf when they were baptized. If they are members of the Roman Catholic or Anglican churches, the promises are made in front of a bishop who will then lay his hands on their heads and pray for them, and perhaps also anoint them with oil. If they belong to a church which does not have bishops, either a senior minister or the local minister may lay on hands or else shake hands with the candidates. After being confirmed the candidate is reckoned a full member of the church, and is allowed to receive holy communion. (In Baptist churches the whole thing happens when an adult is baptized; they don't have confirmation.)

This familiar idea of confirmation bears no relation to the origins of the rite in the early church, and is being widely challenged in many parts of the world today. Just as baptism originally was not a birth rite at all, so confirmation in its earliest stages had no connection with puberty. It was not meant as a parallel to coming-of-age ceremonies which happen in many other countries. In order to understand the issues, it is necessary to examine how confirmation developed.

From the texts that survive, it is known that by the third century the simple immersion in water had become surrounded by a number of other ceremonies designed to express various aspects of what becoming a Christian meant. One such ceremony was to present the candidates to the head of the local Christian community, the bishop, who would lay his hands on their heads and pray that the Holy Spirit would dwell in them. Often he would anoint them with specially perfumed oil (called *chrism*), since oil in the Bible is often used to symbolize the Holy Spirit. At the end of the whole series of ceremonies (which were usually performed at dawn) the new Christians joined the existing congregation, who greeted them with a kiss of peace, before they all shared the holy communion together for the first time.

The Eastern Orthodox churches (in Greece and the Soviet Union, for example) have always kept all the ceremonies together as they had originally been. However, instead of having the bishop physically present each time, the local presbyter anoints the candidate after the baptism with oil that has been previously blessed and distributed by the bishop. So, at the end of the service, the candidate (of whatever age) is a full Christian and able to receive holy communion. Children from their baptism and chrismation have always been communicant members of the church, and grow up receiving the bread and wine. There is

therefore no ceremony for them to go through as teenagers or later.

In the Western church, a different pattern eventually developed. Because bishops could only visit the many churches occasionally, and bishops were thought essential for the laying-on-of-hands, confirmation became separated from baptism.

This of course raised the question as to whether a person who was unconfirmed (especially if it was through no fault of their own) could receive holy communion. In many places people did. So today, in many parts of the Roman Catholic Church, young people may be admitted to communion at about seven years of age but not confirmed until into their teens. The 'first communion' has become a very special occasion.

In England, however, no one could receive communion unless they had been confirmed. Children were also to learn to say the Hail Mary, the Lord's Prayer and the creed before they could be confirmed, usually at or around the age of seven. This was supported by the

Facing: A baptism in the sea off Barbados, held by the Spiritual Baptist church. Baptist churches only baptize adults, and they do it by 'total immersion', as the new believer is lowered right under the water. Baptisms most commonly happen in the 'baptistry' in church, but occasionally in rivers or in the sea.

Above: A baby is baptized. The minister—in this case a bishop—pours water on the infant's head. Often the minister then makes the sign of the cross on the baby's forehead.

idea around at the time that the most important aspect of the rite was the fact that the young person 'confirmed' that they believed the faith into which they had been baptized.

When the Church of England and some of the Protestant churches came into existence at the Reformation, many of them continued this pattern, though they usually raised the age of confirmation (or whatever name they gave it) to twelve, and required the children to learn the answers to a set of questions about the Christian faith: the catechism.

So, from being a brief part of the early church's baptismal rite, confirmation became in most of the Western churches almost a 'reward' for young teenagers for getting the answers to the catechism right, and an entrance ticket to holy communion.

An advantage of this pattern is that if the decision is to baptize babies, they need the opportunity when they grow up to 'stand up and be counted': to say that they themselves believe in Jesus Christ and wish to be his disciples for the rest of their lives. Confirmation provides that opportunity.

But, against this, there are only the barest signs of confirmation in the New Testament, and confirmation historically has nothing to do with puberty or teenage. It is therefore a very unsatisfactory rite of passage, because it is not designed to help a young person into adult life.

As one might expect, the present situation regarding confirmation is very confused. In many places the traditional Roman Catholic and Anglican patterns continue. Some churches stress the importance of adult profession of faith and make people wait until they are seventeen or eighteen before they are confirmed. Others are admitting children to communion (with or without confirmation) at a much earlier age—seven, five, or even lower. Some people are arguing for a return to the early and Orthodox practice of confirming a baby at its baptism by anointing with oil blessed by a bishop, and then possibly having an opportunity for an adult profession of faith many years later.

Sometimes these different patterns are found in different parishes or congregations of the same denomination. One thing seems to be certain: there is more and more dissatisfaction with the traditional practice of confirmation in early teens. It looks as though, whatever else happens to confirmation, its days as a puberty rite of passage are numbered.

Marriage

Unlike baptism and confirmation, marriage is not a uniquely Christian institution. Even within the biblical tradition, there were marriages long before the time of

'First communion', as here at the church of St Severin in Paris, is a very important event in the life of a Roman Catholic child. Children are usually admitted to communion at the age of seven, even though not confirmed until their teens.

Jesus, and, of course, different religions and cultures around the world have their own particular marriage customs, many of them very ancient. Indeed, it is not easy to define precisely what is a 'Christian wedding'. It might be easiest to begin by describing what might be called a typical church wedding in the Western world and then look at the various parts in detail.

The bride and groom's relatives and friends gather at the church, which may well be decorated with flowers especially for the occasion. The priest or minister, sometimes with a choir, waits for the bride to enter the church. The bride is accompanied by her father, or a close male relative or friend, and she walks up the aisle to the front of the church building with her arm through his. She is dressed in a long white dress and wears a head-dress and veil. She will be carrying a bouquet of flowers and will be accompanied by several girls or young women—her bridesmaids—who will also be in special dresses and carrying bouquets. Having arrived at the front of the church, the bride stands on the left of her husband-to-be, still attended by her father. The best man stands on the groom's right, and the bridesmaids line up behind.

The priest then speaks to the congregation about the Christian understanding of marriage. He then asks the man if he will take the woman as his wife and be faithful to her until they are parted by death. The bride is then asked if she will take the man as her husband on the same terms. (In the United States these questions are usually taken up into the 'promises'.) Once they have both publicly given their consent to marry each other, the bride's father 'gives the bride away' by passing his daughter's hand to the priest, who passes it on to the groom to hold. While still holding hands, the bride and groom face each other and repeat after the priest a series of promises to each other, to be faithful and support each other in sickness and health, poverty and wealth. The 'best man', a close friend of the bridegroom, then produces a ring (or often nowadays two rings). The minister blesses these and the couple place one on the third finger of each other's left hand. The minister then joins their hands together and pronounces them husband and wife. The couple then kneel down for a blessing.

A hymn is often sung and prayers are said. In Britain the couple must sign the marriage register. Afterwards, while photographs are being taken, the church bells may be rung. The couple may be showered with confetti (in Britain) or rice or birdseed (in America). Once the photographs are over, the couple and guests usually attend a special meal, the reception, where speeches are made, the wedding cake cut and toasts proposed. Further presents may also be given. After the reception, the couple usually change and leave for the place where they will spend their wedding night. The couple will usually spend at least several days on holiday—their honeymoon—before returning to their new home and beginning 'ordinary' life together.

Most of the above ingredients are present at weddings whether they are small affairs in little village churches or huge ceremonies such as that of the Prince and Princess of Wales in St Paul's Cathedral in London in 1981, which was watched by millions of people world-wide. Indeed, many features are commonly thought to be essential for a 'proper' wedding. Nowadays many marriages take place in registry offices, town halls or private homes (in fact a 'civil wedding' is the rule in many European countries; a church wedding is sometimes held in addition). But quite often features of the church wedding which are not at all necessary for the wedding to be legal—for example, the wedding dress, bridesmaids, best man, flowers, decorated cars—are seen and felt to be very important at registry offices.

Most services performed in church can be traced back directly to the New Testament. Baptism and the eucharist in particular can be traced back to specific commands of Jesus himself and hence their content and the way in which they are understood are unique to Christianity. The same is not quite true of the marriage service, however. True, it does contain a lot of emphases that are uniquely Christian, but much of the service and certainly of the various customs which surround it are adaptations of some of the wedding practices of the Roman Empire. The church had not felt it necessary to scrap the wedding customs of non-Christians completely, except when they were clearly contrary to Christian teaching. Sometimes they did remove offensive practices and replace them with Christian equivalents (see below), but generally they simply continued existing customs, reinterpreting them in the light of the gospel. This approach continues today: in Africa, for example, the churches are trying to find ways to combine the best of local marriage customs with Christian teaching.

Jesus' first disciples were Jews and, as far as we can tell, it was perfectly natural for them to continue to perform events such as weddings just as they had always done, but no doubt with some references to Jesus in the prayers.

Unfortunately, the Bible does not give us a description of a wedding service as it might have been in Jesus' day. All that can be done is attempt to reconstruct what probably happened from scattered references in the Old and New Testaments. The wedding customs of modern Jews give us some further clues, but their customs too have altered over the centuries. Even so, it is interesting how many of the features of the typical wedding described earlier can be found. There were two main stages.

A newly–wed couple sign the marriage register at a wedding service in a London church. Many couples like to make their promises 'before God' in church.

First came the betrothal. This was a little like a modern engagement, but was much more than a private affair between two individuals. Both families were involved—indeed, the parents of the couple may well have negotiated the marriage. As the girl's family were losing the value of the work that she did in the home, the groom's family handed over various goods or money to compensate. A written contract may have been drawn up, setting out the expectations of both sides. Because of all this family involvement, betrothal was seen as binding and could only be broken by a process very similar to divorce.

The wedding itself took place at a variable time after the betrothal. If the couple had been betrothed as children, the wedding might not take place for many years. There was a procession of the bride, dressed in festal clothes and attended by several maidens, to the groom's house. He, too, seems to have had several attendants. A blessing was almost certainly invoked on the couple, and there was a long feast to which guests were invited.

As more and more non-Jews within the Roman Empire became Christians, it was natural that their weddings should show more and more features from their own background. We have already seen how some of the customs of modern marriages go back to Jewish times; even more stem from Roman practice.

This is especially true of the understanding of marriage itself. the Jewish ethos tended to emphasize not only the need for the couple to be faithful to each other but also fertility—the importance of having children to carry on the race of the Chosen People, as they saw themselves. Both these aspects were present in the Roman understanding of marriage, but there was also a much greater emphasis on the idea of contract: marriage was at heart an agreement into which two people entered freely. This is the reason for the basic structure of the marriage service described above. The man states publicly that he will take the woman as his wife, and the woman says that she will take the man as her husband on the same terms. Having heard this, the bride's father can, with a clear conscience, 'give her away'—in other words, hand her over to the man she has chosen. The couple then make promises to each other: 'I, John/Mary, take you, Mary/John, to be my wife/husband...for better for worse...' Strictly speaking, they are not married by the minister at all—they marry each other.

Most of the rites we call sacraments have to be performed by somebody who is ordained (only a priest can celebrate the eucharist and so on) but in marriage it is the couple themselves who perform the sacrament. The minister, however, still has an important role to play. The passing of the bride's right hand by her father to the minister who then passes it to the groom symbolizes the idea that it is God who gives the couple to each other. It is he who has guided their choice and who now brings them together. This is emphasized when the minister joins the couple's hands together after they have made their promises, pronouncing them husband and wife and saying, 'That which God has joined together, let not man divide.' And he blesses them in God's name. Clearly this symbolism makes most sense if the couple are committed Christians and have actively sought God's help in the choice of a life partner.

Many other features of our modern weddings also go back to the practices of the first five centuries or so of the Roman Empire. Like the Jews, the Romans had a betrothal some time before the wedding itself, and it seems that one of the aspects of this ceremony was the giving of a ring to the bride. Once betrothed, a girl would wear a veil to show her new status. The veil was meant to symbolise her virginity, as was the white dress that she

A coffin is borne to the graveside in a Cornish village churchyard; a lifeboatman has died in the course of a rescue.   **The burial service is a focus of the grief of the bereaved, but also of hope in Christ.**

wore. Sometimes, during the actual wedding, a large veil was spread over both bride and groom. The 'giving away' of the bride by her father also seems to come from this period.

Originally, as with the Jews, marriages generally took place in the home but, as time went on, there was an increasing tendency for them to take place in church, and gradually this became an almost invariable rule. This enabled another important development to take place. Pagan couples were expected to offer a sacrifice to the gods on the day of their wedding. Christians instead substituted the eucharist for the sacrifice; and so the wedding in church would lead naturally on, after the blessing of the couple by the priest, to the receiving of holy communion. This custom still continues in the Nuptial Mass of the Roman Catholic Church. At the Reformation the practice virtually ceased in the Anglican and Protestant churches but today some couples still request it, especially in the United States.

One custom which used to form an important part of the marriage ceremonies has now virtually disappeared: in some places and for many centuries the bridal chamber was prepared and blessed. This was the room in which the couple were to consummate their marriage. It was frequently specially decorated, often with flowers, and the couple were escorted there—and sometimes even placed in the bed itself—by the guests. There were then several prayers by the priest before the guests all left and returned to the feast.

Funeral

In recent years death has been the subject that no one wants to talk about. In some ways it is true that what we have today is the opposite of the situation of a hundred years ago. Then, our Victorian ancestors seemed almost to have relished death; they read accounts of deathbed scenes, and had a whole range of customs associated with death and mourning. It was sex that was the taboo subject. Today we live in a society where sex is much more prominent—from advertising to AIDS warnings—but death is certainly not an acceptable topic of conversation. Anyone who mentions it is likely to be accused of being 'morbid'.

In many ways this is because death has become a very private affair. In the old days a person usually died at home with his or her family gathered around, and perhaps the minister also present. The body stayed in the home until the day of the funeral, and friends and relatives might come to 'view' it. The funeral service usually took place in the local church or chapel, and the deceased was buried in the local graveyard or cemetery. The whole village or locality would be aware of what was going on. After the funeral, it was accepted

as only natural that the closest relatives would wear black clothing for several months or more, and would not be ashamed to show their grief by, for example, using black-edged notepaper for writing letters.

Nowadays things are very different. In Western countries most people die in hospital. If the hospital is far from the family home, often the relatives will not be able to get there in time to be present at the actual death. The body will be cleaned and prepared by hospital staff or the undertaker, not by family or local women. The funeral service is quite likely to be conducted at a church, funeral parlour or crematorium which may be far from the deceased's home. If the body is to be cremated, the coffin will simply 'disappear from view' at the crematorium chapel, and, even if it is a burial, lingering at the graveside is likely to be discouraged. After the funeral is all over, the surviving spouse is expected to 'snap out of it' and to 'get back to normal' as soon as possible.

All these changes have of course had a great effect on today's funeral customs. Even the churches have tended to simplify their funeral services to make them 'nicer' and 'less of a strain' on the mourners.

As with the marriage service, the early Christians seem to have taken over many features of Jewish and Roman practice, but with some important modifications. There are even a few points at which Christianity was unable to modify existing customs.

Traditional Christian burial rites tend to have four parts: in the home at the time of death, a service in church, at the grave, and some sort of memorial service some time later. As the body has to be moved from the house to the church and then to the grave, processions form an important part of the ceremonies, though nowadays modern transport has changed things considerably.

The pagan Romans had taken over from the ancient Greeks the idea that after death the soul was rowed across the River Styx to the Underworld by Charon the ferryman, and so they would place a coin in the dead person's mouth as his *viaticum*, the fee that he would need on his journey. Early Christians were accustomed to speak of holy communion as the 'medicine of immortality' and it came to be thought a good thing to receive communion as soon before death as possible, and even to die with the sacrament in one's mouth, very much as the equivalent of Charon's fee. In fact the name *viaticum* came to be used of the last administration of communion to a dying person.

After a person had died, the body was washed and clothed. Both Jews and pagans used to hire professional mourners—'wailing women' who would cry and wail while this was being done. But there are records that early Christians were forbidden to hire them, and told to sing psalms instead. The pagan Romans used to have their funerals mainly at night and to wear black clothes. Again, we know that in some places early Christians were forbidden to wear black, and told to wear white instead and to carry green branches as a sign of their belief in the resurrection. It is interesting that the wearing of black is one custom which the church was unable to change and even today men feel that they should wear a dark suit and black tie, and women dark or black clothes.

In church the service traditionally had a great deal of singing, again a contrast with the wailing of the pagans. The deceased person was commended to God in confidence that he or she was still in his keeping. Any grief was because the separation was hard to bear, not because there was no hope. As time went on it became common to have a celebration of the eucharist at the funeral. At this these words were repeated: *Requiem aeternam dona ei, Domine, et lux perpetua in ei luceat* ('Rest eternal grant unto him, O Lord, and let light perpetual shine upon him'). From the first word of this we get the phrase 'Requiem Mass'.

From church the body was taken to the grave. The Romans used to cremate their dead on an open funeral pyre (as has been done for centuries in India). Christians, however, like the Jews before them, traditionally buried their dead as an expression of their belief that their bodies would be raised at the Last Day when Christ returns to judge humanity. Indeed, in some places the belief in the resurrection of the body has been so strong that old people have saved their teeth as they fell out and had them buried with them so that they would have a full set at the resurrection! However, unlike many pagan peoples who buried various weapons and possessions with the deceased person for use by him or her in the afterlife, Christians usually included no grave goods. Their understanding of the life to come certainly involved their bodies, but it was not simply a new version of life on this earth.

Today, many Western Christians believe that the body's part in God's purposes ends in death, and so they are not particularly concerned that it must be buried. Cremation is therefore becoming an increasingly popular alternative. If God can bring together the scattered dust and bones of long-dead Christians, so the argument goes, he can do the same with the ashes of cremation. However, cremation has only been allowed to Roman Catholics since 1963, and is still unusual among Orthodox Christians.

After the committal, it was usual to have a meal and this continues to this day. Sometimes the immediate relatives might have been fasting since the death, and there was always the need to show hospitality to those who had come to attend. The pagans seem to have believed that in some way the dead person took part in and benefitted from these meals, and they took place at least annually at the grave (the Chinese have a similar custom today). There are even cases where there is a hole in the wall of the tomb into which food and drink can be poured! Often these feasts turned into riotous and drunken occasions, and church leaders condemned them. As a substitute Christians would celebrate the eucharist (sometimes on the tomb itself). This was especially likely to happen if the dead person was particularly holy or had been killed for the faith.

Worship

In most Western countries a significant proportion of people still go to church regularly on Sundays. It is the most visible way of identifying Christians. So important is it to go to church that Christians in some parts of the world will often risk harassment, fines or imprisonment to do so. But what do they go for? What do they do when they get there?

Between the many sections of the Christian church there are great differences in forms of worship. At one end of the range there is rich ceremonial with features such as incense; at the other come extremely simple services with virtually no extras at all. Within this wide range there are a number of common features which occur in the main Sunday worship of virtually all Christian groups, though the proportion and frequency may vary. These common features can be summarized as:

▶ Praise

▶ Word

▶ Prayers

▶ Eucharist

Praise. People all respond to things they find particularly beautiful, lovely or impressive. They are moved by the sight of a huge mountain or a delicate flower; poets write in praise of courage; song-writers compose songs that people enjoy because they say the things they want to say about the people they love.

In a similar way Christians praise God for his greatness and love. Perhaps the most common way of doing this is through 'hymns'—specially composed songs, usually of several verses. Singing can help people express their deepest feelings, and for Christians to sing about God reminds them of what he is like and uplifts them. Christian praise has perhaps one important difference: it is something that Christians believe they owe God, no matter what they happen to feel like. Singing in particular can be something that people do to show they are happy, but for Christians

God is still great and good and holy, even if they are feeling down or are in difficulties, and therefore he deserves their praises even then.

Word. Although the Christian faith is centred on a person, Jesus Christ, the record of his life, the long preparation for it and what happened as a result are contained in a book, the Bible. The Bible is read by millions of Christians in private, but also one or more passages are nearly always read in Sunday worship. In some churches (for example Presbyterian or Orthodox) the Bible may be carried in procession to emphasize its importance. Often it is read from a special stand or 'lectern'. After the reading of a portion of the Bible one of the leaders of the congregation will explain it, trying to draw out its relevance for today. This is called the 'sermon' and in many churches, Protestant ones in particular, it is the 'high point' of the service.

Prayer. Prayer is two-way conversation with God. Christians pray privately, and prayer forms part of all acts of worship. Usually a minister will pray at several points in the service in the name of the congregation (either using his own words or a set form). Many churches also provide the opportunity for the whole congregation to join together in saying a prayer (the Lord's Prayer is usually said this way). Sometimes one or more 'ordinary' members of the congregation may lead in prayer at certain points.

One of the most important types of prayer in Christian worship is 'intercession'. This is praying to God on behalf of other people or situations. Christians are commanded in the Bible to pray for governments and rulers, for the sick and needy, and in fact for any situation. Though it is difficult to explain how prayer 'works', Christians believe that as a result of prayer God's activity in the world can often be more clearly seen.

Eucharist. Many Christians would describe this as the central act of Christian worship. The vast majority of Christians believe that at his last earthly meal with his disciples ('the Last Supper') Jesus commanded them to continue meeting together and eating and drinking two of the ingredients of that meal—bread and wine. By doing this they were to remember for all time his death on the cross for them. He also spoke of the bread as 'my body' and the wine as 'my blood'.

Over the centuries this meal has taken many forms and acquired many different names—Lord's Supper, Holy Communion, Mass, the Liturgy. 'Eucharist' (from a Greek word meaning 'thanksgiving') is now widely accepted. At times the element of eating has almost been lost in elaborate ceremonial and an exaggerated awe of the actual elements of bread and wine. Some Christians talk of a change taking place in the elements, so that they become in a very real sense the Body and Blood of Christ. Others would see the essential change as being a spiritual one in the worshipper, while yet others seem to say that the meal is simply a reminder, and no 'changes' take place at all.

The actual frequency with which different churches hold the eucharist also varies. For many it is always the main Sunday service. Some will also celebrate it daily throughout the week. Others will have it monthly or less. Despite all these differences, however, most Christians would agree that the eucharist is very important to them. In this service they feel close to Jesus who died for them, and are given strength to live their daily lives.

Other church ceremonies

When a new church is built, there is a service of *consecration*, in which the building is dedicated or 'set apart' for its special purpose. When something new is introduced into the church—such as a new organ or new vessels for the communion service—there may be a brief ceremony of *dedication*. (These terms are interchangeable in some churches.)

When a new minister or priest comes to a church, there is a service of *induction* (sometimes *installation*) in which he or she is welcomed and officially installed. It sometimes includes a procession round the different parts of the church in which the responsibilities of the minister are explained.

At an *ordination*, which is held in a church or a cathedral, men and (in several churches) women are ordained to become deacons, priests or ministers. The main part of the service consists in the laying on of hands by the bishops or other ministers as a sign of commissioning for the work they are undertaking. When other church workers are appointed or sent out by a church, there is often a service of *commissioning*.

Healing services are becoming more and more common. People come forward for special prayer for healing, and hands are laid on them. In some cases the priest puts a touch of olive oil on their forehead.

There are also special services associated with the different festivals of the church year. These are described in the chapter on festivals.

Conclusions

Some parts of these rituals have a distinctively Christian meaning, while others have little to do with Christianity. Baptism expresses what it means to be received as a member of the family of God through faith in Jesus Christ. The service of holy communion focuses on the death and resurrection of Jesus and points forward to the time when his kingship will be established over the whole world.

By contrast, what is distinctively Christian about our wedding and funeral services is the words that go with the rituals. In a Christian wedding there is a clear recognition of God as the Creator who has given us the institution of marriage, and of Jesus as the one who reveals the love of God. In a Christian funeral there is the reminder that death is not the end, because Christ through his resurrection has taken the sting out of death.

For many people the words are hardly important. It is the ritual itself that is important, and people feel free to attach their own meaning to it.

Some parents who bring their baby for baptism may not understand all the words that are said or the promises they are making. Many couples who are married in churches would not call themselves Christians, and some might say that they hardly believe in God.

It is important, however, that we don't write off people's desire for a religious ceremony as nothing but 'going through the motions', 'pleasing the family' or '-conforming to tradition'. There are often deeper instincts and desires at work, as Derek Murray, a hospital chaplain, explains about his work in a hospice:

'*It might be suggested that dying, or the involvement with a dying relative, is one of the most religious episodes in any life. Mysterious forces, however explained by the doctors, are at work, and there is about to be a journey into the unknown. Even the hardest and the most cynical feel that it is worth taking out a little insurance, so there is a demand for prayers to the unknown God. But there is more to it than that. There is often a quite genuine desire to commend a soul to its maker, and a real apprehension of the numinous when death is threatened... The subject of dying brings out latent but deeply held beliefs...*'

Questions

▶ *How deep is religious feeling in Western countries?* Today only a small percentage of people in the West claim to be Christians. Yet, for example, in England today approximately 40 per cent of babies are baptized in church, about 15 per cent of people attend church regularly (in the United States this is over 50 per cent), over 60 per cent are married in church, and well over 90 per cent receive Christian burial.

Do we conclude that it is more than tradition and conformity which makes people come to church for these ceremonies?

▶ *How should the church respond to this situation?* Should it discourage people from coming to church for rites of passage, on the grounds that they are 'not sincere' in what they are doing and are merely 'using' the church?

Should they welcome anyone and everyone without asking too many questions about what they believe? As Derek Murray asks concerning the dying, 'Are we able to accept the short-circuiting of normal religious educational processes, and assure the dying of God's love?'

Or should they have a more cautious approach, appreciating the instincts that lead people to come to church, but also trying to lead them to a deeper understanding of the Christian faith?

▶ *What are the alternatives to these rites of passage?* There is no secular alternative to baptism in our Western societies. Giving a baby a name is simply a matter of filling in a form to register the birth; it's as simple as that, and there's no ritual involved. A civil marriage includes the giving and receiving of promises, which are required by law, but there is naturally no mention of God. At a 'secular' funeral, kind words may be said about the dead person. But it is hard to see what, if anything, can be said about the life after death.

▶ *Is worship a waste of time or is it what people were made for?* Some would say that worship is a meaningless exercise because there's no one there to communicate with. Others would say that even if people don't know for certain whether there is anyone there, worship can be valuable because of what it does for *them*, in giving them peace of mind, for example. The alternative to these attitudes is to believe that people are all religious beings, whether they like it or not, and that, as the Shorter Catechism says, 'Man's chief end is to glorify God and enjoy him for ever.'

4 Saints

The original English word for what we now call a saint was 'hallow', which still survives in phrases like All Hallows and Hallowe'en, but in the Middle Ages 'hallow' was replaced by the French word 'saint', which itself comes from the Latin *sanctus*. This was the word which early Christian Roman writers used to translate a word from the New Testament meaning 'holy'.

'Holy' is a very difficult word to define. In the Bible the basic idea is of being set apart, specially reserved for God. To say that somebody is a saint means that they are special because they belong to God.

Nowadays people are used to thinking of only a limited number of people being Saints (with a capital S), but in the New Testament all Christians are described as saints, because everybody who believes in Jesus Christ belongs to God in a special way. In this sense every modern Christian can rightly be described as a saint. Over the centuries, however, the popular understanding of the word changed.

Saints and Martyrs

One major factor which tended to create a class of 'super-Christians' was the persecution which produced 'martyrs'. *Martyr* is a Greek word meaning 'witness', which soon came to be applied in a special way to those Christians who bore witness to their faith by being prepared to die rather than give up their faith in Christ. The popular image of early Christians being persecuted and thrown to the lions does in fact show something that really happened. From time to time over three hundred years, Christians in the Roman Empire were liable to be arrested, tortured and killed by the pagan authorities who tried to make them worship their gods. To the

Christians to die in this way was a great honour, because it meant that they were closely imitating Christ who himself was tortured and killed. Surviving Christians often wrote down accounts of the trial and death of their fellows, and many such accounts have survived.

After this period of persecution the word 'Saint' came to be applied also to Christians who seemed better than others in certain respects. Following the adoption of Christianity as the official religion of the Roman Empire in the fourth century, many people joined the church who were very lukewarm in their beliefs and in the depth of their faith and commitment. Compared to the somewhat lower 'spiritual temperature' that this produced, the lives of those who really took their faith seriously stood out more clearly.

Another factor was the way in which outstanding Christians in some sense took the place of the earlier gods and heroes of pagan religion. Pagan religion in the classical world was full of beings who were either semi-divine (through having one parent a mortal and the other a god), or were granted the gift of immortality. Such figures (often called 'heroes') formed an intermediate group between ordinary men and women and the far-off, powerful gods. Being halfway between mortals and the greater gods, they stood in an excellent position to intervene on behalf of an individual, a group or a city.

In pre-Christian days localities or cities often had their own local deity who was believed to protect and guard his or her own people. Sometimes the supposed dwelling of such a god or spirit was a natural feature, such as a well. With the coming of Christianity, however, the instinctive desire for a local protector was sometimes transferred to a local Christian of prominence—perhaps the person who first preached the Gospel in the area. And not infrequently elements of the old pagan belief became mixed up in the tales of this local figure. This is no doubt the background to the idea that a country needs to have a patron saint.

Tom Corfe's summary of the story of St Bridget provides an example of how this process worked in the years after St Patrick brought Christianity to Ireland:

'Saint Bridget, it is said, was born about twenty years after Patrick's death: but we know almost nothing about her life, nothing that we can be really sure about. What we do know is that the Celts of Britain and Ireland had long worshipped a powerful goddess who was usually called in Ireland Brigid... Men invoked Brigid's help to protect their flocks and herds and bring increase, to inspire poetry and grant wisdom and skill in craftsmanship, to heal the sick and comfort the dying. She was all-powerful and ever-helpful...'

Patrick and his followers could not deny that so useful and helpful a spirit existed. So she came to be identified with a Christian saint. Saint Bridget's festival is celebrated in February, as Brigid's had been. The saint's shrine, with an ever-burning fire tended by virgins, was at Kildare, where formerly there had been a pagan sanctuary; the very name Kildare means 'the church of the oak-tree'. Saint Bridget's miracles took the place of the goddess's magic. Saint Bridget cared for the sick and poor, guided poets, wise men and craftsmen, protected the cattle and made the land productive; and she still does. Saint Bridget's crosses are still plaited out of straw throughout Ireland and set up over the doorways of houses and byres to bring luck and safety.

Once Christianity had become the official religion of the Roman Empire, the number of martyrdoms naturally declined dramatically, though there were still some among the barbarian tribes to the north or in the Persian Empire to the east. By now the church had got used to the idea of 'first-class Christians' who stood out from the rest and began to treat individuals whose lives had been particularly good or holy with the respect which formerly had been reserved for those who had died a martyr's death. This thinking has had both good and bad results:

On the positive side, the example of countless men, women and children down the ages, who have held firm to their faith and overcome all manner of temptations, has undoubtedly been an enormous encouragement to other Christians in their own times of difficulty.

Negatively, the creation of a sort of spiritual hierarchy has tended to encourage 'ordinary' Christians to think that they are not in the same league in God's eyes and to be content with a lower level of commitment. In addition to this, the Saints all too easily become seen as intermediaries between the ordinary believer and God. They seem easier to approach and all too often Christians have contented themselves with praying to a Saint (usually the Virgin Mary) rather than directly to God through Christ. This seems a lower form of spiritual life than that which the New Testament Christians so obviously enjoyed.

It's not surprising, therefore, that at the Reformation the whole concept of Sainthood was savagely attacked by many of the Reformers, who often tore down the shrines of Saints and destroyed their statues and relics. This too had its negative side, since it created a gap between living and dead Christians and cut Christians on earth off from their brothers and sisters in the fuller presence of God. One result of this has been a weaker sense of heaven and the afterlife among Western Christians and Western society in general.

Becoming a Saint

Outstanding local Christians or martyrs were originally venerated only in their particular region. People would

Bernadette Soubirous, St Bernadette of Lourdes, saw a vision of the Virgin Mary. Now Lourdes welcomes more visitors than any other pilgrimage centre, as people from everywhere seek healing.

pray to them and celebrate their feast—usually the anniversary of their death. There was no official process for turning people into saints; the cult of the saints simply grew naturally. That system still operates in the Eastern Orthodox churches to this day. In Western Europe, however, where the church was centralized on Rome, the custom gradually developed of seeking the approval of the pope before a departed Christian was accorded the honour of a Saint. The procedure is as follows:

▶ *The local diocese*. The process begins here. The bishop may make formal inquiries about the cause and extent of the person's fame of sanctity or martyrdom. This might involve questioning witnesses about the deceased's life and any miracles claimed. If enough evidence is available, the case might be referred to:

▶ *The Congregation of Rites*. This body examines each case rather like a court of law, with defence and prosecution lawyers. The Congregation of Rites looks at the evidence and arguments presented by both sides and decides whether or not to recommend to the pope that the case should be taken further. If they agree that it should, they then institute the next procedure.

▶ *The Apostolic Process*. At this stage the case is taken out of the hands of the local diocese and is handled by the appropriate departments in the Vatican.

All relevant medical and scientific evidence is examined. If the findings are positive, and if the pope and the Congregation of Rites agree, then there is another stage.

▶ *Beatification*. The pope officially declares the person 'Blessed'. This means that they can be prayed to, and their feast celebrated, but only in a particular city, diocese or region, or perhaps within a particular religious order.

If, following the beatification, further miracles are reported, then new processes of inquiry may take place. If they conclude that the miracles are genuine, then the final step is reached.

▶ *Canonization*. This requires a solemn ceremony in the Vatican at which the pope declares the person a Saint (with a capital S) and gives official permission for him or her to be venerated throughout the whole Roman Catholic Church.

The Most Popular Saints

St Andrew (died about AD64). Andrew has always been one of the most popular of saints, and is patron saint of countries as far apart as Russia and Scotland. He was the brother of Simon Peter and the Gospels contain several references to him.

St Mark's Gospel tells how Jesus called Andrew and Peter to leave their work as fishermen and follow him. From then on Andrew is described as one of the twelve disciples (later called 'apostles') who were Jesus' closest companions during his earthly ministry.

Very little is known for certain about Andrew after Jesus' resurrection, but because of his importance as Peter's brother many stories were told about him. There are early traditions that he visited southern Russia and Greece, and even Ethiopia. Large numbers of miracles are attributed to him. Andrew is believed to have been put to death at Patras in southern Greece. He had healed and converted the wife of a local proconsul who thereafter refused to have sexual relations with her pagan husband. The husband had Andrew imprisoned, beaten and then crucified by being tied to a cross placed near the sea. For two days Andrew hung there, preaching to the people, before he died.

Eventually his bones were taken to Constantinople when that city was made the second capital of the Roman Empire. (As Rome, the first capital, had the bones of St Peter, it was only fitting that New Rome, as Constantinople was called, should have the bones of Peter's brother.)

One tradition says that at some time in the eighth century Greek monks travelled as missionaries from Constantinople to Scotland, and took the bones of St Andrew with them to protect them from dangers on land and sea. They landed on the coast of Fife in Scotland at the place which is now known as St Andrews. When the Scots in the area were converted to Christianity, they chose St Andrew as their patron saint. His shrine at St Andrews was an important place for pilgrimage and a centre for the church throughout the Middle Ages.

We are told that several centuries later Angus, King of the Picts, saw an x-shaped cross, the emblem of St Andrew, against the sky before he went into battle. When the Scots later won the battle, they believed it was because St Andrew had come to their aid. As a result the St Andrew's cross became the emblem of Scotland. The flag of Scotland includes this white diagonal cross (known as the Saltire cross) against a dark blue background which symbolizes the sea.

St Andrew's Day is 30 November. Before the Reformation it was observed as a religious holiday, and even after the Reformation it remained a day of feasting. Men and boys would go out in the morning 'Andra-ing', wandering through the woods and fields to catch rabbits and squirrels for the Andermas dinner, and spend the rest of the day eating and drinking with their families and friends.

St Augustine (354–430). St Augustine is one of the most influential writers in the Western church. He wrote many works about the Christian faith and his thinking influenced Reformation leaders such as Luther and Calvin. Western theology and practice bear his influence down to the present day.

Augustine was a native of North Africa. His mother, Monica, was a Christian, but Augustine was not. For fifteen years he lived with a concubine, by whom he had a son. Eventually he went to Italy, but became increasingly troubled at his lack of inner peace. One day, while meditating, he heard a child's voice saying, 'Take and read.' He picked up his Bible and read, 'Let us behave decently, as in the daytime, not in orgies and drunkenness, not in sexual immorality and debauchery, not in dissension and jealousy.' This verse 'released' him, and he was instructed in the Christian faith and baptized.

Augustine subsequently returned to North Africa where he became bishop of the city of Hippo. The times were very unsettled, since there were divisions in the church and the Roman Empire was collapsing. Many of his letters and books deal with these situations.

St Benedict (about 480–550). One of the most famous incidents of the Second World War was the assault on Monte Cassino in Italy, where the Allies had a hard fight to dislodge German troops from a strategically-placed hill top. The Germans were in fact occupying one of the most ancient and prestigious monasteries of Europe, and the damage inflicted on it in the fighting is one of the tragedies of the war.

The founder of Monte Cassino was Benedict. Very little is known about his personal life. He was born at Nursia in Italy, and as a young man he decided to follow a life of asceticism and prayer and lived for a time in a cave. Eventually he settled at Monte Cassino, which had been a pagan site until then. There he was joined by others with whom he lived a simple common life. It was to regulate the life of this community that he drew up his famous *Rule*. Communities based on Benedict's Rule—Benedictines—spread all over Europe by the Middle Ages and can be found throughout the world today. Cardinal Basil Hume of England is perhaps one of the most famous Benedictines of modern times. Their traditional dress is black.

St Bernadette (1844–79). Bernadette Soubirous was the daughter of a poor miller, the oldest of six children. In the year 1858 when she was fourteen, she claimed that she had a series of eighteen visions of the Virgin Mary over a period of six months at the well of Massabielle in Lourdes, at the foot of the northern slopes of the French Pyrenees.

In this vision the Virgin Mary told her to drink from the spring (which still produces nearly 4,000 gallons of water a day), and asked for a church to be built on the site. She also emphasized the need for prayer and penance in the Christian life.

After her story was carefully examined by church leaders and accepted as genuine, a basilica was built on the site and consecrated in 1876. Since then Lourdes has become the greatest centre for pilgrimage not only in modern Europe but in the whole world. With approximately four million visitors a year, it receives even more pilgrims than Mecca.

Bernadette herself joined the Sisters of Notre Dame at the age of twenty-two, and remained with them until she died at the age of thirty-five. She was officially canonized by the Roman Catholic Church in 1933.

St Christopher (? third century AD). Virtually nothing is known for certain about the original Christopher. It is likely that a real person called Christopher existed and that stories were later attached to him. The name Christopher in Latin is *Christo-ferens*, meaning 'Christ-carrier'.

The basic story about him is that he was a very large man (even a giant, according to some versions) who lived near a river and used to help travellers to cross. One day a child came to the river and asked Christopher to carry him across. He agreed, but found the child getting heavier and heavier as he waded through the river. At this point the child told him that he was Jesus, and that Christopher was carrying the weight of the whole world and its Maker on his shoulders.

He must have been regarded as a saint from the fifth

In the beautiful story of Saint Christopher, the saint carried the Christ-child across a river. Now travellers in many countries carry St Christopher medallions.

century or even earlier, since the first church known to be dedicated to him dates from AD452.

Travelling in Europe was always dangerous—with bad roads, with many rivers, swamps and forests to cross, and constant danger from robbers. It is easy to understand, therefore, how travellers felt the need of special protection, and St Christopher came to be regarded as the patron saint of all travellers.

Pictures showing him fording a river with the Christ-child on his shoulders were often painted on the wall opposite the entrance to churches so that all who came in would see them. There was a popular belief that anyone who saw an image of St Christopher would not die that day, and people soon began carrying or wearing little pictures or engravings of St Christopher with them, and St Christopher medallions remain popular today.

St David (died AD589). Since the twelfth century St David has been regarded as the patron saint of Wales. His father was a famous prince, and his mother was recognized as a saint. He seems to have become the head of the church in Wales at a very early age.

He founded many churches all over Wales and established an important centre for the church in the place which is now called St Davids. He also founded monastic communities which had a very ascetic life-style: the monks drank only water and no wine, and ate bread and vegetables every day.

His feast day is 1 March, the day on which (according to tradition) he died.

The daffodil, which is at its most plentiful in March, is known as David's flower and has become the emblem of Wales. The name comes from the word *asphodel*, the flower in Roman mythology which grew on the Elysian Fields of the Dead. This may explain why daffodils are so popular in graveyards.

St Francis of Assisi (1181–1226). St Francis is one of those saints everyone has heard of, but few people know very much about! He is generally portrayed in a brown friar's habit, talking to birds and other animals. In recent years a song attributed to him has become popular in churches and schools—'Make me a channel of your peace'. However, there is much more to Francis than that.

As a young man Francis helped his father in the family business for a time, but also served as a soldier and was imprisoned for a year. At the same time there gradually developed in him a love for the poor, and especially for lepers.

One day, in the partially ruined Church of San Damiano in Assisi, Francis heard a voice, as if from the Christ figure on a crucifix, saying, 'Go and repair my church, which, as you see, is falling down.' Francis took the command literally and sold some of his father's cloth to raise money to buy materials to repair the church.

From then on until his death in 1226, Francis lived a life of poverty, dedicated to Christ and his church. Eventually he was joined by a few companions and out of this small group grew the great world-wide Franciscan Order which still exists today. Francis himself was not very good at organization and, even in his own lifetime, the running of the Order was taken over by others. Yet the appeal of a simple, attractive life, devoted to Christ, has been a very powerful one down the years.

Francis' feast day is on 4 October.

St George (died about AD303). The popular picture of St George as a knight in armour on horseback slaying a dragon dates only from the Middle Ages. But behind this legend there is almost certainly a real figure, belonging to a much earlier time.

All that is known of the real St George (who may have been a Roman soldier from Cappadocia in Asia Minor or from Palestine) is that he was martyred for his faith at Lydda in Palestine in the reign of the emperor Diocletian. His popularity quickly spread in both Eastern and Western Europe, and he was known in Britain as early as the seventh century.

Hundreds of years later the simple story was elaborated into a detailed legend. There was a dragon which was terrorizing a certain area and which could only be kept happy by being offered two sheep every day by the local people. Eventually the people ran out of sheep and were going to have to start offering a human victim each day instead. The first person to be chosen was the king's daughter. She wore her wedding dress and waited for the dragon to come. Just in time St George arrived and overpowered the dragon, tying it up with the princess's girdle. He told the people he would get rid of the dragon for ever if they became Christians. They agreed. St George killed the dragon and fifteen thousand people were baptized. Later, when St George went to Palestine, he refused to recognize that the Emperor Diocletian was divine, and was tortured and finally killed by being dragged by horses, burnt and beheaded.

This legend about St George became very popular in the Middle Ages because in it the saint exactly fitted the ideal of the day—a warrior, who was also chivalrous and a champion of the church. King Richard I of England ('Richard the Lion-heart') adopted St George as his saint while on a Crusade, and on his return home made him the patron saint of England (replacing Edward the Confessor). He also brought home the banner of St George, an upright red cross on a white background, which became the flag of England. His feast day since then has been 23 April, and in 1222 St George's Day was declared a public holiday.

Despite being the patron Saint of Portugal as well as

The Debate about Mary

The different opinions about Mary can be illustrated by setting these three quotations side by side:

A Catholic view

'Mary was involved in the mysteries of Christ. As the most holy Mother of God she was, after her Son, exalted by divine grace above all angels and men. Hence the Church appropriately honours her with special reverence. Indeed, from most ancient times the Blessed Virgin has been venerated under the title of "God-bearer". In all perils and needs, the faithful have fled prayerfully to her protection... As it has always existed in the Church, this cult is altogether special...'

The Second Vatican Council

A Protestant view

'Around the fifth century the word theotokos *began to be widely used in Catholic writing—a Greek term meaning "Mother of God"...*

'By the Council of Chalcedon in AD451 there was general acceptance of the title. With this acceptance came the absorption of many pagan strands into the reverence of Mary...

'Influential theologians like Augustine stressed Mary's sinlessness, artists and artisans by the thousand arose to decorate their churches with images and statues of Mary, which became instant focal points of worship...

'By the time the doctrine of the Immaculate Conception was officially proclaimed by Pius IX on 8 December 1954, it had long been articulated by those in the Catholic theological and ecclesiastical hierarchy.'

Tony Cummings

A non-religious view

'In the person of the Virgin Mary the earth goddess—the great mother of ancient religions—succeeded in re-establishing something of her former position...

'She was Mater Virgo, virgin mother, the primal material prior to its division into the multiplicity of created things; Stella Maris, star of the sea, the immaculate womb of the divine font as well as the primeval waters over which the Spirit moved; and the Tree of Jesse, the world-axle, and the branch upon which "the spirit of the Lord shall rest". Inherited attributes though these were... the Church had to come to terms with the cult and legends of the Virgin.'

---

of England, St George was 'demoted' by the pope in 1969 to a local saint.

St John the Baptist (died about AD28). John was a relation of Jesus. He was the son of the priest Zechariah and his wife Elisabeth, who had had no children until an angel told Zechariah in the Temple at Jerusalem that they would have a son who was to be especially dedicated to God's service. Zechariah at first did not believe this could happen and was struck dumb until after the baby was born.

Nothing more is known of John until, as a young man, he is described as living an ascetic life in the Judean wilderness, preaching the coming of God's Messiah, and

Facing: **This triptych by Perugino shows Mary, the mother of Jesus, at the foot of her son's cross. The depth of her sorrow can only be imagined. Sorrowing mothers everywhere always feel a close identity with Mary.**

urging people to repent of their sins and be baptized.

John was imprisoned by King Herod for denouncing his marriage to Herodias, his brother's wife. Herodias had her revenge when her daughter Salome danced for Herod, who was so infatuated with her that he promised her anything she asked for. Prompted by her mother, Salome asked for the head of John the Baptist on a platter.

John is often depicted with a lamb, from his words about Jesus, 'Behold the Lamb of God'.

John the Evangelist (died about AD95). This John was the brother of James with whom (together with Peter) he was one of the 'inner three' of Jesus' disciples. He is mentioned by name in the Gospels of Matthew, Mark and Luke, but in the Gospel attributed to him, he is only spoken of as 'the beloved disciple' which suggests strongly that the Gospel is substantially his work. He was close to Jesus at the Last Supper. The New Testament writings attributed to him, (the Gospel and three letters) stress love as the heart of the Christian faith. The author of the last book of the Bible, the Revelation, is also called John, but is probably a different John.

As Jesus hung on the cross, he entrusted his mother to John's keeping. They may well have travelled to Ephesus together, for in that part of Turkey there are

St John the Baptist, seen here in a sixteenth-century wooden sculpture from a German cathedral, said of his cousin, Jesus: 'Behold, the lamb of God, who takes away the sin of the world.'

local traditions about both of them. Unlike his brother, who was martyred, John seems to have lived to a ripe old age.

His symbol is the eagle, taken from one of the four living creatures in the Revelation. John's Gospel begins with the words, 'In the beginning was the Word' and lecterns for reading from the Bible in churches are often designed as an eagle.

St Mary. No other saint has received as much devotion as Mary, the mother of Jesus. For many she is the ideal, model Christian, rewarded for her acceptance of God's will with the highest place in heaven. But some believe her essential humanity has been obscured by centuries of romantic stories and distortion.

Mary was already betrothed to Joseph when she was visited by an angel and told she would have a son by miraculous means. The baby, Jesus, was born at Bethlehem, then brought up by Mary and Joseph at Nazareth. Mary hovers in the background of Jesus' ministry, and on at least one occasion did not seem to understand his mission. She was entrusted to John's keeping by Jesus at Calvary. For a while she is mentioned with the other disciples after Pentecost, but then fades out of the picture.

Mary's special relationship to Jesus naturally was seen to give her a significance that other saints did not have. This led to a tendency to 'fill in the gaps' about her life. Both the Roman Catholic and Orthodox Churches ascribe perpetual virginity to Mary and attach a great deal of devotional and doctrinal significance to it. Similarly, the Roman Catholic Church officially teaches that she was preserved from sin from the beginning of her existence ('the Immaculate Conception') and that, after her death, she was taken bodily into heaven ('the Assumption'). She came to be viewed as a strong intercessor on behalf of ordinary Christians.

By the time of the Reformation, Mary was seen by many to be, for practical purposes, closer and more approachable than Christ himself. It was this interference with the uniqueness of Christ that led most of the Reformers very much to 'downgrade' her in public and personal prayer. Her position is a source of difference between Christians that has still not been resolved.

St Michael. St Michael is one of the few well known saints who was not even a human being! He is mentioned in the Bible several times as a mighty spiritual being, a leader of the army of angels who fought and defeated Satan. He later came to be called one of the four 'Archangels' (the others being Gabriel, Raphael and Uriel).

Not surprisingly, Christians frequently wanted to pray to such a mighty spiritual warrior, asking for his help. Monks (who saw their lives as a kind of spiritual warfare) often had a particular devotion to St Michael, and Mont-St-Michel in Normandy and Skellig Michael in Ireland are famous off-shore monastic sites dedicated to him.

St Michael's feast day is 29 September, hence the name 'Michaelmas' given to that season.

St Nicholas (fourth century). Like St Christopher and St George, St Nicholas is a saint who was enormously popular in the Middle Ages, but about whom very few hard facts are known. Almost all that can be said about him with any certainty is that he was Bishop of Myra in south-west Turkey in the early fourth century. In 1087, when Myra was captured by the Muslim Turks, Nicholas' remains were taken to Bari in Italy and his popularity seems to have come with him to Western Europe. He is the basis of the Santa Claus or Father Christmas character. The development of the legend is given in the chapter on festivals.

St Patrick (390–461). The patron saint of Ireland was born and brought up in Glamorgan in Wales, where his father was a landowner. At the age of sixteen he was captured by pirates and taken to Ireland as a slave. After six years he escaped, and went to France where he lived in a monastery for a few years. When he returned to Britain, he had the idea of starting a mission to take the Christian faith to Ireland. In order to prepare himself he trained for a further fourteen years at a monastery in France, and eventually landed in Ireland in AD435.

He travelled all over the country, especially in the north, seeking to win over the tribal kings and clan chiefs to the Christian faith, and built churches and monasteries. He was specially concerned to lead people away from the pagan religion of the Druids with all its idolatry and sun worship. He was known for the simplicity of his life and for his pastoral care.

The emblem of Ireland is the shamrock, no doubt because according to tradition Patrick used the three-leafed shamrock as an illustration of how the Father, the Son and the Holy Spirit are one God and not three. Patrick's feast day is 17 March.

St Peter (died about AD65). Peter was one of, and indeed the leader of, Jesus' team of twelve disciples and he is mentioned a great deal in the New Testament.

Peter was not his original name. He was originally called by the Jewish name of Simon (like all the first disciples he was a Jew). Jesus, however, gave him the additional name of 'the rock', *Petros* in Greek. It is from Petros that we get the English 'Peter', French 'Pierre', Russian 'Piotr' and so on.

The New Testament describes Peter as a fisherman with his brother Andrew. From the very beginning he was one of the inner core of three disciples (with James and John) who were particularly close to Jesus and were with him on certain special occasions such as the Transfiguration. Jesus gave Peter along with the other apostles the power of 'binding and loosing' (which includes the forgiving of sins) and spoke of Peter as having the keys of the kingdom of heaven. This probably refers to his confession of Jesus as God's chosen one, the faith which 'unlocks' the saving power of God (-Matthew 16:17-19). Peter is therefore often depicted as

St Michael, the great warrior-angel, has long appealed to monks, who often see their lives as spiritual warfare. The famous Mont St Michel, in Normandy, is an example of the link.

holding one or more keys.

There is a very early tradition that Peter made his way eventually to Rome, and became leader of the church there. It is very likely that he was martyred there during the reign of the emperor Nero. He is reputed to have been crucified upside down, as he said he was not worthy to die in the same manner as Jesus. The great basilica of St Peter's in the Vatican is believed to be built on the site of his grave. The tradition grew that he was the first in an unbroken line of bishops of Rome.

St Thomas. Why do we call a person who is inclined not to believe something 'a doubting Thomas'? The answer is that Thomas, one of Jesus' twelve disciples, refused to believe the others when they told him that Jesus was risen from the dead. 'Unless I put my finger into the marks of the nails and place my hand in his side, I will not believe,' he said. A week went by, then Jesus again appeared to the disciples and invited Thomas to touch him. Thomas was convinced and fell down before Jesus saying, 'My Lord and my God!'

The Bible does not tell us what happened to Thomas, but there are ancient traditions that he travelled East, preaching the gospel. His name is linked with parts of the Middle East, but also strongly with India. In south India there are very ancient communities of Christians (who until recently worshipped in Syriac, similar to the language spoken by Jesus) who claim to have been founded by Thomas himself.

St Valentine. The story of St Valentine is that of an early Christian martyr. It is given in the chapter on festivals.

Conclusions

Saints seem to meet several genuine human needs. These include the need for protection, the need for a human ideal to admire and look up to, the need for someone who can sympathize with us in our troubles, and the need for someone who can communicate directly with God on our behalf.

The idea of sainthood in Christianity has developed in several stages. In the New Testament period 'saint' simply meant 'holy', or 'set apart', and was applied to *all* Christians.

In the centuries after the New Testament was written, the word came to be applied to individuals who were outstanding either because they lived a specially godly life, or because they performed miracles, or because they died as martyrs.

When people were converted from a pagan background, therefore, they may have looked to Christian saints to do what they had previously expected pagan deities to do for them.

The Orthodox Churches and the Roman Catholic Church have accepted the practice of venerating (but not worshipping) the saints, and built it into their understanding of the Christian faith and life.

The Protestant Church has generally been either very cautious or very critical of the whole practice of venerating saints, believing that it has brought in some of the less helpful aspects of popular religion, and obscures basic truths of the Christian faith.

Christians still debate how people can relate to God and to Christians who have died. Benedicta Ward represents one line of thinking.

'*The saints are venerated for their participation in the life of Christ; their lives are imitated as true images of that life; and it is also the custom of Christians to offer prayers to the saints requesting them to continue to pray for their fellow Christians still on earth. The intercession of the saints depends as a concept on the idea of the church as a family united in heaven and on earth as one body, in which all members are "alive unto God" who is their life. Communication is therefore not interrupted but only changed by death.*'

W. Griffiths Thomas voices the other major line of thought.

'*The entire practice reveals an apparently inherent tendency in unspiritual and human nature to fear the holiness of God, and by stopping short of it to seek the influence of an intermediary... When once the soul has entered into a personal experience of what is meant by fellowship with the Father, and with His Son Jesus Christ, there can be no thought of any intermediary.*'

Questions

▶ Is *Mary a special case*? Some Christians would say that the Virgin Mary is in a very special position on her own and that she shouldn't be included in a list of saints. Other Christians have strong reservations about the whole idea of venerating Mary, while many who are not Christians try to find historical or psychological explanations for this practice.

▶ *Who are the modern saints*? Assuming that people accept the idea of saints, even in a limited way, are there any people in our own century who are already popularly regarded as 'saints'? Four people who may come into this category, even if they are never likely to be pronounced officially as saints by the Roman Catholic Church, are Martin Luther King, Mother Teresa, Oscar Romero, and Maximillian Kolbe.

5 Churches

If you come any day between March and November, you will find crowds of men, women and children wandering around, just gazing in amazement. They come from all over the world. Why? Because this is one of the wonders of the world.
The Dean of Salisbury Cathedral

This still is…and with luck always will be (acid rain permitting) a place where first and last things take you by the heart.
John Ezard, writing about Salisbury Cathedral

I was glad when they said unto me, 'Let us go into the house of the Lord'.
Psalm 122:1

A church is a building where Christians gather to worship. The English word 'church' comes from the Anglo-Saxon *cirice*, which itself comes from the Greek *kurikon* meaning 'belonging to the Lord'. The Scottish version, 'kirk', is nearer to the original Greek. The basic idea is of the building as 'the Lord's house'.

But it has to be remembered that the building is a church only in a secondary sense. The real church is the people who meet in the building, people who follow Jesus Christ.

The Origin of the Church Building

Probably everybody at some time or other has been in a place that has made them feel 'creepy', or perhaps peaceful, or where it seemed natural to talk in whispers. It might be on the top of a mountain, by a waterfall, in the middle of a wood, in a cave, or in any number of such places. They feel that there is something special about the place, and that some power stronger than themselves is present. It may make them feel good, or it may make them feel a bit nervous or scared.

Before the coming of Christianity, people often said that such feelings were the result of gods or spirits visiting or living in the place. Sometimes there were particularly unusual features, such as the hot water springs at Bath in England, which were said to belong to the god Sul, or the sulphurous vapours which rose

from a deep hole in the ground at Delphi in Greece, and which were believed by the ancient Greeks to be sacred to the god Apollo. Often such sites became the centre for the worship of the particular god or spirit. Offerings might be left there, or individuals or groups might go there to worship the deity.

The next stage seems to have been to mark the site with special features or buildings. Perhaps the earliest of these were circles or groves of trees or wooden posts, followed later by stone circles. These could be very large, as at Stonehenge near Avebury in England, or else much smaller. Often such circles seem to be arranged in deliberate ways, perhaps in connection with the movement of the stars and planets, but the precise meaning behind most of them is now lost for ever.

Later still, specific buildings were erected in which to worship the gods. These ranged from the splendid temples built by the Greeks and Romans, which were often simply built on a city street and no longer at a natural sacred site, to the much cruder huts in the remote villages where the carved wooden and stone statues of the tribal gods were kept.

When the early Christian evangelists came to different parts of Europe, teaching the faith of the one true God and the superiority of Christ over all supposed gods and powers, one of the most natural ways of demonstrating this was to take over the old temple building or sacred place and convert it for Christian worship. One world-famous example of this is the Parthenon on the Acropolis at Athens, originally built as the temple of the goddess Athena, then converted into a church. But the same thing happened countless times in the villages of Europe: the idols were removed from their building, which was consecrated and turned into a church. In addition, the evangelists might select groves of trees (which were sometimes cut down) as places of worship, or the sacred high point of the village, which had the added advantages of being visible and safe from flooding. The old enclosure thus became the new churchyard. Since the local people already thought of the site as special or sacred, it was natural for them to transfer these feelings to the new church building and grounds.

The Function of the Church Building

At first sight this seems obvious: it's for Christians to worship in. But there's rather more to it than that.

All Christians would agree that the primary function of a church building is to provide somewhere to perform a whole range of specifically Christian activities, such as baptism, eucharist, confirmation, ordination and so on. Most would also use it for activities which are not specifically Christian in themselves, but which Christians usually do in a distinctive way, for example weddings and funerals.

But there are other possible uses: business meetings of the church governing body; shelter and relief for the poor and distressed; secular activities such as concerts and plays.

There is also the question of whether the church building exists primarily to serve the people and so be comfortable for them, perhaps with carpets, comfortable seating and adjacent kitchens, or whether its primary purpose is to express things about God—his greatness, power, majesty, holiness, and so on. How a church building looks will depend on which of these two ideas the architect and congregation think should have the dominant emphasis.

Church Buildings through the Ages

Christian architecture down the centuries has varied as different ideas about the precise range of functions of the church building have come in and out of fashion.

The Early Church

The Acts of the Apostles describes Christians worshipping in three main places: in the temple of Jerusalem, in synagogues and in homes. Within fewer than fifty years of the death of Jesus only one of these was still open to

them. The temple was destroyed by the Romans in AD70, and Acts itself shows how the Christians soon began to be barred from the synagogues all around the Roman Empire. One might expect to find them starting to build similar buildings for themselves, for there is some evidence, such as in the letter of James, that the early congregations saw themselves as synagogues. But by the end of the first century Christianity was beginning to be viewed suspiciously by the Roman authorities and there seems to have been no chance for them to start creating purpose-built meeting places.

So the house continued as the basic Christian centre; these were the first church buildings. What seems to

A church in the United States reminds people of God. Church buildings are found right round the world. More than any other visible entities, they call to mind the spiritual dimension of life.

have happened is that the Christians in a locality would meet in the home of one of the better-off local leaders, whose house would probably be bigger. Their needs were relatively simple: a room for all to assemble in, with places for reading the scriptures and celebrating the eucharist, and somewhere for performing baptisms. In the ancient city of Dura Europos on the River Euphrates, archaeologists have discovered the remains of just such a house. A wall has been knocked down to make two rooms into one, presumably because the local congregation had grown too large, and across the courtyard a small outhouse has been modified so that baptisms can be held in it. Since the early church baptized both adults and children by immersion and naked, baptism was not witnessed by the rest of the congregation.

As the centuries passed and Christianity became more widespread and accepted, specially designed buildings began to be erected. And once the Roman emperors started to favour Christianity in the fourth century there was a great flowering of church building. Most of the ancient churches that have survived are aligned so that the worshippers face east. This seems to have been an adaptation of the Jewish custom of praying facing the temple in Jerusalem. The prophecy of Malachi speaks of Jesus rising as the 'Sun of Righteousness', and the early Christians believed that Jesus would come again from the east.

In parts of Syria and the eastern provinces many churches seem to have been built on a synagogue pattern with a central platform or *bema*, on which the clergy sat for the readings from scripture before processing to the table at the east end for the communion proper.

In most of the Roman Empire the basic shape adopted by the Christians was that of the *basilica*— basically a rectangular building, often with a semicircular extension at one end called an *apse*. The congregation stood in the main part of the building (-standing was the normal attitude for prayer), and there were seats for the clergy around the wall of the apse. In the middle of the semicircle was a special chair called a *cathedra* for the bishop. This chair was a very important sign of his office and he sat on it to preach to his people.

These typical Russian domes are at Zagorsk, the great centre of the Russian Orthodox church. Each country has developed particular styles of church architecture, which feel to its people like 'proper churches'.

Even today the person in charge of a formal meeting is the chairperson and a professor at a university is said to have a chair in their subject.

The Eastern Churches

From this basic design the Eastern and Western branches of the church developed along different lines. The Eastern churches tended to make their buildings squarer and to put a semicircular dome on top. The square was said to represent the earth with its four corners (north, south, east and west) and the dome to represent the dome of the heavens. The two came together in the building because worship is the place where heaven and earth meet. This accounts for the characteristic shape of Greek Orthodox churches to this day. Sometimes the plan is modified slightly—for example the Russian Orthodox tended to alter the shape of the dome to the now famous 'onion-domes' seen at the Kremlin—but the basic idea remained the same.

In the Middle Ages the Orthodox churches were built with a screen that was covered with icons. The screen divided the eastern apse, where the clergy performed their parts in worship, from the nave where the people were. Gradually the explanation grew up that the sanctuary represented heaven and the nave earth, and when the clergy came out of the sanctuary to proclaim a blessing or to administer communion, it symbolized the love and grace of God coming from heaven to earth. Thus the very shape and layout of the building forms an essential part of the way in which the members of the congregation understand what is going on when they meet God in worship.

The Western Churches

In the Western church, the basic basilica pattern developed on very different lines. For a while the pattern remained, though the sanctuary tended to become almost a separate room, reached from the nave only by a narrow arched door, as in some Saxon buildings. Then in the Middle Ages there was a tremendous explosion of church building and a very definite style emerged which even now people associate with 'a typical church'.

Basically, whereas the East sought to create a sense of the holiness of God by using the dome and icon screen, the West sought to do the same by using space. So the old apses became long, narrow *chancels* with God represented as being distant and holy at the far east end of the church, where the laity were no longer allowed to come. Often churches had several priests (and of course monastery churches had many monks) who sat facing each other in the chancel for their many long services. The love of symbolism then led to

Gargoyles carved on the stonework high up on the structure of Notre Dame Cathedral in Paris.

churches being built cross-shaped with two side 'arms' or *transepts*. Baptisms were now almost exclusively of children, so there was no need for a separate building or *baptistery* and instead a large stone bowl or *font* was set up within the church itself, usually at the west end near the door, to symbolize the fact that baptism is the way of entry into the church.

Another very important development at this time in the Western church is of *side chapels*, each with its own altar and frequently dedicated to a different saint from the one to which the church as a whole was dedicated. Originally churches had had only one altar and there had been only one eucharist per week at the gathering of the whole local congregation on Sunday. (This tradition has continued in the Orthodox Church, where an altar cannot be used for the eucharist more than once a day.) In the West the practice grew up of each priest being required to celebrate the eucharist, to *say mass*, daily. Where there were several priests attached to a church, it was useful to have more than one altar so that they could say mass at the same time. It also came to be believed that each mass had a certain 'spiritual value' which could be applied to particular purposes—mainly shortening the time of the souls of the departed in purgatory. This led to the practice of wealthy people paying large sums of money to build little chapels called *chantry chapels* actually inside churches for the sole purpose of providing somewhere for a priest to say mass daily for their souls.

The Reformation and After

One of the most significant of all the changes brought about by the Reformation was the move from seeing the mass as a sacrifice in which Christ's body became present on earth to seeing it more as a communal meal for the faithful. There was also renewed importance given to preaching and teaching from the Bible in the course of worship. The existing churches were rearranged to emphasize these two convictions: screens which separated the altar from the people were removed and pulpits were set up in a prominent position. Often the stone altar was replaced by a wooden 'holy' table, usually set nearer the people at the opening of the sanctuary or in the nave. Pictures, images, statues and stained glass were frequently removed as they were regarded as idolatrous, and sometimes depicted themes which could not be found in the Bible. Within the churches of the Reformation, there were differences over the extent of reordering necessary: Anglican and Lutheran churches were less radical in their changes than the 'Reformed' churches of Holland, Scotland and elsewhere. The first American settlers generally favoured this simple type of church building.

The building of new churches began only gradually following the Reformation, but in England from the seventeenth century onwards a new style of architecture developed. The *auditory church* is best seen in the work of Christopher Wren (1632–1723), the architect of St Paul's Cathedral, London. These churches laid stress upon visibility and participation: their square shape and large windows ensured that all the congregation could see and hear the actions and words of the minister at the front. Their simplicity of design and decoration was inspired by ancient Greek and Roman buildings and led the worshippers to impressions of intimacy with God and one another.

The auditory design influenced most of the Protestant churches, with only minor changes between them. The focus at the top end of the church varied slightly. Anglican churches tended to have short and wide sanctuaries containing a communion table. Other churches had a prominent pulpit in the centre, with a smaller or movable communion table. Baptists built churches with a large submerged tank at the front in which a person could be fully immersed in water when they were baptized. With time other features developed: benches were replaced by more comfortable box pews for the gentry, sometimes even having a little stove! The pulpit developed to have a number of stages—the 'three-decker'—with each stage reserved for leading different sections of the service, the top being for the sermon. Other groups were more radical in their design. For example, the earliest Friends' Meeting Houses (set up by the Quakers or 'Friends') had nothing to distinguish them from ordinary houses except that they had rooms large enough to contain a group of people.

In the wake of the Reformation, the Roman Catholic churches developed an alternative architecture known as *baroque*. Baroque churches tried to stress the authority and dignity of God, and the church, by reflecting the dignity of a royal courtroom. The shape of the buildings was normally oval focusing upon the high altar, with other altars placed in separate chapels set to the side. Classical art and carving decorated the walls and ceiling to create an atmosphere of regal beauty. The ceremonial of the mass became more developed in this time, so that the baroque design worked together with the ornate ceremonial to produce an impression of dignity, order and majesty. The baroque church was seen as a gateway into heaven, where Christ would be regally present in the mass. The artwork of the churches further enhanced this effect, most especially by the ceiling paintings which frequently created the illusion of looking up into heaven.

The Nineteenth Century and Gothic Revival

In the middle years of the nineteenth century, a reaction against the starkness of the auditory design started in England. Architects looked wistfully back to Gothic architecture, thinking of the Middle Ages as a golden age of faith with a unified Christendom. Churches began to be designed to this historic pattern: long and narrow sanctuaries, side chapels, screens and stained glass came back, box pews were replaced by bench pews facing the altar. Many Anglican churches were influenced by the Anglo-Catholic Movement to emphasize ritual rather than preaching in worship, and this fitted the architecture of the Gothic Revival. Before long, other denominations were building churches to this pattern, although among the Free Churches the interiors still tended to give the pulpit a more prominent role. As the nineteenth century was a period of prosperity and population growth in Britain, there was a huge increase in church building. This is why today so many churches in Britain have this architectural style, and many people still regard it as what a typical church should look like.

The Twentieth Century

This century has seen the rise of the Liturgical Movement in both Roman Catholic and Protestant churches. This movement has stressed the importance of full participation by the congregation in worship, the importance of preaching, and the communion service as the central act of Sunday worship. In turn it has influenced the design of churches. The ornate Gothic style has given way to buildings which are designed to be flexible aids to worship, rather than constraints. The development of modern building materials and the rising cost of fuel has in turn led to a move away from stonework and high ceilings. In the early years of the century, these factors led churches to be simple and functional, often in plain rectangular shapes with low ceilings, sometimes using abstract art and stained glass as decoration. However, functional church buildings can also be regarded as drab and lacking any sense of the mystery of God. In recent years, architecture has wrestled with the balance between styles which are functional yet which also retain a sense of the 'numinous'.

With the contemporary stress upon flexibility in worship, many existing churches have been reordered or modified to allow for modern styles of worship. Narrow chancels have been turned to other uses, the altar or communion table has been brought forward to a dais at the front of the nave to encourage more participation by the people at communion, pews have been replaced by movable seating. Such rearrangement is often a sensitive issue within a particular church. But it is worth noting that ancient church buildings have always been rearranged periodically to serve the particular needs of Christian worship as it has evolved down the ages. From the churches of earliest Christianity to the present, church buildings have not been monuments, but living records of the beliefs and worship of the people who have built them and used them.

Decoration and Symbolism in Churches

One of the qualities which seems to make human beings different from animals is a sense of beauty. In all societies people are not simply content with the functional, but have desired to design buildings and objects in a way which may have little or no practical use, but which adds a sense of importance, of occasion, of solemnity or of joy.

Among many groups, decoration is very important. Often such decoration is designed to convey information or give a message—in other words, it is symbolic. Today's world is full of symbols. Business companies, schools and civic authorities all use logos at the head of their notepaper. This may take a traditional form such as a coat of arms, or it may be a specially designed symbol or a design created from the initial letters of the name of the institution. It is meant to be attractive, to give a sense of importance, and to enable the institution or product to be instantly recognizable.

Sometimes, of course, a symbol is meant to be a 'secret sign' rather than a means of public identification. Members of a club or society may wear a lapel badge which identifies them to other members but not to the world at large. Some early Christian symbols originally had this aspect. In the early centuries when antichristian persecution kept flaring up in the Roman Empire, Christians adopted some symbols which enabled them to recognize each other but not to be identified by the state authorities. Perhaps the most famous of these is the fish (*See* Visions of Glory). Early Christians often had fishes painted as wall decorations in their houses, or

inlaid in mosaic on the floor. Pagan visitors would see in it simply a piece of decoration; other Christians would recognize its meaning. In the same way the phoenix, a mythical bird that was believed to set fire to itself every few hundred years and then rise again from the ashes, was used as a symbol of the resurrection of Jesus Christ from the dead.

Gradually, as Christianity became more accepted, more explicitly Christian symbols began to be used. The cross was of course one of the most important of these. In the days of persecution it would obviously have identified people as followers of the crucified one. Also, crucifixion was a real possibility for Christians themselves and the cross was not simply a nice piece of ornamentation or jewellery; it was, after all, an instrument of torture and death. A modern equivalent might be to consider whether people would like a representation of a noose or an electric chair as decoration in their living rooms. However, once crucifixion was no longer a possibility, the cross was widely used in church life and, indeed, usually became the focal point of the church building on the holy table or east wall. In medieval churches there was often a crucifixion scene with carved figures of Jesus, Mary and John in the chancel arch. This tableau was called the *rood screen*, from *rood*, the Old English word for 'cross'. In Britain most of these were destroyed at the Reformation, but a few have survived or been restored, and there are many modern examples in existence.

Once Christians in the Roman Empire were free to

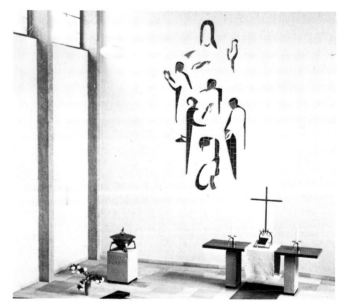

A communion table and a font in a church in Germany. The words on the font translate as: 'One Lord, one faith, one baptism.' Other important features to look for inside churches are pulpits, from which sermons are preached, and lecterns, where the Bible stands open to be read.

practise their religion and decorate their own churches, they did so with great enthusiasm. For most of them the incarnation of Jesus meant that it was allowable to depict sacred figures in paint, wood and stone, and even small village churches were often rich with carving and artwork. The purpose of this was not simply to beautify the building, however, important though this was. In an age when very few people could read, one of the primary aims was education. Even if people had been able to read, Bibles were few and far between, handwritten and very costly. Not only that, but they were in Latin, once the common language of the Roman Empire.

By the Middle Ages, however, Latin was understood only by clergy and scholars. Ordinary Christians learned the stories of the Bible and the lives of the saints from the walls and windows of their churches. Stained glass windows often depict such scenes; but in medieval Europe the insides of many churches were often brightly coloured and covered with a whole host of wall paintings. These could be life-sized and were often very vivid and moving. The crucifixion was of course a common subject, as were depictions of the last judgment with spine-chilling details of what was believed to be the fate of those in hell.

At the Reformation there was a violent reaction in some parts of Europe against the use of pictures or images in church (*See* Visions of Glory). Many of these stained glass windows and wall paintings were judged to be distractions or superstitious and were destroyed or whitewashed over. Some churches still do not hold with them. But in recent years some have been discovered and restored.

Medieval churches were not only full of colour; they often contained statues. These were usually of Mary or other saints. Often stone carvings of the saints were incorporated into the fabric of the building itself, for example the placing of a statue of the church's patron saint in a stone niche over the main door. Others were of wood and painted. Candles were lit before them by worshippers asking for the saint's prayers, and at special festivals they might be carried in processions. Again, most of these were destroyed at the Reformation on the grounds that Christians could pray directly to God through Christ and therefore did not need the saints to pray for them; and also because the statues themselves were being treated as having miraculous powers. Empty niches in old churches often show where the statues of the saints once stood.

Conclusions

The need for some kind of 'sacred place' or 'sacred space' seems to be almost universal. All religions have their own sacred places which are set apart for some special religious purpose. It has been suggested that these sacred spaces act as a kind of 'focusing lens', because they bring into focus the most basic ideas in each religion.

▶ They are places for communication and meeting with God, or the gods or the supernatural;

▶ They are places of divine power which can transform human life;

▶ They provide a kind of model of the world, i.e. they express something.

All church buildings are attempts to say something about the Christian faith. The features that are given most attention reveal what the church architects felt to be most important. For example, when the altar is the focus of attention in the building, it is a reminder of how important it is for Christians to remember the death and resurrection of Jesus. What is considered important can change over time.

Changes in society affect the style of church buildings. Architectural styles influence church building in an obvious way. The importance of Christianity to its society is revealed in the way a church is built.

Questions

▶ *How can the attraction of churches and cathedrals to so many people be explained?* Why is it that people who don't go to church to worship often have a fascination for church buildings? Is it just a question of the architecture and an interest in old things?

Ralph Whitlock describes visits to churchyards with his daughter:

'We read the inscriptions on the gravestones, speculate on the age of the yew trees and open our minds to the mysterious aura that pervades the place. We both have a strong sense of the past and find that the past of a parish is epitomized in its churchyard.'

What is it that makes up this 'mysterious aura'?

▶ *What if there were no churches in Western society?* If this sounds a strange question, at least it makes the point that the existence of so many beautiful churches in the Western world is an indication of the important place which Christianity once had in the life of the whole community. What if all the Christian churches in our countries were to disappear? Would their place be taken by places of worship of other religions? Or would a new religion or new religions be created, with their own 'sacred places', to fill the vacuum?

6 Visions of Glory

...the history of Western art is largely the history of Christian painting...
Sarah Jane Checkland

I sketch and paint Christ and the sufferings of Christ...so that people may see them plainly, may remember them and not forget them... I mean to embrace Christ Himself and to do Him reverence... We Christians, by bodily kissing an icon of Christ, or of an apostle or martyr, are in spirit kissing Christ himself or His martyr.
An early Christian icon painter

What is a religious artist?... As I see him he is someone who brings his skill and understanding to bear on the problem of giving expression to the tenets of an organised belief... Those who have done this best in the past have gained...from their belief. But they seem to have excelled especially because, in addition to this they were good artists... Bad or superficial religious works in the Church are not religious at all.
Graham Sutherland

Art inevitably reflects the beliefs of any culture, including its religious beliefs. All forms of art in one way or another express what an individual or a community believes about the nature of the world.

Art in Society

In the Western world art developed out of the classical tradition of Greece and Rome, and then for many centuries was associated with the Christian tradition. It was used to express beliefs about God, about Christ, and about the universe, to decorate places of worship, and to provide aids to worship and devotion. These are the most obvious ways in which religion has been associated with art in the Western world.

But it is not only the art which has something 'religious' as its subject matter that can be classified as religious art. Any work of art can be religious in a broader sense if it communicates something about the meaning of life. Art isn't simply about paint and perspective! As Jane Dowling, a British Christian artist,

has said, 'A study of an onion on a plate could be as ''religious'' as a painting of the Crucifixion.'

Religious Art in Western Culture

This chapter is primarily concerned with art that is very obviously connected in the broadest sense with some religious theme, with particular emphasis on Christian art in the West. But it also aims to highlight other ways in which art in the Western tradition has been associated with the bigger questions of life which are raised by religion.

These are the questions to be answered:

▶ *How does art express religious feelings and beliefs?* How has art been associated with religion in the Western world— from prehistoric times to the twentieth century?

▶ *How did Christian art begin and develop in the first few centuries?* If most European art has been deeply influenced by Christianity, where can the influence of Christian beliefs be seen? And what *other* influences have been at work?

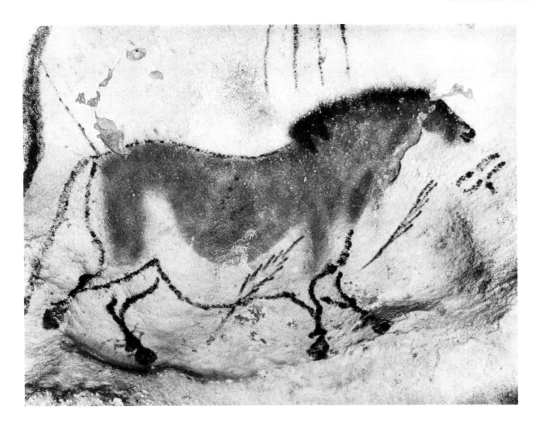

This horse was painted on the wall of a cave at Lascaux, France, many thousands of years ago. Did these paintings have a magic or religious meaning?

▶ *How can the changes and developments in art at crucial periods be explained?* What lay behind the new movements of the Renaissance, the Reformation, the Enlightenment and the twentieth century? To what extent were they connected with changes of culture and religious belief?

▶ *How do people interpret the symbols in Christian art?* What do these mean, and how do people decode them?

▶ *What is distinctive about art in the Western world?* What makes it different, for example, from Islamic art, African traditional art, or Japanese Buddhist art?

Prehistoric Art

Early prehistoric tribes used art to decorate themselves, their implements and their jewellery; but they also seem to have attributed magical properties to their art. The two basic needs of primitive people were food and fertility—both for themselves and the earth.

Cave paintings of animals and birds may have represented a primitive kind of magic. The idea may have been that if the people painted the animals, they would be more successful in going out to hunt; by drawing them they would have control over the spirits of natural things. Many of the painted animals have hand prints or the marks of spears on them, probably indicating signs of capture.

Many of the early cave paintings are found confined to just one wall, deep inside the cave. This may have been thought to be nearest to the womb of the Earth-Mother. Pictures on it are often superimposed on one another, implying that it was considered to be a very important position.

Images of women with huge breasts and wide hips have also been found inside the caves. These were probably fertility symbols, intended to ensure not just that women would be fertile and produce children, but that 'Mother Earth' would also be fruitful.

Art in Primal Religions

In primal religions all over the world, gods and spirits are thought to live in trees, streams, the sun and animals and birds. These spirits are often represented in images, which are thought not to be the gods themselves but to represent the god and to have the spirit of the god living in them.

Votive offerings and sacrifices are made to the images in places of special religious significance. These include symbolic representations of the petitions of the worshippers which are hung around the idols. This sort of belief or symbolic gesture has continued into many of the more developed religions. Even around Christian shrines some pilgrims hang small wax images of parts of the body that they want to be healed and pieces of cloth to receive blessings and be used in healing. They light candles to represent their prayers.

Art in Greek Religion

The early art of the tribes who later made up the great empires of Greece and Rome consisted of stylized decoration and votive offerings. They progressed towards art and architecture of a high standard of technical and naturalistic excellence.

In ancient Greece each city state had its own god or goddess who lived in a temple and was represented by a statue. This statue would be brought out of the temple for religious celebrations like festivals or games, and a statue of the deity might also be placed in the stadium or the theatre. A temple like the Parthenon on the Acropolis in Athens was the house for a deity (in this case the goddess Athena, the patron goddess of the city) not just a place of worship. The Parthenon stood high above the city, guiding ships to safe harbour in Piraeus. Unlike the small domestic altars in the corners of homes and private sanctuaries, the temple was the common property of all the citizens. But a temple was also a monument to the community and what they thought about themselves. So the Parthenon, designed by Phidias, with its huge free-standing statue of the goddess covered in beaten gold, and the friezes depicting centaurs, Amazons, deities, maidens and horsemen, expressed the pride of the Athenians in their city as well as their devotion to Athena.

Greek sculptors aimed to achieve correct proportion and anatomical accuracy as far as possible. But they also tried to depict nature in an idealized way, and aimed to create the 'perfect' human form. For a long time, therefore, the young adult male was one of their main subjects of study, and they tried to depict a well-built but not overly developed figure—an athletic gentleman rather than a specialized athlete. It was this ideal of human beauty which was felt to be appropriate for representing divine beings.

As the Greek Empire became more self-sufficient, the beliefs became less superstitious and more philosophical. The art of this later period was less idealized and more centred on the human being. Clever elaborate works were produced, more for the glory of the artist than for the glory of their gods.

Art in the Jewish Tradition

From around the nineteenth or twentieth century BC the ancestors of the Jewish people were surrounded by peoples who worshipped representations of their gods, believing that the idol was itself a god or that the god was somehow present in the image.

The second of the ten commandments, which were given around the thirteenth century BC, spells out very clearly the belief that Yahweh their God is the *only* true God, and that he will not tolerate any images or idols: 'You shall not make for yourself a graven image, or any likeness of anything that is in heaven above, or in the earth beneath, or that is in the water under the earth; you shall not bow down to them nor serve them; for I the Lord your God am a jealous God.' (Exodus 29:4–5)

The ban on images, however, did not mean that everything in their worship had to be completely plain. In the tabernacle, for example, which was constructed around the same time that the ten commandments were given, there was embroidery, carving and metalwork. The geometrical plan, and even the materials from which the tabernacle was constructed, seem to have had special symbolic meaning. The people believed that God's spirit actually inspired the artisans with the design and gave them the skills for the work and for training others (- Exodus 35:30–35).

The Jewish tradition for decorative work has been maintained right down to the present day. In

Greek sculptors tried to represent the ideal human form, such as would call the gods to mind.

synagogues, for example, there are no pictures or stained glass windows depicting God, angels or any human beings. Some strict Jews today even refuse to have their photographs taken, believing it to be breaking the commandment against images. But other kinds of decorative arts are encouraged, especially embroidery, patterned ornament, metalwork and calligraphy. It is interesting that many of the great artists, musicians and artisans of the twentieth century and before have been Jewish.

Early Christian Art

The early Christians agreed with Jews that God cannot be seen or represented in any picture. But they believed that Jesus of Nazareth was God in human form, a full human being. Paul described Jesus, for example, as 'the image of the invisible God' (Colossians 1:15). In other words, the Christians were saying that if you want to know what God is like, look at the nature and character of Jesus.

In the light of this, Christians soon began to modify the traditional Jewish interpretation of the second commandment which forbids the making of images. They believed that people no longer have to guess at what God is like, because he has shown himself to people in a human form. Human flesh and matter are important, because the incarnation (God coming 'in the flesh') has shown that they can convey the divine. If the disciples could describe Jesus as a real person by using words, then surely they could use paint and ink to describe what he meant to them? In this way it seems that the early Christians gradually overcame their hesitation about religious images, and started to paint pictures of Jesus.

For nearly 300 years after the time of Christ, the Christians in the Roman Empire were an insignificant minority, often persecuted by the authorities. Evidence of their art is therefore found not in magnificent

Once Christianity became the official religion of the Roman Empire, the basilica shape of official Roman buildings became the norm for church buildings. This basilica-style church is in Ravenna, Italy.

churches, but in tombs, on jewellery, as household decorations such as wall frescoes and mosaic floors, and in secret meeting places like the catacombs in Rome.

Their art during this period expressed what was most significant about their faith. Most of it concentrated on Christ, and portrayed his triumph over all powers in the world and over death. For example, pictures of the Magi coming to worship the Christ child pointed to Jesus as the one who is to be worshipped by all the kings and rulers of the world. Pictures of healings and other miracles showed his powers over sickness and the natural world. Pictures illustrating stories from the Old Testament also said something about Jesus: Jonah and the whale was a picture of Christ's triumph over death, and the three friends of Daniel who were rescued from the fiery furnace were a reminder of Jesus being raised from death. The emphasis was on Christ's triumphant resurrection rather than on his death; and pictures of this kind in the catacombs therefore expressed the Christian hope in the face of death.

As long as the Christian movement was rather like an underground movement, symbols were very important. One of the best known secret symbols which was used to distinguish Christians was the sign of the fish. The Greek word for 'fish' was *ichthus*, and this sequence of letters indicates the first letters of a Greek phrase meaning '-Jesus Christ, Son of God, Saviour'. Another favourite symbol was the *Chi-Rho* sign, which is the first two letters of the Greek word 'Christ'. The anchor which also included a cross was also used late in the Roman period as a symbol of the security of the believer of Christ.

When the emperor Constantine adopted Christianity as the official religion of the Roman Empire in AD313, Christian art became much more public, and was required on a much larger scale. When people started building churches, therefore, they copied the basic structure of official Roman buildings, which was the origin of the basilica shape. Another significant development was that instead of simply giving hope and comfort to a persecuted minority, art could now be used much more widely to teach the large numbers of people who were being baptized and coming into the church. So Eusebius, speaking of the cathedral in Tyre, could say, 'The evidence of our eyes makes instruction through the ears unnecessary.'

When the Christians therefore started to decorate the walls of their new churches, they began to develop a whole new set of symbols. Some of them came straight from the Bible. The vine, for example, stood for the Jewish people in the Old Testament and for the church in the New Testament: just as the branches are part of the vine, so every Christian believer is joined to Christ. Other symbols, such as the peacock, were new; here the idea was that just as the peacock hides its splendour in

Eastern Orthodox Christians make use of icons in their worship, as windows to the spiritual world. This icon of Mary and Jesus is from the Novgorod school. The virgin's three hands have a spiritual meaning.

its tail when it is lowered but reveals it when it is raised, so Christ concealed the splendour of his deity when he became man, but has now revealed it in all its glory.

Other ideas were borrowed from contemporary Roman art. If the Greek god Apollo, for example, was represented in sculpture in a particular stance, why couldn't Christians depict Jesus in the same way as the Good Shepherd? In pagan Roman art the shepherd with a lamb on his shoulders was a symbol of philanthropy. This same image or 'iconography' was used by Christians to depict Christ as God bearing human nature to show his love for the world. In cases like these the Christians weren't worried about the 'pagan' origins of the art forms they were copying. They believed that the art forms of the day could be borrowed and transformed to express their faith in Christ, although they rejected many other aspects of pagan religion and culture.

On this same principle, when they looked for other ways of portraying Christ, they remembered that in painting on ivory carvings and manuscripts, Roman emperors and dignitaries as a sign of honour were given a halo behind their heads, or a special lozenge shape of light, called a 'mandorla'. They then used these to portray the risen Christ as ruler of the universe, enthroned in glory as 'Ruler of All' (*Pantocrator*). This was one of the most popular ways of portraying Christ, and it became very common in paintings or mosaics which dominated the dome or apse in churches. In Sancta Maria Maggiore in Rome, for example, Christ is depicted as a young emperor seated on his throne. Similarly the popular Greek figure of the philosopher seated with a scroll in his hand was taken and made into a symbol of Christ as the 'True Philosopher' and source of all wisdom. And to encourage people to worship Christ rather than the sun, Christ was portrayed as the Sun God. Images of Christ on the cross didn't appear until around AD400, and weren't very common, because Christians had previously been persecuted and they wanted to emphasize the resurrection of Christ and his rule over the earth more than his death.

Icons

The Greek word 'icon' simply means image or picture, but it came to be used for stylized paintings of Jesus, characters from the Bible, or saints. These paintings were widely used in churches where they were displayed especially on a large screen (*iconostasis*) which separated the congregation from the sanctuary and which represented the link between heaven and earth. They were also used in homes as a way of encouraging meditation and devotion to Christ. They were developed especially in Egypt, Ethiopia, Turkey and Greece, from where they later spread to Russia. They became popular in the Orthodox and Coptic churches, which separated from the church of the Roman Empire over doctrinal differences and developed a different teaching on images. The idea behind the painting of icons was that, as God has revealed himself in human form in the person of Jesus, he has made himself known through material things; and if his revelation can be heard in the words of the gospel by the ears, something also needs to be seen with the eyes. As one writer said, 'If merely mental contemplation were sufficient, it would have been sufficient for him to come to us in a merely mental way.' An icon therefore becomes a door of perception, a door into the spiritual world; if people look at an icon in the right spirit, it is thought that they enter through that door and become part of that spiritual world. They see through the picture to the real thing for which it stands.

It is not difficult to see, however, that icons could be abused. Pope Gregory said, 'Paintings are the Bible of the illiterate.' This could easily develop into a situation in which people who were uneducated or didn't have a strong faith could not see the difference between the

image and what it represented. They couldn't understand the deeper, spiritual meaning of icons, and worshipped them almost as idols or treated them superstitiously as objects containing some kind of magical power.

Many of the Church Fathers, especially in the Western church, were aware of these dangers. The Synod of Elvira in Spain, for example, declared in AD300, 'There ought to be no pictures in the church lest what is worshipped and adored be depicted on walls.'

Those who were against the use of images were known as 'iconoclasts', and some of the Christian emperors and church leaders did their best to use their power to stamp out the use of icons completely. They weren't entirely successful, however, and the controversy continued for several centuries, with many people killed on both sides. Church councils met from 629 onwards to debate this issue among others. In 787 a council was held in Nicaea (in modern Turkey), at which icons were approved for use in the church. It was not, however, until the Council of Constantinople in 843 that they were officially accepted and restored.

The Medieval Church

Celtic monks on the borders of the Roman Empire kept Christian teaching alive when much of Europe was ravaged by warring tribes and the empire was beginning to dissolve. The Celtic monasteries of Iona, Lindisfarne and Ireland developed their own kind of icons. Their symmetrical, interwoven patterns came from Viking styles of decoration. Using intertwined mythological figures and intricate patterns of precious colours including beaten gold leaf, they enriched the pages of manuscripts. They prized these very highly both for their spiritual content and as glorious works of art produced to celebrate their faith.

The late medieval world, when European society had begun to stabilize politically, was the great age of cathedral building in the West. Architecture was developed to the highest level in order to glorify God in places of worship. The form of cathedrals developed from the pattern of Roman basilicas. Most cathedrals were linked to monasteries and became focal points not only for monks and nuns, but also for the whole community.

But how splendid should churches and cathedrals be? Bernard of Clairvaux (1090–1153), the founder of the Cistercian order of monks, believed that rich art could be a distraction in worship and preferred plain churches, full of light. He discouraged images and used simple, decorated stone. He also protested about spending too much money on church buildings while doing nothing for the poor:

'The church is resplendent in her walls, beggarly in her poor; she clothes her stones with gold, and leaves her sons naked; the rich man's eye is fed at the expense of the indigent. The curious find their delight here, yet the needy find no relief.'

St Francis had similar ideas about the wealth of the church, although many of the greatest works of art come from Franciscan monasteries.

The Benedictines were founded in 480 and the Cluniacs in 910. These two orders wanted to inspire religious awe in worship through majestic architecture, art and music. Someone who accepted this view was Abbot Suger of St Denis in Paris, who believed that only the best is worthy of God, and that beautiful objects could lead to spiritual awareness and understanding. He wanted the whole building to reflect the vision of the heavenly Jerusalem described in the book of Revelation (chapter 21) with its coloured walls and symbolic sacred geometry. Suger's building was the first of the great Gothic cathedrals. The plan was based on the geometry of the 'Golden proportion' which was then thought to be the proportion that God, the 'Great Architect', used in designing the perfect world. Windows of stained glass and objects encrusted with precious stones and jewels added to the whole feeling of glory. His words are inscribed on the cathedral door:

'Whoever thou art, if thou seekest to extol the glory of these doors,
Marvel not at the gold and the expense but at the craftsmanship of the work.
Bright is the noble work; but, being nobly bright, the work
Should brighten the minds, so that they may travel, through the true lights,
To the True Light where Christ is the true door.
In what manner it be inherent in this world the golden door defines:
The dull mind rises to truth through that which is material
And, in seeing this light, is resurrected from its former submersion.'

During this period there were several significant developments in art and architecture which enabled churches and cathedrals to reflect the particular beliefs and needs of the time. The invention of *ribbed vaulting* made it possible to build churches higher and wider than before, thus creating more space and light. Added to this, another new development, the *flying buttress* enabled architects to use thinner supporting walls, leaving room for large stained-glass windows which added to the feeling of transcendence.

By the end of the thirteenth century plagues and wars ravaged Europe. The crusades brought an even greater awareness of death. This led to a great emphasis in church teaching on fear and confession, and in art there are many reminders of death and the transience of human life, especially in tomb sculptures and murals.

Rich patrons seeking penance or blessing provided wealth for the enrichment of cathedrals and churches. Chantry chapels and altarpieces were donated by patrons to ensure that prayers would continue to be said (or chanted) for the repose of their souls. This helps to explain why places of worship sometimes look today like mausolea and glorious displays for important families.

Alongside the emphasis on doom and judgment, the art of late medieval times portrayed more than ever before the humanity of Christ. He was portrayed as a fully human person who identified with human beings in their suffering. This can particularly be seen in paintings of Jesus as a human baby suckling at his mother's breast, in the 'Man of Sorrows' image of Jesus' sufferings, and 'Pieta' paintings of the Virgin mourning

A neglected aspect of medieval Christian art is the craftsmanship in wood and stone to be found inside churches. This bench end from a church in Somerset, England, symbolizes the battle between good and evil.

her dead son. Christ was no longer just the divine 'Ruler of All' as seen in Byzantine church mosaics.

The Renaissance

The term 'Renaissance' is used to describe the 'rebirth' or renewal of learning that took place in Europe between about 1300 and 1550. It was a period marked on the one hand by curiosity and creative adventure, and by a fascination with antiquity on the other. As people began to rediscover the literature and ideas of the classical period, they came once more under the spell of the art of ancient Greece and Rome.

In art it was a period of rapid change and development of new techniques and styles. The invention of oil paint and systems of perspective allowed for new ways of achieving realism. Artists also worked with the philosophers and thinkers of the time to put deeper meanings into their work.

Early Renaissance painters worked mostly for the church on religious commissions. Later, secular patrons became equally important. The work of an Italian artist named Giotto represents a significant development towards realism in art. Whereas the Byzantine tradition sought to create a flat, two-dimensional world, Giotto experimented with light and shade to make his figures appear solid. He tried to set his scenes in a three-dimensional world of landscape and buildings, although the figures always remained larger and more important than their surroundings. He found new ways of representing figures and tried by their gestures and expression to show his saints and angels experiencing real emotions.

As painters like Mantegna and Piero della Francesca invented systems of proportion and perspective, their representations of Christ showed figures in more and more complicated positions. They used symbolic geometry in their works and made references to classical prototypes. Sometimes the artist's cleverness seemed almost as important as the subject. Mantegna, for example, painted the dead Christ in the tomb foreshortened, with his feet towards the viewer, and Masaccio represented God the Father, in his *Trinity Altarpiece* as a man standing on the earth. Previously he would only have been shown as a symbol or as a hand reaching out of the sky.

Deeply religious painters like Fra Angelico and Botticelli seem to have deliberately simplified their style from what was fashionable at the time, in order to make the religious feeling in their work stronger. In about 1490 Botticelli was very much affected by the teaching of the monk Savonarola, who spoke out against corruption in the church and was eventually burned at the stake.

As great Italian families like the Medici grew in wealth and influence, secular patronage for the arts became more common. Patrons vied with each other to commission the most celebrated artists to work for them and produce more and more magnificent works of art. Raphael's *Stanze* in the Vatican, Michelangelo's sculptures for papal tombs and the Sistine Chapel frescoes were partly commissioned to impress visitors by the power and learning of the pope, and partly to rival the great commissions made by past popes from different influential families.

With the excavation of Roman archaeological sites, great classical works of art were discovered, and artists began to compete with each other to make references to past works in their own paintings. Christ was sometimes portrayed like a Roman god, a classical hero living in a world of beauty and nobility, modelled on the writings of Plato and Aristotle which were thought to prefigure Christ's teaching. Pagan themes using classical myths became more common in works of art. Often these were interpreted as representing Christian truths or ideals of spiritual beauty and love. This also reflected new teaching about traditional Christian beliefs. The increased veneration of Mary, for example, led to more frequent painting of events from her life and depictions of her beauty and serenity. Raphael's smooth and serene representations of Christ and the saints as perfect beings in paintings that have order, harmonious colours and proportions have greatly influenced the way in which Jesus has been portrayed and thought of up to this day.

The art of northern Europe, where a similar renaissance of learning developed, was very different from that of Italy. Paintings were less dramatic in size, with a greater emphasis on the real world. Christ and the saints were represented as real people, sometimes in contemporary clothes, with no divide between the natural world and the supernatural.

The Reformation

The Reformation represented a protest against many of the practices and beliefs that had been added to the basic Christian faith since the times of the early church. The Reformers believed that God wanted a direct relationship with his people which did not depend on the traditions and practices that the Roman Church had developed.

They believed that the Christian message was better communicated through words rather than through pictures. Images, they thought, could distract from a direct communication with God, and could be idolatrous and encourage wrong doctrine. Consequently there were few paintings in Reformed churches, and shrines and devotional images were removed or destroyed. The interior arrangement of churches was often changed. Less emphasis was placed upon the sanctuary, altar and places of religious rites, because the Reformers believed that these rites had been corrupted by superstition. There was a stronger focus upon the pulpit where the Bible was expounded in the language of the people, and upon the spaces where the congregation participated in singing and prayers.

Some Reformers wanted to remove the arts altogether from worship. Henry VIII spoke against the use of images in churches as part of his attack on Rome. The Puritans in the sixteenth and seventeenth centuries followed this lead, and many sculptures and other artefacts in cathedrals and churches were destroyed. As a result the visual arts virtually dropped out of English religious life for a time, except among the nobility and royalty. Sadly this also contributed to the lowering of the standard of art in Britain except within the field of secular portraiture.

Lutherans, however, were more open to the visual arts than many other Protestant groups, because of the attitude of Luther himself:

'Now there are a great many pictures in those books (of the Bible), both of God, the angels, men and animals, especially in the Revelation of John and in Moses and Joshua... Pictures contained in these books we would paint on the walls for the sake of remembrance and better understanding, since they do no more harm on walls than in books.'

In Nuremburg, the painter Dürer became dissatisfied with Catholicism and followed the teaching of Erasmus and Luther, although he never actually made the break with the Mother Church. He painted in a style influenced by Italian art rather than the style of his Protestant German and Dutch contemporaries. But Dürer's works were full of new subjects, many of which were directly derived from his reading of the Bible.

The increased emphasis on the scriptures, preaching, and the development of new techniques of mass printing encouraged an increase in religious illustration for books and tracts. Dürer produced beautiful woodcuts and copper engravings of biblical scenes, such as his vivid illustrations of the Book of Revelation. Both Reformers and Catholic Counter-Reformers used powerful artworks in books and tracts to teach and to denounce each other. Cranach, for example, produced grotesque cartoons of the papacy, and a Catholic artist, Erhard Schoen, represented Luther as a pair of bagpipes being played by the Devil.

Calvin saw a place for the arts in the church, but insisted that they should be 'fitting' according to Protestant principles, and thought that they were more suited to secular life than to places of worship:

Facing: **The baroque splendour of St Mark's Basilica in Venice shows the cumulative effect of many images, giving a true 'vision of glory'. Notice also the galleries at different levels, from which separate choirs would blend in performances of music by composers such as Monteverdi.**

'Even if the use of images contained nothing evil, it still has no value for teaching... Sculpture and painting are gifts of God...for His glory and our good...but their practice is to be kept pure and legitimate... Only those things are to be sculpted or painted which the eyes are capable of seeing; let not God's majesty, which is far above the perception of the eyes, be debased through unseemly representation.'

Following Calvin's ideas, artists in Protestant countries such as Holland frequently produced works of art for private purposes rather than large church commissions or overtly religious subjects which might look too much like Catholic paintings. (This was particularly important in Holland since the province had only recently broken free politically from Spanish Catholic rule.) Paintings were of scenes from the world of their day and often contained objects such as skulls, flowers, moths and spilled glasses which were symbols to remind viewers of the transience of human life and the need for a true relationship with God. Protestant art thus began to express a Christian world-view instead of concentrating on specifically religious subjects.

As Reformation art stressed the meaning of faith rather than the transcendent qualities of the church and sacraments, the Roman Catholic Church responded to the Protestant call for reform. The Council of Trent in 1545 and 1563 encouraged the removal of all that was extravagant and difficult to understand, and reaffirmed the teaching role of the arts in the church.

Baroque Art

The word 'baroque' is derived from the term for a twisted or irregularly shaped pearl. It is used for the style of art that flourished throughout Europe from the end of the sixteenth to the early eighteenth centuries. Like many movements in art its name comes from its critics, who saw its works as reactionary and distasteful. They used it to mean 'absurd' and 'grotesque' (just as the term 'Gothic' was used to mean 'barbaric'). It was, however, a movement which was concerned with wholeness and balance. Every part of the picture needed to be in harmony, and there was a concern for reality of appearance, through creating space and using light and dark in a dramatic way. Artists like El Greco, Bernini and Caravaggio sought to represent religious emotion and devotion by elongating and twisting figures and

Rembrandt's painting represents the risen Jesus, two disciples and a servant in the village of Emmaus. The disciples have just realized who their guest is. Rembrandt set his biblical scenes in the context of the everyday Dutch life of his time.

creating a dramatic play of light and colour to enhance the emotional feeling of their paintings.

The Jesuits of the Counter-Reformation were trying to strengthen the power and image of the Roman Church in order to stem the tide of reformation and criticism of the Catholic faith. They therefore encouraged the adoption of this style of art and architecture, because it was so dramatic and commanding. The designs were meant to impress worshippers who might be tempted to leave the Mother Church. In Italian churches are spectacular ceiling paintings of ecstatic visions of saints and angels rising up, as it were, into the heavens. They were designed to stress the pageantry and importance of Catholic traditions, the central importance of the Mass, and the doctrine that the church itself was the way by which believers found salvation and blessing—elements that were being criticized by the Reformers.

In Spain, where the church had also had a long struggle with the Muslim Moors, Baroque art was especially dramatic, richly decorated and full of emotion. Velasquez, Zurbaran, Ribera and Murillo painted devotional art that was both impressive and filled with emotion, expressing the teachings of the Jesuits and of the Inquisition.

In northern Protestant countries, the Baroque style was also influential and fashionable, but had a different emphasis. There were fewer representational scene-paintings on the ceilings of the churches, but they were often richly and elaborately decorated to enhance the space for worship. The focus was often still on the pulpit rather than the altar, and now also on elaborate housings for organs. These were used to enhance with inspiring music the Protestant emphasis on the meaning of words. The rich choral music of Johann Sebastian Bach (1685–1750), emphasized biblical words and faith and added Baroque splendour and intensity of meaning.

Rembrandt van Rijn (1606–69) used the dramatic light and shadow of Baroque art and its search for realism to express his strong religious faith in intensely meaningful and technically brilliant paintings. Many of his major commissions were for portraits in which he shows the inner value of his sitters, both wealthy and poor. All his painting reflects his world-view, which was deeply influenced by his Christian faith. Although paintings of biblical scenes were mostly out of fashion by his time in Protestant Holland, Rembrandt seems to have produced many of his 160 religious paintings and 600 drawings of religious subjects as personal meditations inspired by his reading of the Bible. His paintings and etchings became prized and started a new vogue in religious art.

The Age of Enlightenment

During this period in the eighteenth century, European thinkers developed a spirit of critical enquiry emphasizing logic and knowledge rather than emotional understanding and faith. As a result, there was much questioning of traditional beliefs.

Religious art became relatively unpopular, and elegant 'society' art was fashionable. The Christian faith was no longer seen as the main influence and inspiration behind the arts. Instead, much emphasis was placed on beauty in nature, which was often expressed in religious terms.

This meant that artists felt much greater freedom in choosing their subject matter, and religious paintings were no longer thought to be superior. There was much more scope for artists to begin to paint their personal thoughts and the subjects that they found most inspiring. There was a new interest in the study of nature and painting from life, and landscape painting became popular—especially views of the places which people visited in the quest for knowledge and education.

William Blake, the mystical English painter and poet, protested against the worship of intellect and reason that he thought had come with the Enlightenment. He considered himself to be a Christian, but drew his inspiration from wider sources, using his vivid imagination to create a spiritual mythology through which he expressed his beliefs. He was very conscious of the corruption of the society and religion of his day, and wanted to bring about religious and moral redemption in society. Science, he believed, could not help people in understanding questions of ultimate truth and value which lay beyond the physical world. He held the Enlightenment's emphasis on reason as responsible for the spiritual death of society in his day, and wanted his art to make people aware of this and to awaken their spiritual sensitivity:

'To see a World in a Grain of Sand
And a Heaven in a Wild Flower,
Hold Infinity in the palm of your hand
And Eternity in an hour.'

The Nineteenth Century

Doubt and scepticism continued into the nineteenth century, fed by new discoveries and criticism. In spite of this crisis of faith, however, there were several periods of religious revival.

The evangelical revival at the end of the eighteenth century resulted in a flowering of church architecture. There was a strong emphasis on the art of preaching, and congregational hymn-singing flourished; but very few works of great religious art came out of it. The revival did, however, influence the general social and moral

The English artist and poet William Blake had a highly individual vision of spiritual reality. The sufferings of Job, in the Old Testament, meant a lot to him.

climate of Victorian England. This in turn led to the religious content in the works of people like Charles Dickens, George Eliot and Samuel Palmer, the Pre-Raphaelite movement and to the social and artistic ideas of John Ruskin.

The Pre-Raphaelites wanted art to return to a style that was simple, moral and true to nature in colour and form. They rejected the sophisticated techniques that they felt had corrupted the serene meaning of art since early Renaissance religious art. Many of their paintings seem sentimental to modern viewers, but they were thought of as revolutionary and too realistic when they first appeared. Holman Hunt's *The Light of the World* portrays Christ in rather a romantic way, typical of the sentiments of his society. Other paintings contain simple moral Victorian stories and symbols, and religious paintings influenced by them were used widely to illustrate Christian books and in religious prints. These have influenced the popular view of Christianity in British society up until today.

The Oxford Movement from 1833 brought a revival of a high-church style of worship and this influenced the design of more elaborate churches, particularly the flourishing of 'Gothic Revival' architecture.

The Catholic Church also experienced revival and growth in the nineteenth century. This was particularly after the first Vatican Council of 1870 which emphasized the doctrine of the church's 'infallibility' in order to guard against the heretical trends of the times. Much great art came out of this revival. The Jesuit poet, Gerard Manley Hopkins, who originally wanted to paint, expressed his spiritual understanding through symbols of his faith which he found in nature. In Germany the painter Caspar David Friedrich expressed similar ideas to those of Hopkins in serene symbolic landscapes. The 'Nazarenes' were a group of religious German painters, originally from a Protestant background, who worked in a style close to that of the Pre-Raphaelites in England. They moved to a monastery in Rome because they thought that to paint Christian subjects in a pious way was a moral duty.

This century also saw a great search among artists to express mystical meanings in art. The Romantic movement, for example, looked more to nature and to mythological and historical subjects than to Christianity for inspiration. Romantics like Turner, Delacroix, Wordsworth and Wagner often preferred powerful subjects to more subtle ones, and travelled widely in search of inspirational experiences. Sometimes they expressed their experiences and ideas about art and nature in almost religious terms.

The post-impressionist painters at the end of the century were dissatisfied with impressionist art that just imitated the surface of nature and of their society.

Following the example of the Romantics they wanted to reflect the inner meaning and spirit of their age. Van Gogh, for example, had a crisis of faith that led him to question his Christian faith and Dutch Reformed Church background. He turned to art and tried to paint the relationship between God and ordinary people in the working of nature. Emile Bernard, Maurice Denis and Paul Gauguin, working in Pont Aven in Brittany, tried to record the simple faith of Breton peasants in a simplified style of painting. They studied the profound works of the religious painter of peasants, Jean-François Millet. Denis went on to become a committed painter of Catholic religious images. Gauguin moved to the South Sea Islands where he painted the primitive legends and superstitions of the natives. His return to primitive life was an early example of the fashion of trying to find universal truths which were uncontaminated by the sophisticated beliefs that had developed in the West. Of his painting *Where do we come from? What are we? Where are we going?* he wrote:

'*Then lastly, an old woman nearing death appears to accept everything, to resign herself to her thought. She completes the story. At her feet a strange white bird holding a lizard in its claws, represents the futility of empty words… So I have finished a philosophical work on a theme comparable to that of the gospel.*'

The Twentieth Century

There have been very few major artists who have been committed to a traditional Christian faith, and fewer who have expressed their faith in explicitly religious works. In literature T.S. Eliot, and in music Olivier Messiaen managed to express their faith directly in works which stand in quality alongside the greatest twentieth-century exponents. Georges Rouault, the French Catholic painter, is the prime example in the visual arts. Using rich colour and texture he employed expressive marks, trying to capture spontaneous and profound religious emotion. He worked over each picture for many months,

managing to create images that have the simple intensity of icons, and the freedom and personal expression of modern works of art.

Much of the religious art of this century has been commissioned for particular church buildings. Canon Walter Hussey, for St Matthew's, Northampton and Chichester Cathedral, sought to continue the historic tradition of the church commissioning great works of art for places of worship. Three notable churches were specifically designed to contain pieces by some of the most important contemporary artists: Coventry Cathedral, Notre Dame de Toute Grace, Assy and the Matisse Chapel, Venice. Artists were chosen, not usually because of their personal faith, but because the style and feeling of their work was in sympathy with the intentions of the project. Both Henry Moore and Graham Sutherland (a mid-life convert to the Catholic faith) have written about the unusual challenge they felt in designing a work of art for a specifically religious setting. Henry Moore's *Madonna and Child* (1943–44) has been described as 'the most important carving to be placed in a church this century'. The sculptor said this of it:

'It has, I think, a quiet dignity and gentleness. I have tried to give a sense of complete easiness and repose, as though the Madonna could stay in that position for ever.'

A number of artists have used Christian subjects and themes as vehicles for expression in their work without actually having a Christian faith themselves or intending a religious message. Picasso and Francis Bacon painted the crucifixion as a representation of the suffering of humanity, particularly after the horrors of the great wars. Chagall, the Jewish painter, often painted the crucifixion of Jesus to express the sadness and glory of a great representative of the Jewish people. Other artists have used the resurrection and the incarnation as titles for abstract paintings but have used them as forms and concepts rather than as statements of Christian faith.

Rather like William Blake in the previous century, many of the artists who have made religious claims in the twentieth century have been rather unorthodox in their beliefs. Stanley Spencer, Eric Gill, Salvador Dali, Emile Nolde, Carel Weight, Norman Adams and David Jones have all used religious subject matter or mystical ideas. Sometimes, as in the Renaissance, they have represented biblical subjects in contemporary settings.

Facing: **The art of craftsmen in stained glass has a special clarity. This nineteenth-century window in Suffolk, England, shows a nativity scene.**

Salvador Dali's *Christ of St John of the Cross* is to many a very moving picture; others feel that it says more about Dali's own particular brand of mysticism than about the meaning of the death of Christ as Christians understand it.

These then are some of the significant developments that we can notice in the arts as they relate to religion in this century:

There have been many new movements in art. The variety of different movements reflects the different ways of searching for meaning. More than in any other century, there has been a passion for innovation and the discovery of different methods and styles of expression. Expressionism, cubism, surrealism, conceptualism, minimalism, and different forms of abstraction have all been developed by artists reaching out to find new ideas and ways of representing them. This has sometimes made it difficult for artists to develop styles of religious art, since artists have been accused of relying too much on the past. A personal traditional faith has often been claimed to be irrelevant to the production of great 'modern' art.

There has been an increasing interest in art from cultures and religions other than Christian. Picasso and many other artists were deeply influenced by African and other tribal art. They often looked for styles that were uncorrupted by Western cultural sophistication, in order to produce works that were more pure and universal in expression. Other artists such as the American abstract expressionists Mark Rothko and Jackson Pollock turned to Zen Buddhism and Shinto to find ways of making colour and shapes hold an intense meaning and have a hypnotically intense effect on the viewer.

There has been increasing interest in other philosophies and ideologies. A large number of artists developed ideas and subjects under the influence of theosophy, the occult and spiritualism. Mondrian and Kandinsky, for example, turned directly to the theosophical teachings of Madame Blavatsky to learn about the symbolic use of colour and to find a subject for their art that was loaded with deep meanings. Joseph Beuys believed that the artist was a sort of alchemist, 'shaman' or witch-doctor working with symbolic materials.

With this there has also been a strong interest in the spiritual element in art. People speak freely about the 'spiritual' effect of art, and for some people art has almost become a substitute for religion. Kandinsky, who wrote a book entitled *Concerning the Spiritual in Art*, tried to induce 'vibrations' in the soul of the people looking at his paintings. He described the responsibility of the artist in this way:

'His *actions, thoughts and feelings…constitute the spiritual atmosphere, in such a way that they purify or infect the spiritual air; and these actions and thoughts and feelings are the material for his creations, which likewise play a part in constituting the spiritual atmosphere.'*

Religious art has taken on a broader meaning. Artists who talk of art in religious terms are often not interested in Christianity specifically, but are concerned with religion in its broadest sense as part of art's concern with truth.

Adrian Wisniewsky, for example, who was brought up as a Catholic, in a painting entitled *Toying with Religion* paints what he describes as 'two non-believers bored with being atheists'. The figures are turning their backs on the traditional Christianity of the churches, in order to investigate 'religion' which he symbolizes in the picture as a giant opium bud. This is a rather obvious reference to Marx's famous saying that religion is 'the opium of the people'.

The American abstract expressionist painter Barnett Newman wrote as follows:

'*I am concerned not with my own feelings, nor with the mystery of my own personality but with the penetration into the world of mystery. My imagination is therefore attempting to dig into metaphysical secrets. To that extent my art is concerned with the sublime. It is a religious art which through symbols will catch the basic truth of life… The artist tries to wrest truth from the void.'*

Much modern Western art expresses a profound despair. Negative philosophies and feelings about the meaning and value of life have influenced the subject matter and style chosen by many artists. Francis Bacon, who calls himself an atheist, tries to show ugliness and meaninglessness in his work. Others have shown the loneliness, lack of dignity and isolation of modern society.

Religious art has had more support from the Roman Catholic Church. The Roman Catholic Church in this century has generally had a more positive attitude towards the arts than Protestantism, although there have been several significant exceptions. Protestant artists have tended to work more with expressing a Christian world-view in paintings of secular subjects. Anthony Green, for example, celebrates human relationships in a way that is not obviously 'religious' but is very positive. The second Vatican Council in 1963 called officially for a wider use of the arts and this deliberately encouraged church art and explicitly religious subject matter:

'*All artists who, prompted by their talents, desire God's glory in holy church, should remember that they are*

The paintings of Georges Rouault resemble stained-glass images. The bold lines and single construction give them great spiritual strength and directness.

engaged in a kind of imitation of God the creator… Of their nature the arts are directed towards expressing in some way the infinite beauty of God in works made by human hands. Their dedication to the increase of God's praise and of his glory is more complete, the more exclusively they are devoted to turning men's minds devoutly towards God.'

There was a revival of popular religious art in the 1980s. This revival affected both the Catholic and Protestant churches. It developed out of the 'folk art' tradition which has always been in the Western church. It can be seen, for example, in banner-making, frescoes, sculpture, altar-pieces, pilgrim souvenirs, flower-arranging, embroidery, wood-carving, stone-carving, metal work and glass work.

One critical observer describes much of this art as little more than 'little pious things in little pious places—decorative and nothing else'. But the establishment of art festivals, Christian art centres, study groups for professional artists and the like suggests that standards are being raised all the time, and that much serious thought and reflection is going into this contemporary revival of religious/Christian art.

Art in Other Religious Traditions

In the Hindu religion, just as in the developed religions of many ancient cultures, as its mythologies became more complex, so did the sophistication and richness of its artworks. Temple architecture, sculptures and frescoes became immensely rich and detailed. They vividly re-enact the stories of the faith, the Vedic and later gods (all representing functions or attributes of the one supreme God), and the ways to knowledge. There is a lavish, often frightening, atmosphere in which to worship. The statues are symbolic of the divine presence, and receive food and gifts. Shrines with images of the favourite deity are also used in individual Hindu homes.

In the Japanese Shinto religion animist belief reached rich sophistication. Large, impressive symbolic gates (*torii*) command the entrance to shrines where charms and paper tokens are a feature of worship. The sense of perfection in proportion is particularly important in Japanese Buddhism. Raked sand-gardens and carefully chosen symbolic stones and plants are positioned to create a mood of wholeness and peace to aid meditation.

Buddhist temples elsewhere are more dramatic. Large statues of the Buddha (The Enlightened One who attained the divine by paths that his worshippers seek to emulate) dominate shrines. The faithful worship and pray for enlightenment in an atmosphere heavy with meaning. The 'mantra', a repeated magical saying, is sometimes written in richly decorated prayer wheels which are set in motion to send the power of the phrase out into the furthest limit of the universe. Worshippers will also contemplate the 'mandala', a meditation circle representing spiritual and cosmic relationships. They believe that concentration on the powers that emanate from it leads to an experience of the divine.

A Zen Buddhist painting a mandala would seek to be in tune and in contact with spiritual forces, in order to produce a work. The patterns endlessly repeating within the wheel shape are supposed to induce a feeling of knowledge. Both Hindus and Buddhists also use 'tantras', or paintings with complex symbolism, as sources of meditation which are supposed to induce inner ecstasy and bring wisdom and spiritual understanding.

Muslims have kept even more strictly than the Jews to the Old Testament exclusion of the use of images in places of worship. The Qur'an teaches that an object and its image are magically united. To protect against idolatry, representational art is therefore not allowed in mosques. Muslim buildings are far from austere, however, as Muslims have a high regard for the arts and crafts and for the enhancement of their worship. The architecture, like the woven prayer-mats, brass objects, and manuscripts, is richly patterned with coloured, abstract and stylized floral decorations. Coloured glass, domes and minarets, ceramic tiles and pierced patterns in the walls and window decorations all take on variations and characteristics of the particular cultures in which they are produced. Especially rich decoration is made with calligraphic patterns using phrases from the Qur'an.

Christian Art in Other Cultures

The development of Christian images in art has not been confined to the Western world. The Christian faith has spread throughout the world, and as a result believers of different nationalities throughout the world have expressed their faith in images that relate to their own situations. Sometimes Christ has remained as a Western figure through the influence of nineteenth century illustrations used in teaching; but often he is portrayed as being of the same racial type as the painter. This has helped believers to identify with Jesus as one of them. It also means that by coming in human form he is seen to have identified with the people of each particular time and nation, and lived and died for them.

Some types of pagan or pre-Christian art of other cultures are associated with witchcraft and superstitions. At times ethnic Christian groups have deliberately rejected the styles of artefacts that are obviously related to beliefs that are at odds with Christian beliefs. At other times, as in early Christian art in ancient Rome, Christians of different countries and cultures have used their own native styles of art to depict their understanding of great Christian themes. Sometimes this seems incongruous to Western eyes that have been brought up to identify Christ as a white Caucasian (which he was not). Occasionally it has led to doctrinal misunderstandings or corruption, as in the portrayal of Christ as a South American revolutionary freedom-fighter, or in the influence of voodoo on the Christian religious art of Haiti. More often it is really creative and can give us insight into new aspects of the Christian faith and challenge traditions that we have taken for granted.

Conclusions

Art in most cultures has been closely associated with religion and deeply influenced by it. Apart from art which has a purely utilitarian purpose (such as advertising and design), artists have always tried to express what they see and what they feel and believe about what they see. Even when art is not explicitly religious, it is in one way or another expressing ideas, feelings and convictions about the significance of the world and the meaning of life. Art has frequently been associated with the search for truth.

Art conveys its meaning in many different ways. This meaning is expressed through the many choices that artists make: the kind of art-piece; the subject that is chosen and represented; the style, medium, colours and forms chosen to give the work a particular feeling; the hidden symbolic meaning of a work that may be contained in its geometry, the meaning of symbols and images, or the metaphorical allusions in the subject of the work. The meaning is also affected by how the viewer relates to the feeling or aura of a particular piece, or the place in which it is seen.

Art in the Western world has been deeply influenced by Christianity. It has been said that 'the history of Western art is largely the history of Christian painting'— with the possible exception of the late nineteenth and twentieth centuries. Different aspects of belief have been given different emphases at different periods, and this has meant that worshippers and artists have varied their practices, using the arts in different ways. But for many centuries it was the Christian faith which provided the main source of inspiration for Western art.

Artists have persistently looked for some kind of spiritual foundation. When Western art has turned its back on the Christian faith as its main source of inspiration, artists have looked in other directions, such as classical art, Eastern art, primitive art, spiritualism and the New Age and other philosophies.

The Christian faith can be expressed in different cultural contexts. While certain styles of art have suited the expression of faith in Europe, Christ's teachings and life are valid for people in all different societies and ages. Western styles are not the only ways of portraying Christianity. After all, Christ was himself from a very different Middle-Eastern culture, with different social customs and with ways of expressing his faith which Westerners today would find foreign.

Art plays an important part in popular religion. The painting of a saint, the crucifix with the body of Jesus, the statue of the Madonna and child, or the nativity scene on a Christmas card—all of these contribute to the religion of an individual or a community. Those who are already committed may find that this kind of art feeds their faith and proclaims it to the world. Outsiders may find it pleasant, or they may reject it as distasteful or unintelligible. And for those who find themselves somewhere in between it sums up a great deal of what folk religion or popular religion is all about.

Questions

▶ *Why is it becoming easier for people to associate art with religion?* Michael Day, chaplain to the London Art Colleges says, 'When I first started going to the Royal College of Art twenty years ago, people said, "Who the hell is he?" Now there are young artists in college who actually want to be religious painters.' Why has the situation changed?

▶ *Why is there increased public interest in art in a secular and scientific age?* Attendance at museums and art galleries has been increasing rapidly over the last few years, with 57 million people attending in one year recently in Britain. What is the explanation?

▶ *Can art be a substitute for religion?* It feeds the emotions, talks about meaning and value, and gives us a sense of the past. So is it taking the place of religion for some people?

▶ *Why do many of the same themes recur again and again in art?* And why do artists constantly return to Christian themes, even if they themselves are not Christians? Is it simply that Christian themes are part of Western culture, and that this is therefore a kind of common language which most people still seem to understand? Or is there a deeper reason? Do past beliefs, myths and legends have an inner significance that people respond to?

▶ *Why is there such a fascination with the Madonna, the Virgin Mary?* Is she a symbol of femininity, motherhood, fertility, submission, or holiness...or something else? Has she taken the place of the ancient Mother Goddess, the 'Queen of Heaven'? Does she represent the idea of God becoming man in the person of Jesus?

▶ *Why has the crucifixion been described as 'the most prevalent symbol of all' in modern religious art?* This is an intriguing development, especially when it was not so in the early church. Is it that people identify more today with a suffering man than they do with a triumphant figure in glory? What does the crucifixion of Jesus mean to people today, and is this different from what it meant to Christians in the past? Is there something about the idea of the dying and rising God which appeals to people?

7 Heavenly Music

Music leads the soul to the highest realm. It enables us to bridge the gulf between man and God.

A Sufi saying

Let the ears of a Christian girl be deaf to musical instruments, let her not know why the flute and the lyre were made.

Jerome AD345–420

It is possible to taste with wonder…God's wisdom in his wondrous gift of music… Those who are the least bit moved know nothing more amazing in the world. But any who remain unmoved are unmusical indeed and deserve to hear a certain filthy poet or the music of pigs.

Martin Luther 1483–1546

If there has been a 'common religion' in England in the last hundred years, it has been based not on doctrine but on popular hymns.

James Obelkevich

Music is a different form of communication from the one offered by the consumer society. The task of restoring music to its role as a communicator of beautiful things to society…comes under the heading of human rights.

Miguel-Angel Estrella, founder of Musique Espérance

Music, like poetry, drama or sport, is hardly essential for keeping human beings alive. But it seems to be an almost universal phenomenon and to exist in one form or another in every society.

The Origin and Function of Music

Anthropologists say that from the very beginning human beings have felt the need to come to terms with nature— the change of seasons; the growing and harvesting of crops; birth, life and death in people and animals. They have therefore spent time on unnecessary activities like ritual, play, drama, art and music. The acting out of these things through ritual and sacred play enabled them to cope with the course of nature and their life within it.

If this is true, then perhaps music stems from a basic urge to get to grips with human experience and to express feelings about life. It is part of how people cope.

Religious Music in Western Culture

In exploring music as one aspect of popular religion, therefore, these are some of the questions to be answered:

▶ *What does music have to do with religion?*

▶ *How has music been associated with religion in the Western world?*

▶ *What part does music play in popular religion?*

▶ *Has most European music been deeply influenced by Christianity, as would appear to be the case with art?*

▶ *How important was the influence of the Jewish tradition and of Greek music in the first centuries of Christianity?*

▶ *Why have Christians in the past had such different attitudes towards music?*

▶ *Is there anything in common between 'secular' music and 'religious' music in the present day?*

Music in the Old Testament and the Jewish Tradition

The worship that took place in the temple at Jerusalem, the most important shrine of the Jewish people, involved singing as well as playing a large number of musical instruments. The singers and instrumentalists who served the temple numbered 288 in all. Compare this with the choir of eighteen boys and twelve men at Canterbury Cathedral!

The book of Psalms in the Old Testament can justifiably be described as the oldest songbook and hymn book in the world that is still in use. In these 150 sacred songs, and in others in different parts of the Old Testament, are examples of almost every kind of song that has been sung since then. There is scarcely a twentieth-century song that doesn't have a parallel in the Old Testament. For example:

▶ The blues are similar to the psalms of lament like Psalms 42 and 43.

▶ Protest songs are close to psalms of protest like Psalms 74 and 79.

▶ Songs about the joys of romantic or sexual love are parallel to the Song of Solomon.

▶ Songs about broken relationships are very common today and are also found in the Psalms, although there the theme is usually broken trust between man and man rather than man and woman.

▶ Songs about personal anxiety and despair are found in Psalms 42, 43 and 69.

▶ Songs celebrating the joys of life include Psalms 104 and 127.

▶ Songs of regret are like the psalms of repentance, such as Psalm 51.

This explains why it has been said of the Psalms, 'All human life is there.' The people of Israel felt they could bring all their personal and national anger, anxieties, joys, prayers and praises to God in music. The Psalms show, therefore, that in Israel's life music was used to celebrate and come to terms with every aspect of life—in precisely the way that anthropologists have described.

This rich tradition came to an end when the temple at Jerusalem was destroyed by the Romans in AD70. The music of the Jewish community which survived became much simpler; and the synagogues which sprang up wherever the Jews were scattered developed only vocal music.

Greek Music

The word 'music' comes from the ancient Greeks, although their word, *mousike*, covered a wider range of activities—including poetry, history, tragedy, comedy, dancing, astronomy, as well as what people today mean by music. Their philosophers thought that just as athletics provides training for the body so music provides training for the mind. And they tended to judge music by the good or bad effect that it had on people. So, for example, one kind of music was thought to make people lazy, while another was regarded as dangerous for pregnant women; and the Spartans believed that a proper musical education could make people more law-abiding!

The ideas of the Greek philosophers influenced Christian attitudes to music for centuries. Aristotle, one of the most famous of these philosophers, believed that every adult should enjoy and understand music, because it could do three things: promote education and influence morality; purify the emotions; and provide relaxation. He also picked out the pipes (which probably sounded similar to the flute) as an instrument which was specially emotional and could excite people to a drunken frenzy. It was probably because he singled out the pipes in this way that they were never used in churches for centuries. So the fact that Schubert in 1828 didn't use flutes in his E flat Mass was to some extent a result of Aristotle's influence. Christians have often fallen into the trap of regarding certain musical instruments and types of music as being bad in themselves. It is surprising that of the two main influences on Christian thinking in the early centuries—Jewish and Greek—it was this Greek influence, which came from outside, which was stronger.

Music in Early Christian Times

There are very few references to music in the New Testament. One of these is found in Mark 14:26, where it says that Jesus sang a Passover psalm with his disciples before he went out after the Last Supper, knowing that he would be arrested and crucified. Revelation, the last book of the Bible, paints a picture of heaven as a place where

Facing: **These musicians portrayed on a Greek vase remind us that music was important to the Greeks. It was believed to uplift the mind and spirit as well as the senses.**

there will be both vocal and instrumental music. And Paul mentions music as an antidote to all sorts of depravity when he says:

'*Do not get drunk on wine, which leads to debauchery. Instead, be filled with the Spirit. Speak to one another with psalms, hymns and spiritual songs. Sing and make music in your heart to the Lord, always giving thanks to God the Father for everything, in the name of our Lord Jesus Christ.*' (*Ephesians 5:18*)

He must have thought that music could be a very powerful tool!

For many centuries after this—in fact right up to the Reformation in the sixteenth century—Christians mostly sang the Psalms or other texts from the Bible. People regarded hymns as human inventions and therefore not suitable for worship. One notable exception, however, was Ambrose, Bishop of Milan (339–397), who was accused of bewitching half of Europe with his powerful hymns. At least three of them are still in use today: '-Come thou Redeemer of the earth', 'Creator of the earth and sky', and 'O strength and stay upholding all creation'. Another exception were the Arians, a heretical group in the fourth century who popularized their teachings by writing songs.

Since those early centuries, there have generally been three different kinds of attitude to music among Christians:

Negative attitudes. Many church leaders were afraid of importing the corruption associated with certain kinds of instruments into church life, and they tried to avoid those kinds of music which were played in society around them. Whenever most of the Early Church Fathers wrote about music, they condemned contemporary music and warned about its dangers.

The Apostolic Constitutions, for example, written in about 380 by a Syrian Christian, mentioned the *aulos* (flute) player in a list of people who were not allowed to become members of the church by baptism unless they gave up their job. One fourth-century Christian writer regarded music as a useless art:

'*Now among the arts which are necessary to life, the goal of which is plain to see, there is carpentry and the chair, architecture and the house, ship building…weaving…forging; among the useless arts are cithara (a string instrument) playing, dancing, aulos playing and all others whose product ceases when the activity ceases.*'

Total disregard. Others regarded worship as something spiritual, and totally excluded music from church services because they thought it was entirely human in its origins.

Cautious approval. There were a few who believed that the human ability to make music is part of the creativity people inherit from being made in the image of God. St Augustine, for example, commended the use of music—but with much caution. He believed that nothing is worthy of being used in worship except the inspired text of the Bible, and he warned people against being moved by the beauty of the voice or the music rather than by the words being sung. He also said that some instruments were suitable for accompanying worship while others were not: 'Let none turn his heart to theatrical instruments.'

Tertullian, a Christian writer living in Carthage around 170–225, and John Chrysostom, Bishop of Constantinople (389–407), thought that singing was more valuable than instrumental music of any sort. Basil the Great (330–379), while warning against the evils of certain types of music, was one of the first to note that melodies are a help in remembering words. He said that melodious settings of the Psalms are given by the Holy Spirit to help weak, erring humans to retain the words in their memory.

The Christians of this era reconciled these views with the fact that there was so much emphasis on vocal and instrumental music in the Old Testament by interpreting all references to music in the Old Testament as allegory. This, for example, is how Clement of Alexandria explained Psalm 150:

'''*Praise Him on the strings and instruments*'' *refers to our body as an instrument and its sinews as strings from which it derives its harmonious tensions, and when strummed by the Spirit gives off human notes.*'

Another answer is that they saw musical instruments as a concession to human weakness:

'*Just as God allowed sacrifices, so too did he permit instruments, making concession to their weakness.*'

The many cautions and prohibitions of the Early Church Fathers seem to indicate that in reality several varieties of vocal and instrumental music gained a firm foothold in church life from the very start. Music has a way of taking the law into its own hands!

The Middle Ages

Song schools. These probably first appeared in Rome during the time of Pope Sylvester in the fourth century. Before the eleventh century there was no exact way of writing down melodies, and monks spent up to nine years learning them by heart. These schools sent out 'missionaries' to teach people the chants of the church. So, for example, in 680 Benedict Biscop brought a skilled singer back with him from Rome to teach the monks at Wearmouth Abbey in England the music that was sung at St Peter's in Rome.

Plainsong. The singing of a simple, unaccompanied melody line had been used from the very beginning of the church. Plainsong melodies from the very earliest times are still in use today, and embody the traditional ritual melody of the Western church. Gregorian chant is one category of plainsong that developed in the sixth century during the reign of Pope Gregory. The emperor Charlemagne's insistence on its use to the exclusion of all other plainsong chants ensured its survival, and it is still used today.

This is how Bernard of Clairvaux (1090–1153) commented on the use of plainsong chants:

'*Let the chant be full of gravity, let it be neither worldly, nor too rude and poor... Let it be sweet, yet without levity, and, whilst it pleases the ear, let it move the heart. It should not contradict the sense of the words, but rather enhance it. For this is no slight loss of spiritual grace to be distracted from the profit of the sense by the beauty of the chant, and to have our attention drawn to a mere vocal display, when we ought to be thinking of what is sung.*'

Harmony. Many scholars think that it was the famous monk Hucbald, 'the one legged' (840–930), who introduced harmony, when he suggested that some of the congregation should sing the melody at a lower pitch—a fourth or a fifth lower—in order to improve the quality of the singing. This marked the beginnings of singing in parts and harmony in Western Europe, although there is some evidence that singing simultaneously at different pitches occurred in ancient Greece, the Far East and probably elsewhere too.

Music notation. Guido of Arezzo (ca. 995–1050) invented a system of writing down music which superseded all others, and on which all later developments, including the present system of notation, are based.

Carols. These were originally danced as well as sung, and several well-known Christmas carols come from the Middle Ages. 'The Holly and the Ivy', for example, was originally sung as a dance between 'lads and maids'. The symbolism was of pagan origin, with the holly symbolizing masculinity and the ivy femininity. In the Christian version of the carol, different features of the holly were linked with the life and death of Jesus. A large number of other carols owe their origin to the introduction of the crib in churches at Christmas, a practice that was introduced and popularized by St Francis of Assisi.

The carol was important for the development of religious music because it abandoned the timeless plainsong chants of earlier centuries and, by using dance melodies, helped to usher in the era of modern music. This is how Percy Dearmer sums up the significance of carols:

'*Carols are songs with religious impulse that are simple, hilarious, popular and modern... Carols were moreover always modern, expressing the manner in which the ordinary man at his best understood the ideas of his age, and brought conservative religion up to date; the carol did this for the 15th Century after the collapse of the old feudal order, and should do the same for the 20th.*'

The organ. It is thought by some that the organ (or its primitive predecessor) was introduced into church worship by Pope Vitalian in the seventh century. It survived many storms of theological debate and death sentences pronounced on it at various times, and lived on to be described by Mozart as 'the king of instruments'. In 1619 Michael Praetorius said of the organ:

'*Almighty God...can never be given sufficient thanks for having granted to man...such gifts as have enabled him to achieve such a perfect...instrument of music as...the organ; and to play on it with hands and with feet in such a manner that God in heaven may be praised, his worship adorned, the man moved and inspired to Christian devotion.*'

The pipe organ was (and is) an extremely versatile instrument, and in modern terms was the first polyphonic synthesizer to be invented. It is capable of being used in all styles of music, from Bach to rock and pop, but sadly few are still used in this way.

The Reformation

The leading figures of this era had differing views on the value of music in Christian worship.

Luther

After a time of personal spiritual crisis, Martin Luther (1483–1546) came to understand the nature of God's righteousness and forgiveness in a new way, and it was this experience that set the whole Reformation in progress. His ideas spread like wildfire across Europe, and led to a revival in religious music in Germany. This music drew not only on the older traditions of church music, but also on secular music of the time, including folk songs and the music of ordinary people. Luther himself wrote a large number of hymns, and it was said

---

'Amazing Grace'

It's strange that a religious poem written over two hundred years ago should not only reach the pop charts in Britain in 1970 but stay there for at least a year.

▶ John Newton, the author of the hymn, was brought up in a Christian home. At the age of eleven he went to sea and began an infamous career as a slave trader. He endured many adventures and hardships, including surviving a near shipwreck. This encounter with death prompted a dramatic conversion to Christianity, and he wrote 'Amazing Grace' as a reflection of his own life experiences.

▶ What is it that makes this song so appealing? Is it simply the tune—a very moving old American folk song? Or is it also that the words express a longing for something that might be able to change human nature?

Amazing grace (how sweet the sound)
That saved a wretch like me!
I once was lost, but now am found,
Was blind but now I see.

Through many dangers, toils and snares
I have already come;
God's grace has brought me safe thus far,
And he will lead me home.

---

that he did more harm to his enemies through his hymns than through all his sermons and books.

It isn't surprising therefore, that once the Lutheran Church was established, hymn singing and instrumental music, especially organ music, began to flourish. And this was the tradition into which J.S. Bach (1685–1750) was born. He is still regarded as the greatest composer of organ music and one of the greatest composers of all time, and his influence on music right up to the present day has been incalculable. He died in relative poverty, and his works were largely ignored at the time in the flood of new music being written, and remained so for almost a century.

Zwingli

One of the Reformers in Switzerland, Ulrich Zwingli (1484–1531), had a much more negative attitude towards music. He believed that worship was a spiritual activity, and that music was a human invention which had no place in the worship of God. He therefore banned all forms of music and singing from his church services.

Calvin

Protestant churches which came into existence through the influence of John Calvin (1509–64) rejected the use of any musical instruments. In Scotland, for example, the Presbyterian Church, which was established in 1560, permitted only unaccompanied singing until late into the nineteenth century. Books were even published condemning the organ (such as The Use of the Organ...Indefensible, by James Begg, 1866) and to this day in Scotland, England and other parts of the world there are churches of various denominations in which instrumental music of any sort is not allowed.

In spite of this ban on musical instruments, however, Calvin was concerned that everyone in the church should be able to join in the singing, and not only the choir. He also wanted people to sing in their own language, and to understand what they were singing. He therefore put the Psalms and other passages of the Bible into a simple poetical form with a metre and stanzas. These 'Metrical Psalms' soon became very popular, and spread quickly throughout Europe. For example, John Knox (1505–72), a minister to the English-speaking refugees in Geneva, brought the Anglo-Genevan Psalter to Scotland, where it was revised before being used in Scottish churches. It has been revised several times since then, and is still part of the hymn book of the Scottish Presbyterian Church.

This Scottish Psalter was important because it enabled the ordinary people of Scotland to sing with ease paraphrased texts from the Bible. The most famous of these is the paraphrase of the twenty-third Psalm, 'The Lord's my Shepherd,' which is found in every major hymn book in the English language, and is usually sung to the tune *Crimond*.

The Puritans and the Dissenters

Widely differing attitudes to religious music persisted through the seventeenth century.

The Puritans

In the reign of Oliver Cromwell (1649–60), Puritan values held sway throughout England. The conflict that this created can be illustrated by the story of the Puritan soldier who was trying to climb up into the organ loft in a church to smash up the organ, when the organist dropped a millstone on him from the organ loft and killed him.

This soldier was simply trying to carry out a law passed by the House of Commons in 1644, prohibiting organ playing in church services and demanding 'the speedy demolishing of all organs...in the cathedrals...or parish churches...throughout the kingdom of England and...Wales, the better to accomplish the blessed reformation so happily begun and to remove offences and things illegal in the worship of God'.

The Puritans did not, however, object to every kind of music. They usually accepted music outside the church, and some had organs in their homes. Many organs that were banished from churches were bought by tavern keepers and used for entertainment. It's very probable that what later became 'music hall' can be traced back to the time when Puritanism was at its height.

Oliver Cromwell himself was a great lover of music, and he removed the organ from Magdalen College in Oxford to his own palace at Hampton Court. He even employed his own private organist, paying him a huge salary of £100 per annum, and when one of his daughters was married he entertained his guests with a large orchestra.

A vast quantity of secular music was published during the time of Cromwell's rule. One of the most famous publications is Playford's *Dancing Master*. String fantasias, rounds, madrigals, music for lute, viola and violin, books on musical theory and other music books of every possible kind were published.

The Dissenters

The Dissenters were those who felt unable to conform to the practices and beliefs of the Church of England in every point. They therefore chose to leave, or were forced to leave it in 1662. They set up churches all over the country, and soon began to develop a musical tradition of their own which was quite distinct from that of the Church of England. Many of the major hymns of the seventeenth and eighteenth centuries came from the pens of Dissenters.

Richard Baxter (1615–91) was appointed chaplain to King Charles in 1660, but refused the offer to become Bishop of Hereford. His decision to step down from the Anglican ministry and to continue preaching led to two terms of imprisonment. He wrote a number of hymns, a few of which still find a place in our hymn books today. His best known hymn is 'Ye holy angels bright who wait at God's right hand'.

Isaac Watts (1674–1748) has been called 'the father of English hymns'. His career as a hymn writer began when he complained about the poor quality of the hymns in the church services he attended at Southampton. His father promptly suggested that he should try to write something better himself, and the following Sunday his first hymn, which was sung at the evening service, delighted everyone. His first collection of hymns became a best-seller, and the hymn writers who followed were greatly indebted to him.

He also turned his attention to the Psalms, which he regarded as totally unsuitable for Christian worship because they expressed unchristian sentiments. In his *Psalms of David Imitated in New Testament Language* he aimed to 'see David converted into a Christian'. It has been said of Watts that he 'saw with the clear intuition of genius what needed to be done and alone he did it'. In total he wrote over 600 hymns; two of the best known are 'When I survey the wondrous cross', and 'Jesus shall reign where'er the sun'.

The Evangelical Revival

With the birth of John Wesley (1703–91) and his brother Charles Wesley (1707–88) the river of English hymn writing became a flood. John's preaching all over the country brought a great spiritual revival, and he became one of the founder members of the Methodist movement.

Ever since the days of John and Charles Wesley in the eighteenth century, hymn singing has been central to Christian worship around the world. This Korean choir benefits from the Wesley tradition.

Handel's *Messiah*

The man who composed the best known sacred oratorio in the Western world had a quick temper and a gift for languages. He is said to have shouted and sworn in at least five languages at singers who didn't come up to scratch! He was also very generous and had a clear faith. Percy Scholes says that 'he used his art on many occasions during his life time for the assistance of charity. Like Bach, he was a sincere Christian and (within the limits which human nature commonly attains) a consistent one.'

► He wrote *Messiah* at a point in his career when most other mortals would have given up. His earlier success in opera had faded when the Italian style went out of fashion. He was heavily in debt, because his last theatre company owed £12,000. King George had withdrawn his patronage, and he was caught up in feuds and vendettas with rivals both past

and present. And he had suffered what is thought to have been a stroke or a form of paralysis. He therefore withdrew from the public eye between February and November in 1742, and in some quarters it was thought that his days of greatness were past and that he had burnt himself out. But in spite of all this his spirit wasn't broken.

► It was at this point that Charles Jennens provided Handel with the libretto of *Messiah*. Jennens was a rich, self-opinionated bachelor, who was nicknamed by his colleagues 'Solyman the Magnificent'. On 22 August Handel started work on Jennens' libretto and twenty-four days later, on 12 September, he had finished the entire work. This must rank as one of the greatest feats of musical composition of all time.

► The story goes that when Handel had just finished writing the momentous 'Hallelujah Chorus', his servant found him at the table with tears streaming from his eyes.

Handel exclaimed: 'I did think I did see all Heaven before me, and the Great God himself!'

► The first performance of *Messiah* took place in Dublin, because Handel was out of favour in fashionable London. The first performance was a charity concert for 'the Society for relieving prisoners, the Charitable infirmary and Mercer's Hospital', and was a great success. Jennens, however wasn't so pleased, and wrote to a friend:

'I gave Handel Messiah which I value highly and he has made a fine entertainment of it, tho' not near so good as he ought to have done. I have made him with great difficulty correct some of the grossest faults in the composition but he has retained some passages...obstinately...unworthy of Messiah.'

► When Handel planned to perform *Messiah* on his return to London, he was warned of opposition from the church on theological grounds. Audiences didn't greatly enjoy the work, and there were only

three performances that season. King George II attended one performance, however, and was so moved by the 'Hallelujah Chorus' that he rose to his feet, and didn't sit down until it was over. Thereafter it became a tradition, and for over 200 years people have stood during that part of the work.

The 'oratorio' takes Christian music into the concert hall, as choir, soloists and orchestra make music to words often taken from the Bible. Handel's *Messiah* is the best-known example.

'Negro spirituals' often took the theme of Jesus setting us free from slavery. When slavery was abolished, the celebrations were ecstatic, as here on the West Indian island of Reunion in 1848.

When John was sailing to Georgia in 1735, he found a group of Moravian Christians from Germany on board ship. They seemed to sing throughout the journey, in good weather and bad, and John was so moved by their singing that he set about learning German in order to be able to join in their worship. Before the journey was over, he had started to translate these Moravian hymns into English, and his main contribution to hymn writing was through these translations.

As a result of this experience he came to believe that hymns could be used to raise the level of teaching and of personal devotion in the life of the church. He hated slow, drawn-out hymn singing, and demanded that hymns be cheerful and taken at a good pace.

It was his brother Charles, however, who had the greater gift for writing, and many think of him as one of the greatest, if not the greatest, English hymn-writer. Two of the best known of his 6,000 hymns are 'Love divine all loves excelling', and the Christmas hymn 'Hark, the herald angels sing'.

The Nineteenth Century

In this era music was received much more enthusiastically by Christians. The music created in this period came from diverse sources.

The Oxford Movement

The next great stimulus to hymn writing came in the first part of the nineteenth century with the Oxford Movement, which was a revival of the Catholic tradition within the Church of England. Among the founders and hymn writers of the movement were John Keble (1792–1866) who wrote 'Blest are the pure in heart', and John

'And did those feet'

William Blake (1757–1827), the author of this poem which has now become a popular hymn, was influenced by his unorthodox Christian beliefs, by his political beliefs, and by his interest in mysticism. It has become almost an alternative National Anthem for the British.

▶ In this poem, Blake is referring to an ancient legend that Jesus visited England during his childhood, and he gives the impression that the soil of England is almost sacred if Jesus actually walked here. When Blake asks, 'And was Jerusalem builded here...?' he is probably referring to a belief about a past Golden Age which was widely accepted in his day. According to a popular legend, England played an important part in this Golden Age, because the British nation was descended from the giant Albion, who was a descendant of Noah's son Ham, who had settled in England after the Flood. The 'dark satanic mills' are not part of an industrial landscape, but the mills outside the gates of hell.

▶ The hymn remains a favourite in Britain because it combines a strong patriotism with a desire to work for a better future 'in England's green and pleasant land'.

And did those feet in ancient time
Walk upon England's mountains green?
And was the holy Lamb of God
On England's pleasant pastures seen?
And did the countenance divine
Shine forth upon our clouded hills?
And was Jerusalem builded here
Among those dark satanic mills.

Bring me my bow of burning gold!
Bring me my arrows of desire!
Bring me my spear! O clouds, unfold!
Bring me my chariot of fire!
I will not cease from mental fight,
Nor shall my sword sleep in my hand,
Till we have built Jerusalem
In England's green and pleasant land.

Abide with Me

Henry Francis Lyte was the vicar of a small church in Marazion, Cornwall. It seems that the hymn was written at a time when there was deep division in his church, and when most of his choir had left to join the Plymouth Brethren. Lyte was deeply troubled by these events, and when he retired to his study one Sunday evening he sat down and wrote the hymn. The time of day is referred to in the words 'fast falls the eventide', and his sadness over the division in his church is reflected in the lines 'when other helpers fail and comforts flee'.

▶ The tradition of singing the hymn at the Cup Final match of the Football Association in Britain started in 1927. It was selected as part of the pre-match entertainment by the master of ceremonies because it was known to have been a favourite hymn of Queen Mary. The tradition has been kept ever since then without a break, except for one year. In 1959 it was replaced by a display from the girls of the Coventry Keep Fit Association. But by popular demand of the crowd, the singing of the hymn was reinstated the following year.

▶ The idea that God can provide comfort even in the face of deep despair is one that has enduring appeal, even to people who do not regard themselves as religious. This is how Erik Routley sums up the popularity of the hymn: 'There is no need to emphasize what this hymn has meant to the Englishmen... In it this humble curate has ministered to a parish as wide as the English-speaking world.'

Abide with me; fast falls the eventide:
The darkness deepens; Lord, with me abide:
When other helpers fail, and comforts flee,
Help of the helpless, O abide with me.

Swift to its close ebbs out life's little day;
Earth's joys grow dim, its glories pass away;
Change and decay in all around I see:
O thou who changest not, abide with me.

Henry Newman (1801–90), who wrote 'Praise to the holiest in the height'.

The Oxford Movement had a remarkable effect on church music, by helping to spread the use of cathedral-type choral services, including the singing of Psalms to chants by the choir, to almost every parish church. Another example of this revival can be seen in the service of Nine Lessons and Carols, which was first devised by the Bishop of Truro in 1860, and later used at King's College in Cambridge.

Negro Spirituals

Negro spirituals are undoubtedly one of the most influential kinds of music to emerge from the nineteenth century. Amid the sordidness, cruelty and inhumanity of slavery, the meeting of African and American culture produced something quite remarkable and beautiful.

Negro spirituals were therefore part of the response of African slaves to the culture of Christianized America.

The words of these songs were adaptations of Bible passages and stories, and made great use of repetition. They contained a large element of improvisation, and often no definitive version of a song can be said to exist. It is thought that many spirituals were composed when the black congregations seized on one particular powerful phrase from a sermon and then began to repeat it over and over again in song. They often used these spirituals as work songs.

This is how one writer comments on the significance of negro spirituals:

'A European coming fresh to the subject would expect to find among a race that had suffered for a quarter of a thousand years of slavery a good many rude poems of revenge allied to vigorous music. But in Negro song slavery is barely mentioned and overt hostility was until recently entirely absent... Instead of it is a spirit of gentle, patient melancholy and of longing...of a confidence in triumph in another world—both of these feelings largely expressed by the use of incidents and images from Scripture.'

American Hymns of Social Liberation

The struggle to win emancipation for the slaves in nineteenth-century America produced hymns that have remained classics to this day. One such hymn is 'Stand up, stand up for Jesus', which was written in 1858 as a result of a tragic accident. An influential young Episcopalian clergyman, the Rev. Dudley Tyng,. had spoken out strongly against slavery, which was still supported by many churches in the United States. His outspoken sermons produced strong opposition, and he was forced to resign. Some of his friends, however, were keen that he should continue preaching, and hired the largest hall available in the city. Here he conducted a mission, and on one occasion preached to 5,000 people on the verse from Exodus 10:11, 'Come now, ye that are men serve the Lord.' Hundreds responded to his call to follow Christ—but this proved to be his last sermon.

A few days later he was involved in an accident, when part of his clothing was caught in winnowing machinery as he was patting a donkey. His arm was wrenched from its socket and he died soon after. When a Presbyterian minister, George Duffield, came to visit him before he died, Tyng asked him to preach in his place the following Sunday. 'What message shall I send them from you?' asked Duffield. 'Tell them to stand up for Jesus,' was Tyng's reply.

From these words Duffield penned the famous words of 'Stand up, stand up for Jesus, ye soldiers of the cross'. He had no idea that his poem would become a hymn, but

The worship of the 'charismatic movement'—for renewal in the Holy Spirit— gives full vent to the emotions. Upraised arms, repeated choruses and a deep sense of togetherness make such singing very distinctive.

quite by accident it found its way into a church newspaper and was then set to music. The hymn swept through the churches in America and soon afterwards arrived in England. People who sing it today generally have no idea that the words were originally a call to stand up and fight against evils in society!

The Christmas hymn 'It came upon a midnight clear' also came out of the same struggle for liberation before the American Civil War broke out. It was written in 1849 at the time of the 'forty-niner' Gold Rush, and one of its verses refers clearly to the tyranny of slavery:

> 'And ye, beneath life's crushing load,
> Whose forms are bending low,
> Who toil along the climbing way
> With painful steps and slow...
> O rest beside the weary road
> And hear the angels sing.'

Revivalism and Gospel Songs

Ever since the successful use of negro spirituals to accompany preaching during the Kentucky Revivals of 1797–1805, evangelists had realized the importance of music in mass evangelism. The evangelist D.L. Moody used the hymns of his colleague Sankey, and the final edition of their music, entitled *Sacred Songs and Solos*, contained well over 1,000 hymns and songs. The style of these songs was similar to the music of the day, and has been described as 'the folk-music of the music-hall'.

Although some have criticized the poor quality of much of the music, it helped to bring life and hope to thousands of people, many of whom were poor and scarcely literate. Some of these songs, like 'What a friend we have in Jesus', 'Man of sorrows', 'I will sing the wondrous story' and 'Revive thy work, O Lord' have survived and are regarded as classics of their kind.

One of the greatest writers of this kind of revivalist mission hymn was Frances van Alstyne, known as Fanny J. Crosby. She was blind from birth, but she wrote over 8,000 hymns and songs before she died at the age of eighty-four. Among her best known and best loved hymns are 'To God be the glory' and 'Blessed assurance'. Many of these gospel songs have been used widely in mission services in Baptist and Free churches, in the Salvation Army and in missions led by Billy Graham and other evangelists.

The Twentieth Century

The range of music used in worship in the twentieth century has been enormous.

Hymns

The stream of hymnody which started with the Reformation continued through the twentieth century. The classic collection known as *Hymns Ancient and Modern*, for example, which was first published in 1861, was revised and expanded twice in this century. One major departure, however, was the attempt (as in *Hymns for Today's Church*, 1982) to modernize the archaic language of older hymns—including the great classics—in order to make them intelligible to non-churched people.

Folk

The popularity of folk music in the sixties and seventies soon led to a new kind of Christian folk song. Sydney Carter's 'Lord of the Dance', for example, put some powerful words into the mouth of Jesus, in which he invites his followers to join him in a joyful dance. In another of his songs, 'Friday Morning', one of the two criminals being crucified with Jesus says to him, 'It's God they ought to crucify instead of you and me.' The irony in these words is that, without realizing it, he is expressing in a very bold way what Christians believe was actually happening in the crucifixion.

Pentecostalism and the Charismatic Movement

Pentecostalism is a stream of Christianity which emphasizes the need for a personal experience of the Holy Spirit, and the use of all the spiritual or 'charismatic' gifts which are mentioned in the New Testament. It became so significant during the twentieth century that it has been described as 'a fourth major strand in Christianity—alongside Orthodoxy, Roman Catholicism and Protestantism'.

The Charismatic Renewal Movement, which grew out of the Pentecostal Movement in the early 1960s, developed a distinctive style of worship, using lively, contemporary music. From this movement issued a veritable torrent of new worship songs and other musical material during the 1970s and 1980s. One of the chief features of these songs is their simplicity: the tunes are easy to learn, and the words are written in the pop/folk style of the 1960s. The worshipper expresses their personal feelings to or about God without the complex ideas and doctrines found in some of the traditional hymns. And in this style of worship people feel free to open their hands, raise their arms, or to dance. The musical instruments used are those that are used in the contemporary pop scene. Graham Kendrick is one of the best known writers of this kind of song.

Music in Other Religions and Cultures

It is helpful to contrast the use that has been made of music within the Christian tradition with its uses in other religions.

In many ways Islam has had a higher view of music than Christianity. At the beginning Muhammad (570– 632) restricted the use of music to the accompaniment of the Qur'an and to family celebrations. He felt that using music in any other context would detract from religious devotion and attitudes. But as Islam spread and Muslims met people of other nations, Islamic music lost its exclusively devotional nature, and began to be used in other ways. Some of the Sufis, the mystics of Islam, believed that music could be a means of bridging the gulf between man and God, and the Sufi belief that music 'leads the soul to the highest realm' had a great influence in the medieval courts in India.

The power of music in Hinduism is very apparent to anyone who witnesses the *puja* (worship ceremonies), where the overwhelmingly powerful noise is intended to awaken the deity. In Hindu thinking sound conveys power; all kinds of percussion instruments are therefore used at worship ceremonies—especially brass plates, gongs, drums, conch shells and bells, all of which are played at the same time. The thinking behind the use of *mantras*—words or sounds without meaning—is that they help to control the vibration of the body and make it easier to meditate.

Some Hindu philosophers had the idea that all vibrations and sounds in the universe, both audible and inaudible, have their origins in *nada brahma*, meaning 'sound God'. Sculptures of the dancing figure of the god Shiva are a visual way of expressing the importance of sound, and symbolize the drumming of the cosmos into existence.

The contemplation of sound is an important feature of Buddhist meditation, although some Buddhist writings underline the distracting and sensual side of music and dancing, especially for those in monastic disciplines. The accounts of the life of the Buddha are filled with music imagery; his residence in paradise, for example, is said to be a place where 84,000 musical instruments play, and the melodies played by the daughters of the gods are accompanied by the tinkling of thousands of bells.

Conclusions

Music plays an important part in all religions and cultures. Individuals and groups have always made music as a way of coming to terms with life and all its experiences. In both the Psalms and contemporary pop songs, people are celebrating the joys and lamenting the sorrows of life and trying to express in words and music the meaning that they see in life.

In several religions, music is closely associated with worship: it's a vehicle for words of praise and prayer— but the music often expresses something that goes beyond the bare words. Even where music has nothing to do with religion in any narrow sense, it touches on things that can be called religious in a wider and deeper sense.

Music has played an important part in religion in the Western world. This survey of music within the Christian tradition in the Western world began with the temple worship in Jerusalem and continued to popular music of the present day. It's obvious therefore that the Christian faith has been a major source of inspiration in Western music; and music has played an indispensable part in communicating the Christian faith.

Christians have had different attitudes to music at different times in history. The way Christians have thought about music has depended on their attitude to the music around them, their beliefs about humankind, and their ideas of worship.

Music plays an important part in popular religion. The majority of people in English-speaking countries are familiar with some of the hymns and songs mentioned in this chapter. They appeal even to people without a strong personal faith.

Questions

▶ *Is it just tradition and sentiment that make people want to sing on religious occasions?* Or does music express something that bare words can't convey? And is it that certain words set to music express religious instincts that are there in all people?

▶ *How important are the words in religious music?* Is it an accident that so many of the words in Western music are Christian words? Could the music with the power of the masses, the passions, the oratorios, and the requiems have been written to words that had no religious content at all?

Many people who have no personal religious convictions happily sing and listen to hymns that affirm God's presence, his protection, and his assurance of life eternal. But do these things have any substance? Perhaps those who cannot sing such words with real conviction are expressing the wistful longing that it might be so.

▶ *What is there to sing about?* The Psalmist had something to sing about because he could look back to the way God had acted in history to save his people. Because of his own experience he could say, 'He put a new song in my mouth' (Psalm 40:3). He could encourage others with the words, 'Sing to the Lord a new song, for he has done marvellous things' (Psalm 98:1).

8 Myths and Legends

A mythology is the comment of one particular age or civilization on the mysteries of human existence and the human mind...

H.R. Ellis Davidson, *Gods and Myths of Northern Europe*

Change continues to occur and the forms taken on by myths will remain endless: yet the issue is fundamentally the same as it has always been in distant times and in distant places.

Kees W. Bolle, Eliade's *Encyclopedia of Religion*

Myths are like music. They both express an idea and trigger off our response to it.

Douglas Davies, *The Lion Handbook of World Religions*

The greatest mythical tales make a direct appeal to the unconscious; they work through intuition. Their power is the flash of insight that illuminates the narrowness of matter-of-fact explanation and compels the intellect to acknowledge the need for a more adequate understanding. Myths possess an intensity of meaning that is akin to poetry.

Kees W. Bolle, Eliade's *Encyclopedia of Religion*

Popular religion has always been full of myths and legends. All over the world people have told stories about the beginning of the world, about heroes and saints, gods, spirits and demons, and about how the world will end.

Those who have told these stories have attached a great deal of significance to them, and have believed that in some sense they were true. In some cases, no doubt, they believed that the events really did happen. But in most cases they weren't interested in whether or not the event described in the story actually happened, because the important thing for them was that the myths and legends expressed important truths about themselves and their society, or about the world.

Before looking at examples of these myths and legends, it is important to define what is meant by the terms, to establish their relationship to so-called fairy tales, and to understand the part they play in religion— remembering that these definitions are simply an outsider's attempt to describe them.

Myths. The word 'myth' comes from the Greek word *'muthos'*. It originally meant 'word' or 'speech', and came to be used for stories about gods and superhuman beings. These stories described both imaginary and historical events in such a way that they were given religious meaning.

Legends. Legends are stories that have some basis in history and are told for entertainment and for education. The legends of King Arthur, William Tell and Hiawatha properly fall into this category.

Fairy tales. These are different from both myths and legends. They are different from myths in that they tell stories of things that happened in our world as it is. They begin with the words, 'Once upon a time...' implying that they happened in this world long ago. By contrast, myths describe what happened in a time before our present time. They are also different from legends, in that they don't make any attempt to describe real people who lived in history.

The Function of Myths and Legends

Myths and legends have several important roles in human culture.

They explain how things began. Myths answer the basic questions that all children ask: Who made the world? Why is the world as it is? The most fundamental myths of all, therefore, are those which describe how the universe came into being, and how things began to go wrong in the world.

They reflect on the annual cycle of nature. Plants die—but they come to life again in the spring, and myths in many cultures try to explain why this happens.

They reflect on the ultimate problems of existence. Human beings have always asked big questions: Who are we? What are we here for? What's the point of life? Why do people suffer so much? Answers to these questions have often taken the form of myths.

They reflect on the struggle between good and evil. Some myths reflect the inner struggle in all of us between good and evil. Others describe a great cosmic struggle. Sometimes this personal or cosmic struggle is tied up with the sequence of the seasons. Thus spring, with its new life coming after the death of winter, represents the victory of good over evil.

They provide models for human activity. Every culture has its own models for people to look up to. What kind of person is most admired? What are the most important qualities a man or woman should have? What are the worst crimes in a community? The myths of each culture give some indication of such qualities.

They explain our history. They explain different traditions, rites and customs in any society. Robert Graves, for example, has described myth as 'a dramatic short-hand record of such matters as invasions, migrations, dynastic changes, admissions of foreign cults, and social reforms'.

They justify the social order. They explain why society is structured in a particular way, and why people must not do anything to upset this order in society. In this way some myths explain the relations between a king and his wife, or between the king and the officials at his court.

The Origin of Myths and Legends

There are basically four different ways of explaining the origin of myths and legends:

Mythology is related to prehistory. This view draws attention to the fact that the earliest myths known today were created and written down in the Euphrates-Tigris Valley. They reflect a situation in which there was a

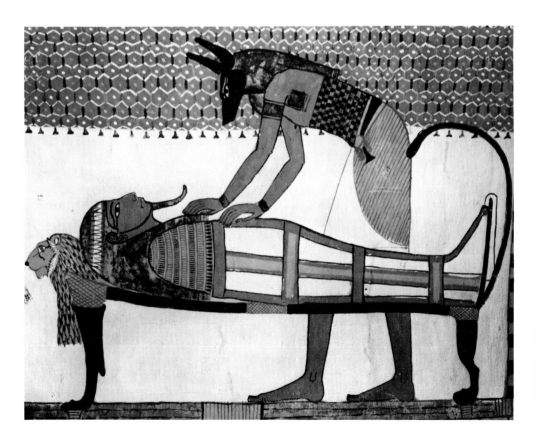

In Egyptian mythology Anubis, the jackal god, was patron of the art of embalming. He conducted souls to judgment. Here he is pictured preparing a dead man for mummification.

certain amount of stability in the country, and suggest that this was because of the way the gods ordered the universe; but life was a constant struggle because of the uncertainties of water and agriculture, invasion and civil war. If this view is correct, it is important to try to understand the historical situation in which myths were first created.

Mythology is related to folklore. One way of explaining some myths is to say that they are a development of folklore. This was the view expressed by the Inuit who said, 'Our tales are men's experience, and the things one hears of are not always lovely things... When I narrate legends, it is not I who speak, it is the wisdom of our forefathers, speaking through me.'

Myths can be explained psychologically. This is the view that has been popularized by Sigmund Freud (1856–1939), and has deeply influenced the way some people now want to interpret the myths of the past. In one of the most famous Greek legends, Oedipus unwittingly killed his father and married his mother.

The people of Canaan are famous from the Old Testament as dwellers in the land which the Israelites battled to occupy. Their myths concerned Baal, a fertility god.

When they discovered the truth, his mother committed suicide, and Oedipus blinded himself before going into exile. From this story Freud coined the expression 'the Oedipus complex' to describe the sexual feelings of a boy towards his mother and his aggressive feelings against his father—feelings which are repressed and are therefore unconscious. He believed that this Oedipus complex is the source of many if not all the creative images within the individual. A Freudian interpretation of myths, therefore, assumes that they tell us more about the individuals who tell them than about the way things are.

Jung (1876–1961) disagreed with Freud over this point. Instead he believed that the individual has a *personal unconscious*, which contains everything related to that person, and a *collective unconscious*, which includes the whole experience of humankind. It includes the archetypes or primordial images which 'bring into our ephemeral consciousness an unknown psychic life belonging to a remote past. This psychic life is the mind of our ancient ancestors, the way in which they conceived of life and the world, of gods and human beings.' He therefore believed that myths tell us something about our collective unconscious, which goes back to the experience of our ancestors thousands of years ago.

Mythology reflects present human experience. Bronislaw Malinowski, writing in the early part of the twentieth century, wrote like this about the Trobriand islanders of Melanesia:

'The myth in a primitive society, that is in its original form, is not a mere tale told but a reality lived...the assertion of an original, greater, more important reality through which the present life, fate and the work of mankind are governed.'

According to this theory, therefore, myth provides a link between the past and the present, because it says something about human experience which doesn't change from age to age.

World Mythologies and Their Influence

Many myths and legends arise from the past, but they continue to influence people today. What part have world mythologies played in popular religion? The questions can be broken down into several more:

▶ *What are the different mythologies of the past which have had an influence on the way Western civilization has developed?*

▶ *What were some of the most important myths of the Egyptians, the Greeks, the Romans, the Norsemen etc? What did they mean to the people who believed them?*

▶ *In what ways have they left their mark on Western culture?*

▶ *If myths and legends are found in all religions, what part do they play in Christianity?*

▶ *Even if today people don't believe in myths about giants and gods, are there other myths—in the sense of stories, ideas or ideals—which have the same kind of power in people's imagination as the old myths used to have? What are the modern myths by which the Western world lives?*

Egyptian Myths

One of the best known myths from ancient Egypt is the story of Osiris, Egypt's greatest king, who became king of the underworld and judge of the dead. One version of it goes like this:

While Ra was reigning as the first pharaoh of Egypt, Nut, the lady of the heavens, gave birth to five children: Osiris, Harmachis, Seth, Isis and Nephthys. When they grew up, Osiris married his sister Isis, and Seth married Nephthys. Later, when Ra had ceased to reign as a king on earth and had taken his place in the heavens, Osiris became pharaoh of Egypt with Isis as his queen. They ruled wisely, teaching the Egyptians agriculture, giving them laws, and building temples to enable them to worship the gods.

Seth, their younger brother, became very jealous and plotted to kill Osiris. So he invited him to a feast and tricked him into lying down in a chest made of cedar wood from Lebanon. He then locked the lid of the chest and threw it into the Nile, which was then in flood. Eventually it was cast ashore at Byblos in Syria, the oldest city in the world.

Isis searched everywhere for the body of her dead husband, Osiris, and when she found the coffin she brought it back to Egypt. Unfortunately Seth found them, and snatched the body of Osiris before it could be buried; he cut it into fourteen pieces, and sent them to different places all over Egypt. Isis then went in search of the pieces, and buried thirteen of them with the proper burial ceremonies wherever she found them, in order to enable the spirit of Osiris to pass to Duat, the land of the dead. There he became king of the dead and, as he sat on his throne, judged all the dead who were summoned before him.

After this Isis did all she could to prepare her son Horus to avenge the death of his father. Eventually there was a long, fierce battle, in which Seth was killed. His body was dragged up and down Egypt and cut into fourteen pieces just as the body of Osiris had been, and in this way the death of Osiris was avenged. At last, therefore, there was peace in Egypt, and Horus reigned as pharaoh for hundreds of years.

The Egyptians believed that Osiris and Horus would one day return to earth and fight the last and greatest battle against Seth to defeat him for ever. When that happened, all the dead who had lived good lives would return to earth with Osiris, return to their bodies once again, and live happily for ever in Egypt, free from all evil.

Mesopotamian Myths

The myths of the Sumerians, who lived in the Fertile Crescent from about 3000BC, and the later myths of the Babylonians and the Assyrians were different from those of Egypt. They told, for example, of how the gods created humankind in order to obtain food for themselves each day. People were therefore created to serve the gods; but in return the gods ensured the renewal of the world each day. Their myths also described a great cosmic struggle going on all the time against evil powers.

One of the best known myths from Mesopotamia is the story of Gilgamesh, and this is one version of it:

Gilgamesh, the proud king of Uruk, had a human father, but his mother was a goddess. He was therefore thought to be two-thirds divine and one-third mortal. One day he struggled with a wild, grass-eating man called Enkidu, who had been sent by a god to punish him for his arrogance. But Gilgamesh defeated him, and they became close friends.

The two heroes then joined together in a series of adventures. First they killed the fire-breathing giant Huwawa, and then they killed a Bull of Heaven which was sent to ravage the earth. But by this time the anger of the gods had been aroused, and they killed Enkidu as a punishment for his arrogance.

Gilgamesh then set out to seek immortality for himself, because he was haunted by the fear of death. He found one of his ancestors who told him, 'The gods appointed death for humans, and kept life for themselves.' Gilgamesh then found a ferryman to take him across the waters of death, but was told that he had no chance of avoiding death, unless he could find a magic plant called 'Never Grow Old' which grew at the bottom of the sea. He dived into the sea and found the herb, but later, while he was sleeping on his way back to Erech, lost it to a serpent. When he woke up he realized what had happened, and he wept, because he knew that he couldn't avoid death.

Here is a myth that says something about human pride and about the frustration that people feel in the face of death.

Canaanite Myths

One of the main features of the myths of the Canaanites was their intense interest in fertility. A favourite myth described how Baal, a fertility god, disappeared and died and was later restored to life:

When Baal had defeated the sea god Yam, he built a house for himself on Mount Tsaphon. He then announced that he would no longer accept the authority of Mot, the god of death, and that if Mot wanted to visit the earth, he could only visit the deserts. In response to this challenge, Mot invited Baal to the land of the dead. When Baal went to the underworld, Athar the irrigation god was put on Baal's vacant throne.

Baal's wife, Amat, naturally missed her husband desperately and pleaded with Mot to restore Baal to life—but without success. In the end she attacked Mot herself, tearing him to pieces with a sharp knife, and scattering his remains over the fields.

In spite of all that had happened, however, El the High God had a dream in which he saw that Baal was not really dead and that fertility had been restored to the soil. Baal therefore regained his throne, and Athar had to flee. By this time Mot too had come back to life, and he now launched another attack. In the battle that followed, all the other gods supported Baal, but neither Baal nor Mot could win. In the end El the High God intervened and sent Mot away, leaving Baal in control.

It's not hard to see how a myth of this kind reflects the changing of the seasons in this area of the Mediterranean.

Greek Myths

The Greek gods who lived on Mount Olympus in the north-east of Greece were a superior race of beings. Nevertheless, they had the same passions as human beings; they were born like men and women, but were ageless, free from disease and pain, and never died. Supreme among the gods was Zeus, 'the father of gods and men', who brought rain, thunder and lightning, embodied the cosmic order and upheld moral law. Here are some examples of the myths of the ancient Greeks about the Olympian gods:

The origin of the universe. In the beginning there was Chaos. Then came the appearance of Gaia, the earth, and finally Eros, love. Chaos gave birth to Erebus and Night and, when these two came together, they gave birth to Ether and Hemera, the day. Gaia bore Uranus, the Sky, and then created the mountains and the sea. This then is how the universe came into being.

Gaia and her son Uranus then came together and produced the first race—the twelve Titans. They then gave birth to the one-eyed Cyclopes and three monsters. Uranus was horrified with his offspring and shut them up under the earth. His wife Gaia, however, was so angry with her husband that she planned to take vengeance on him. She therefore got her son Chronos to come to

Uranus while he was asleep one night, cut off his genitals and throw them into the sea. From the black blood which came from the wound and fell to the earth were born the furies, giants and nymphs. And from the debris which floated on the waves of the sea Aphrodite, the goddess of love, was born.

The origin of the human race. Prometheus was the son of one of the Titans, and had been admitted into the circle of the Immortal Gods at Olympus, the home of the gods. But he nursed a grudge against the Olympian gods because they had destroyed the Titans.

It was Prometheus who created humankind, by bringing earth and water together to fashion the body of the first man, who had a soul breathed into him by the goddess Athene. The first human beings lived in a Golden Age and, as the poet Hesiod said, 'they lived like gods, free from worry, and fatigue; old age did not afflict them; they rejoiced in continual festivity.' This age was followed by the Silver Age, the Bronze Age and the Iron Age, which has continued to the present and in which the human race degenerated into the condition that it is in now.

The gods and Fate. This incident from Homer's *Iliad* illustrates just one way by which the Greeks could explain the delicate relationship between the gods and Fate:

During the Trojan War the Greeks, under their leader Patroclus, won a great victory over the Trojans, who then launched a counter-attack. They were again defeated, and their warrior Sarpedon was killed by Patroclus. But before the battle actually took place, Zeus the High God looked down on the battlefield and was concerned about what was happening, since Sarpedon was his own son. He therefore asked Hera his wife whether he should remove Sarpedon from the battlefield to save his life or allow him to be killed. Hera's answer went like this: '- Although mortals are doomed by Fate, you can do as you wish. But if you intervene to save your son, then every other god will do the same to save his sons in battle. So it is best to allow Sarpedon to be killed by Patroclus.' This is one way, therefore, of explaining the relationship between Zeus and Fate: Zeus remains in complete control, but accepts Fate. Fate is independent of the gods to a certain extent; but Zeus doesn't have to give in and be subordinate to Fate.

Roman Myths

Some of the myths of the Romans were their own; but most of them were borrowed from Egypt, Greece and other parts of the Mediterranean which came within their great empire. Many of their gods were therefore the gods of the peoples they had conquered.

The Larousse Encyclopedia describes their pantheon

This cleverly-constructed troll in the Norwegian countryside reminds us how many figures from our childhood imagination come from the old paganism of Norse legends.

of gods as a 'catalogue in which those who were interested could find the names of protective powers with special functions attributed to them and the rites which must be performed in order to purchase their favours'. It goes on to explain why religion was such a practical business for the Romans:

'Their gods were protectors for whose services they paid; and in case of failure their wages were withheld. Do ut des: I give to thee so that thou givest to me; such was the cynical profession of faith that one might inscribe above the entrance of the Roman Pantheon.'

Even though Roman myths are hardly remembered today, many people know the names of some of their gods:

Janus. Janus was the god of all doorways, including public gates as well as private doors. With his two faces he watched the outside and the inside of the house, and the entrance and exit of public buildings. Thus he became the god of departure and return, and was thought of as the god of all 'beginnings'. He therefore presided over daybreak, and played an important role in the creation of the world. The month of January is named after him, because it marks the departure of the old year and the beginning of the new.

Mars. Originally a god of agriculture, he later became the god of war, whose help was sought before any battle.

Romulus and Remus. These boy twins were sons of Mars and Rhaea Silvia. When they were born they were placed in a winnowing basket which was then left to float on the River Tiber. When the river overflowed and left the basket on the bank beside a grotto, a she-wolf came to suckle the twins who were brought up by a shepherd and his wife. When they grew up they decided to found a new city, but while they were engaged in divination to decide where to build the city, Romulus killed Remus. Soon after this he built the first Rome on the banks of the River Tiber.

Jupiter. Originally the god who hurled thunderbolts to punish or to warn people, he became the protector of the city of Rome, the warrior god, who symbolized justice and honour. Later still he became the protector of the whole Roman Empire.

Saturn. Saturn was originally a god of agriculture, who had been king of Italy during the Golden Age and was driven from the sky by Jupiter. The feast in his honour, known as the Saturnalia, lasted from 17 to 23 December, and was a time for festivities—with a huge feast often lasting all day. As a reminder of the Golden Age, masters waited on their slaves at table, and slaves could say and do what they liked. Shops, schools and law courts were closed, and public life closed down completely (see the section on Christmas).

Norse Myths

These are the myths of the people of Scandinavia, Iceland and Germany before the coming of Christianity. These peoples included the Angles and Saxons, who took possession of parts of England, as well as other people such as the Franks, the Vandals and the Visigoths. Information about their gods and myths comes from Roman writers such as Tacitus (writing about AD100) and from Christian monks writing two or three hundred years after the coming of Christianity.

The following are the best known of the Norse gods. Some have a Germanic name as well as a Scandinavian one.

Woden or Odin. Woden was the god who decided each person's fate. He held his court in a huge hall called Valhalla, where dead heroes spent their time engaged in warlike games and feasting. He was assisted by the Valkyries, supernatural women who acted as guardians and servants, and who mingled invisibly among warriors in battle. When Woden appeared among human beings he was often disguised as a traveller. In addition to being a god of war, he was a god of wisdom, poetry and magic. One myth tells of how he hanged himself on the World Tree (see later) and was raised to life again in a kind of resurrection. In one of the poems he is made to say, 'For nine nights, wounded by my own spear, consecrated to Odin, myself consecrated to myself, I remained hanging from the tree shaken by the wind, from the mighty tree whose roots men know not.' When he fell to the ground, he was brought to life again by the magic power of runic stones.

Donar or Thor. He was greatly feared as the god of thunder, and in some countries such as Norway was the most powerful of the gods. He was generally depicted wielding a stone axe which represented his thunderbolts. He was portrayed as the ideal warrior, simple yet noble, courageous and sometimes brutal. Many stories were told about his exploits.

Tiw or Tyr. He was a god of war (like the Roman Mars), but seems to have been pushed into the background at an early stage.

Loki. In Scandinavian mythology Loki was regarded as a mischief maker, a kind of *enfant terrible* among the gods. He was constantly using intrigue and treachery to undermine the power of the gods, and it was he who eventually caused their downfall.

In addition to these gods there was a whole range of other superhuman beings:

Spirits. These included the souls of the dead, who had magic powers, and also evil demons.

Norms. These were female spirits who were mistresses of fate.

Valkyries. These goddesses rode on flying horses and fought in battles, giving victory to one side or the other and deciding who must die.

Elves. The elves were spirits a little smaller than human beings, who lived in water, woods or mountains. They were generally benevolent, but could often inspire fear.

Dwarfs. Dwarfs were a special class of elves, nearly always ugly and deformed, with hunched backs, big heads, pale faces and long hands. They usually lived underground and engaged in mining.

Giants. Giants were similar to elves and dwarfs, except for their huge size. They could be benevolent or hostile, and generally people were afraid of them. They lived in the clouds, in the mountains or the sea, and would sometimes defy even the gods.

These are some of the best known of the Norse myths, which have influenced Western culture in several important ways:

The beginning of all things. At the beginning of time, a world of clouds and shadows formed to the north of the great abyss which stretched throughout space. Then came fountains, glacial rivers and hoar frost; and as warm air from the south melted the ice, a giant called Ymir was formed out of the drops. He was the first of all living beings and the father of all the giants.

Out of the sweat under his left arm were born a man and woman—both of them giants. Other giants who were born later gave birth to the gods Odin, Vili and Ve. These three gods killed the old Ymir and all the older Giants, except two of them who escaped and gave birth to a new race of giants. Out of different parts of Ymir's dead body were formed the earth, the sea, mountains, sky, sun, moon and stars.

Other gods, who were known as Aesir, came into existence and joined Odin in building Asgard, the home of the gods. The rainbow acted as a bridge between their home and the world of human beings. Dwarfs were formed out of grubs living in the rotting corpse of Ymir, while humans were formed out of two dead tree trunks. When they died, they went to the abode of the dead under the earth, a misty, cold and damp place, presided over by the goddess Hel.

The universe was also pictured as a huge tree, the Tree of the Universe or Tree of the World—an ash tree known as Yggdrasil, whose leaves were always green. Its roots reached down to the world of the dead, and its branches reached the sky. Near the trunk of the tree was a special place where the gods met each day to dispense justice.

At the beginning of time the gods led peaceful lives in Asgard, busily engaged in building, making tools and playing together. Things started to go wrong, however, on the day that the gods tortured a messenger who had been sent by the Vanir, the second race of gods. This led in time to dishonesty, violence and war among the gods and among humans.

The end of the world and its rebirth. The murder of Balder triggered off the final conflict. For several years the whole world was caught in the grip of a terrible winter, and war broke out all over the earth. The gods and giants gathered from each corner of the world and killed each other without mercy in a great battle. Even Odin and Thor were killed during the time which was known as the '- Twilight of the Gods', and so the whole human race was left without protection and swept off the face of the earth.

The universe was set on fire and became an immense furnace. Out of this destruction of the universe, however, a new world came into being. A new generation of gods appeared, who had not been guilty of the same crimes as the earlier gods, and they set about renewing the world. Human beings also reappeared, for some had been protected from the fire in the World Tree, and they gave birth to a new race.

There are several reasons why Norse myths are specially significant for our study:

▶ Although these myths were suppressed during the time when the north-west of Europe was being converted to Christianity, they continued to exist alongside Christianity for several centuries. Pagan beliefs continued for many centuries, and aspects of this mythology persist to this day.

▶ Several of the days of the week are named after Norse gods—namely Tuesday (Tiw's Day), Wednesday (Woden's Day), Thursday (Thor's Day), Friday (Frey's Day).

▶ The German composer Wagner used some of these myths (like the 'Twilight of the Gods') in his operas, and Hitler tried to revive the old paganism as part of his National Socialism. The swastika, for example, had been a sign of the god Thor.

▶ Children's stories are full of tales about elves, dwarfs, giants and trolls, many of which come originally from these Norse myths. C.S. Lewis, a writer well known for his children's books about the land of Narnia, was deeply influenced by images of the Norse myths.

Christian Legends

In the category of Christian legends come stories which have become part of certain Christian traditions, but which are not based on the Bible itself. Many of the earliest ones come from what is called the apocryphal literature, which was written during the first few centuries after the life of Christ, mostly in Egypt and Syria.

These books have titles like 'The Gospel of Thomas', 'The Gospel of Peter'—not because they were written by these apostles, but because the authors believed that they would be more widely accepted if they had the name of an apostle attached to them.

They include stories about Jesus and Mary, and other characters mentioned in the New Testament. Even after church leaders declared at important Councils in the fourth and fifth centuries that these books did not have the same authority as the books of the New Testament, they continued to be popular.

There were at least three motives in the minds of the authors:

To satisfy people's curiosity. There were many subjects of interest on which the New Testament itself was silent:

What was Jesus like as a boy? How did he spend his early life? What happened to the disciples after the death and resurrection of Jesus? This literature did for many people what books and films like *The Robe*, *The Big Fisherman* and *Quo Vadis?* did for many people in the 1950s and 1960s. It was also the equivalent in the early centuries of some of our popular paperbacks, in that these books fed people's appetite for the extraordinary, the sensational and the miraculous.

To defend orthodox Christian teaching about Jesus. In order to defend, for example, the belief that Mary the mother of Jesus was a virgin, stories were invented about her birth, life and death, simply to show that she was an extraordinary person. In cases like these, the writers had the best of motives; but they added many fanciful details to the simple accounts in the Gospels.

To teach heretical ideas about Jesus. Some of these gospels, for example, taught that Jesus wasn't fully human, and that he didn't suffer physically when he died on the cross. Although this teaching was condemned by church leaders, it continued to be popular in some circles for a long time and was spread through this kind of apocryphal literature.

Most scholars agree that, while some of these writings may contain some traditions about the life and teaching of Jesus which could be genuine, most of it was sheer fabrication. Some of the details in the stories seem quite ridiculous to us today, while others are grotesque and sometimes even repulsive.

These legends have contributed much to popular religion. Many of them survived well into the Middle Ages, and some of them inspired a great deal of Christian art and poetry. Even today people are relying on some of these legends, without realizing it, when they tell the Christmas story. Many traditional carols, Christmas cards and nativity plays tell us, for example, that Jesus was born in the middle of the night (-sometimes in a cave); that dazzling light radiated from the face of the baby Jesus; and that the animals bowed down to worship him. None of these details comes from the accounts of the birth of Jesus in the New Testament; they all come from one or more of the apocryphal writings, and people gaily repeat them as if they were part of the original story.

In some cases these legends influenced the development of Christian beliefs. Stories told about the Virgin Mary, for example, encouraged people to revere her and eventually even to worship her.

Legends about Jesus. The legends about Jesus concentrate mainly on his birth and childhood, and on his last days on earth. Here are examples of such legends.

Fact and Fiction in the Christmas Story

The story of the birth of Jesus which people know from Christmas cards, carols and nativity plays goes like this:

▶ Mary and Joseph arrived in Bethlehem during the night after their long journey from Nazareth.

▶ They went round every inn in the village looking for a room, but were turned away each time—until at last a friendly inn keeper took pity on them and offered them his stable, since his rooms were already occupied by guests.

▶ Jesus was born that same night in the privacy of the stable.

Unfortunately there are several problems with this version of the story which have recently been pointed out.

Historical. It's most unlikely that there would have been an inn in Bethlehem at that time—certainly nothing like the hotels or inns that are common today. Bethlehem was a small village in the hill country, and wasn't on an important route.

Cultural. Since Mary and Joseph were going back to the village from which their families originally came, they must have had some relatives in the village, and would have gone *first* **to them. Anyone who understands the culture of the Middle East (or, for that matter, of most of the Two-Thirds World) will recognize that Mary and Joseph would expect to be able to stay with some of them, and would not be turned away.**

Linguistic. The key verse in Luke's Gospel (2:7) is usually translated like this: 'She wrapped him in swaddling clothes (-meaning strips of cloth) and placed him in a manger, *because there was no room for them in the inn.'* **But the Greek word** that is translated 'inn' here (*'kataluma'*) **is also used by Luke in 22:11, where it refers to the** *guest room* **where Jesus ate the Passover with his disciples. And the normal Greek word for what we mean by an inn (*'pandocheion'*) is used by Luke in 10:34 in the parable of the Good Samaritan: 'Then he put the man on his own donkey, brought him to** *an inn* **and took care of him.' So Luke doesn't use this usual word for 'inn' for the place where Jesus was born.**

Is it possible to reconstruct the story of what really happened? This is the suggestion that has been put forward by Kenneth Bailey, an American New Testament scholar who has lived most of his life in the Middle East:

▶ Mary and Joseph may have arrived in Bethlehem two weeks or a month before the baby was due. Joseph should be credited with some intelligence and concern for his wife!

▶ They would probably have gone to stay with Joseph's nearest relatives. If they couldn't have the couple to stay, Mary and Joseph would have gone to the *next* nearest relatives. If none of them could help, they could have gone to Mary's relatives who were living not too far away.

▶ A simple peasant home in Bethlehem would have had one main room, with a lower section for the animals during the night. If the family were a little better off, they might have had a guest room off the main room.

▶ At the time of the delivery, the local midwife would be called in, and all the women of the family and of the village would be in attendance, helping Mary.

▶ The manger would have been one of the troughs carved out of the stone at the edge of the living room. It would normally hold food for the animals, who were brought in for the night, not just for protection but also to keep the house warm.

▶ The correct translation of the verse in Luke's Gospel should probably be, '...and laid him in a manger, *because there was no room for them in the guest room.'* Luke is saying that Jesus was born in the main room of a peasant home—not in the guest room because that was already occupied.

This isn't debunking the whole Christmas story— it's simply peeling away the layers of mythology and legend which have grown up round the Christmas story, and perhaps getting a little nearer to what may have actually happened.

The mysterious atmosphere of England's Glastonbury Tor has been connected with the legends of King Arthur, and also with Christian legends that Jesus visited Britain. In recent years the nearby town has become a New Age centre.

Dragons came out of the cave in which Jesus was born in order to worship him. This idea probably came from the verse in the Old Testament—'Praise the Lord from the earth, you dragons' (Psalm 148:7).

▶ Wild animals accompanied the Holy Family during their flight to Egypt, and palm trees bent down to Mary to enable her to pick their fruit. This may have been influenced by the vision of a peaceful creation described Isaiah 11.

▶ Jesus worked miracles while he was still a boy at home in Nazareth. There are many stories: he made birds out of clay and brought them to life; he carried water from the well in his cloak because his pitcher had broken; he cursed a boy who accidentally bumped into him, and made him fall dead on the spot; he cursed his teacher and made him fall down in a swoon; he had such supernatural knowledge that one of his teachers at school said, 'This child is not earth-born; assuredly he was born before the creation of the world.'

It isn't hard to see how different these miracles are from those recorded in the Gospels. In these legends Jesus performs miracles simply to meet his own personal needs or to get himself out of difficult situations. He appears as a spoilt, selfish, arrogant and vengeful child.

Legends about Mary. No doubt all these legends were developed to show that if Jesus was fully human and divine, and if his mother was a virgin at the time of his birth, he must have been a very special person:

▶ Her parents, Joachim and Anna, were childless; but then, in answer to prayer, Mary was born. At the age of three, she was taken to the temple, where she lived until she was twelve, and was fed by the hand of an angel.

▶ The priests had her married to Joseph, who was by then an elderly widower with children of his own. When she was sixteen, an angel came to tell her that she would have a child. After this Joseph went away from home to do his work as a builder, and when he returned after six months found that Mary was pregnant.

▶ Mary remained a virgin to the end of her life. The '-brothers of Jesus' mentioned in the Gospels were children of Joseph by his previous marriage.

▶ She didn't die a natural death, but was taken up to heaven. This is what came to be known as '-Assumption of the Blessed Virgin Mary'. Eventually she was crowned as the Queen of Heaven.

While noting the role of legend in encouraging the veneration of Mary in some forms of popular religion, it is also important to notice how some in the Western world react to these legends. Marina Warner, for example, grew up as a Catholic, but later rejected her Christian faith. In a book called *Alone of All Her Sex: The Myth and the Cult of the Virgin Mary*, she describes how in some Christian traditions Mary has come to represent 'an eternal ideal of mortal beauty', and to be regarded as a model of chastity, humility, gentleness, and even as 'the culmination of womanhood'. She points out that Catholic teaching about Mary has deeply influenced attitudes towards women, because she reveals such qualities as 'yieldedness, softness, gentleness, receptiveness, mercifulness, tolerance, withdrawal'.

Legends about the saints. There are many other legends related to the Christian religion that focus on the lives of saints. These are dealt with in the chapter on saints.

The Arthurian Legend

The reason for including the Arthurian legend in this book is that it includes several religious themes. Also, for many years it played an important role in the culture of Europe and the English-speaking world.

What seems to have happened is that the memory of a great military leader came to be combined with older Welsh myths about gods and their exploits. Then at a later stage legends concerning the coming of Christianity to Britain were added.

These are the main stages by which the legend developed:

The historical Arthur. The original Arthur (who may have been called Ambrosius Aurelianus) probably lived in the century following the collapse of Roman rule in Britain. He was a Romanized Briton who commanded a force of cavalry against the Saxon invaders.

Cadbury Castle (which is situated about twelve miles from Glastonbury in Somerset, and has been excavated by archaeologists) could have been his headquarters while he was defending the area against the Saxons who were attacking from the east.

Geoffrey of Monmouth's rewriting of history. In 1138 Geoffrey of Monmouth wrote his *History of the Kings of Britain*. He was a Norman Welshman, in touch with the Norman world but fiercely Welsh. In his book he wrote the history of Britain in such a way as to pour scorn on all those who had defeated the Britons in the past, and to make the British race out to be as ancient and glorious as the Greeks and Romans.

He claimed, for example, that the Britons are always victorious over their enemies. He even went as far as to suggest that the Romans never conquered Britain, and that the Britons conquered most of Europe and almost captured Rome itself! In this story Arthur was the greatest British hero, and under him the military glory of Britain reached its heights. Any defeats the Britons suffered were explained as the result of treachery or disunity among the Britons. Although Geoffrey of Monmouth can be described by historians today as a 'reckless forger', it was 600 years before people realized that his work had little to do with real history.

The creation of the basic legend. The poets and bards of Britain and especially of France took hold of the ideas found in Monmouth's *History*, and developed them into a vast body of legends and romances about King Arthur. One of the earliest books in which the legend is found is a poem called *Perceval* by Chrestien de Troyes, which dates from between about 1180 and 1190. This was the basic core of the legend:

Arthur became king at the age of fifteen. He married Guinevere, and held his court at Camelot. While he was fighting in a war at Rome, he heard that his nephew Modred, whom he had left to rule the kingdom in his absence, had betrayed him and abducted Queen Guinevere. Arthur immediately returned to Britain and defeated Modred, but was mortally wounded during the fight. He was then taken to the Isle of Avalon to recover.

In the earliest form of the legend Arthur's kingdom was an imaginary one, an invention of pure fantasy. Camelot wasn't intended to be a real place, and Avalon was the paradise of Celtic myths.

The addition of further elements. Gradually other elements were added to the basic legend:

▶ *The fellowship of the Round Table.* This referred to the circle of Arthur's best knights who formed the Knights of the Round Table.

▶ *The idea of a future reconquest.* It was said that Arthur would one day return from Avalon and rule Britain once again.

▶ *Magical elements.* The chief practitioners were the magician Merlin and the sorceress Morgan le Fay, Arthur's sister.

▶ *Individual heroes.* Legends devoted to telling of the brave exploits of individual knights such as Lancelot, Perceval, Gawain and Galahad arose.

▶ *The story of Guinevere's adultery.* The intrigue concerning the queen's adulterous relationship with Lancelot and the consequences of this behaviour were developed in stories.

▶ *Features from Celtic mythology.* Arthur's mighty sword Excalibur, which he alone could pull from the stone, derived from ancient mythologies. The Round Table itself may originally have been associated with magic in Celtic myths.

▶ *The quest for the* Holy Grail. The idea of the Holy Grail probably came originally from the 'cup of plenty' in Celtic mythology, which symbolized the source of all life. Then, some time before 1200, the Grail came to be associated with the chalice which Jesus had used at the Last Supper and was said to have given to Joseph of Arimathea. According to this new legend, Joseph collected the blood of Jesus in this chalice as it fell from his body during the crucifixion, and in this way the blood was miraculously preserved. The Grail thus became a kind of talisman which would bring

prosperity to anyone who was able to find it.

Once the Holy Grail had become part of the Arthurian legend, it became the aim of all his knights to go in search of it. Although the addition of the Holy Grail meant that the legend developed a more moral and religious flavour, church leaders weren't at all happy with the myth, because it savoured too much of magic.

The history written by the monks of Glastonbury. In 1191 the monks of Glastonbury were faced with the problem of how to finance the rebuilding of their abbey which had been damaged by fire. They hit on the ingenious idea of claiming that they had discovered the grave of King Arthur and Queen Guinevere beside the abbey. The scheme was successful because they were able to raise the necessary money!

Some years later the monks of Glastonbury decided to rewrite a history about the kings of the English which had been written around 1130 by William of Malmesbury. In their history they added many new legends which were not in the original history and presented them as historical fact.

Historians today would say that the first Christians to

The 'Wild West' still flourished a century or so ago. But already it has become an American legend.

come to England may have come to the south-west of the country from Gaul (France). It's possible that they could have come as traders before AD200. Soon after this time Tertullian in North Africa claimed that Christ had 'conquered' parts of Britain inaccessible to the Roman army. And the Christian writer Origen spoke as if Christianity was strongly established in Britain before AD250. It's possible that Glastonbury could have been the first important centre of Christianity in Britain. Celtic saints no doubt visited Glastonbury at various times, and the first monastic community may have been organized by Irish missionaries some time in the sixth century.

Although this is all that historians are able to claim with any confidence today, the monks of Glastonbury had no qualms about the new details of the coming of Christianity which they presented in their new history:

▶ The first Christian missionaries came to Britain in AD60, led by Joseph of Arimathea, and several others (whose names were given!). They built the first church at Glastonbury, as they had been instructed by the Virgin Mary, and established a community. Joseph of Arimathea was therefore the founder of Glastonbury. They also said that he brought two cruets with him containing the blood and sweat of Christ, which were buried with him in his tomb.

▶ Many years later St Patrick came to Glastonbury, re-established a community there, and led it as abbot until he died. After that time Glastonbury became an important centre of pilgrimage and was visited by many saints, including David and Columba.

▶ King Arthur became a benefactor and patron of Glastonbury and died there. The monks could now, of course, show pilgrims the actual tomb of Arthur and his queen!

Later additions. In the fourteenth century the Glastonbury Thorn first appeared on a seal. But it is not until the sixteenth century that there is any evidence in writing of the story about Joseph's thorn which budded at Christmas time when he first came to Glastonbury.

In 1367 a writer in East Anglia claimed that the body of Joseph of Arimathea had been found in Glastonbury. Soon after this the crypt of the Lady Chapel became St Joseph's Chapel, and an image of Joseph was placed there in 1382. The chapel then became a place of pilgrimage, with people coming to pray there and seek healing. Thus, according to historian R.F. Treharne, 'By the end of the Middle Ages Joseph of Arimathea had become completely Anglicized...and had become Glastonbury's greatest asset.'

The result of this process was that the whole Arthurian legend became 'the greatest and most widespread theme of the brilliantly flowering literature of the age'. In 1469 it was popularized by Sir Thomas Malory's Morte d'Arthur, which has been described by scholar and writer C.S. Lewis as 'the English national epic'.

The development of the Arthurian legend over so many centuries, therefore, has much to tell us about popular religion:

▶ It shows us how patriotism and nationalism are often tied up with popular religion.

▶ It reflects the hunger in many people's minds for the supernatural and the miraculous.

▶ It illustrates the kind of role played by saints in popular religion.

Modern Myths and Legends

This category does not deal with myths about gods and supernatural beings, nor with legends about superhuman heroes. It is about myths and legends which are part of our culture—even today. They provide themes which underlie much popular literature and are the foundation of many films and TV programmes. They embody assumptions which people take for granted, never stopping to challenge them or to wonder where they came from. Here are two examples of such myths and legends:

The legend of Robin Hood. The famous outlaw of Sherwood Forest who robbed the rich to help the poor is a British hero with an international reputation.

It's almost impossible, however, to be sure if there ever was a historical character with this name. The earliest form of the legend can be traced back to the thirteenth century; but the original Robin—if there was such a person—must have lived some time before that. There are several people who could have been 'the real Robin Hood', and even in the earliest stories it's impossible to distinguish between fact and fiction.

As time went on the legend was adapted, with new tales and new characters being added. Robin himself went through many changes: at first he was a yeoman, but then he became a nobleman who had lost his inheritance unjustly. At a later stage he appeared as a patriotic Englishman defending his country against the Normans. In the end he became a rebel who took the side of the peasants in their struggle against their cruel and oppressive overlords. And throughout these different stages there was a darker side to his heroic exploits: at times he was simply a common criminal, guilty of theft and murder. Nevertheless, his appeal lies in the fact that he is a hero, with superhuman powers, who is bound always to outwit the villains of the story.

The western. Westerns had a profound attraction for several generations of cinema-goers. Here was a world where there was a clear moral code with a strong sense of honour, and where justice was *seen* to be done. Barry Norman, a film critic, explains the appeal that westerns had for him in his childhood:

'There was a beautiful simplicity about the western. At its best it was a modern morality tale, the clash of good versus evil, with one well-aimed bullet settling the issue and good always triumphant. Never mind that life is not like that: life should be like that. And what saved the western from being little more than a muscular fairy tale was that it was rooted in fact, in the astonishing history of the USA during the last 50 years of the 19th century.'

Since the days of the old-fashioned western, some films have continued with the same kind of themes in a different guise, while others have introduced new themes with a different set of values:

▶ *Rambo* and *Star Wars* are similar to the old westerns in that there's still a clear distinction between the 'good guys' and the 'bad guys', and there's never any doubt that 'our' side will come out on top. The violence is now on a much grander scale, because the weapons are much more powerful than those of the cowboys and Indians or of the marshal.

▶ In *James Bond* the violence is often so spectacular that it simply becomes funny—and there's the added attraction of all the beautiful women he can enjoy on his daring missions for his country to liquidate 'the enemy'.

▶ 'J.R.' in *Dallas* is even further removed from the old-fashioned western. He is the hero who will stab *anyone* in the back and use every dirty trick in the book in order to get his own way in his private and business life— and still come up smiling, asking for admiration.

Conclusions

Myths and legends reveal something of the nature of popular religion.

▶ The idea of Fate or Destiny which is found in the Greek myths is still very much part of the popular religion of many in the Western world.

▶ Magic seems to play an important part in popular religion all over the world. People have always been looking for ways of ensuring that their crops will grow and of controlling their destiny.

▶ Heroes and saints seem to meet a deeply felt need— the need for models to look up to and intermediaries

Sir J.G. Frazer, a British anthropologist, wrote a famous book, *The Golden Bough*. In it he studied many myths from the folklore and religion of different tribes and cultures, and pointed out comparisons with Christianity.

through whom we can make contact with the supernatural.

▶ Nationalism plays an important part in popular religion. As the Athenians looked to Athena as protector of Athens, and the Romans turned to Jupiter, so in popular religion today people think of God as the protector of their nation and believe that he is bound to be on their side in time of war.

▶ Popular religion is basically very practical and human-centred, because it is concerned with the needs of the individual and the community.

▶ When life seems intolerable or simply dull and boring, it's natural that many people hunger for something supernatural.

Myths appeal to the imagination. Myths are never intended to be straightforward stories. They compel an emotional response because the stories have a ring of truth that 'feels' right.

Questions

▶ *Do stories about Jesus in the Gospels come into the category of legend?*

▶ *How do the accounts of the life of Jesus in the Gospels compare with the legends about Jesus and Mary in the apocryphal literature? Do they have anything in common with the legends about King Arthur and Robin Hood?*

These are the conclusions of two writers who studied the Gospels alongside other literature of the first century:

'In none of these various testimonies to the fact of Christ is there any slightest hint or idea that he was not a real

historical person... Indeed it has been argued—I think very rightly—that myth theories of the beginnings of Christianity are modern speculative hypotheses motivated by unreasoning prejudice and dislike.' (Roderick Dunkerley, Beyond the Gospels)

'If the ordinary canons of history, used in every other case, hold good in this case, Jesus is undoubtedly an historical person. If he is not an historical person, the only alternative is that there is no such thing as history at all.' (T.R. Glover, a former lecturer in Ancient History at Cambridge University)

▶ *Do Christian beliefs about Jesus come into the category of myth?*

The idea of a god dying and rising again is found in several ancient myths. The story of the death and resurrection of Jesus therefore does have something in common with this important theme in pagan mythology. The main difference, however, is that in the Gospels the death and resurrection of Jesus are described as events that took place in history.

▶ *If myths and legends can be thought of as 'shadows of the supernatural', do they provide any clues as to what the substance might be?*

Having seen the role that myths play and the questions that they answer, what remain are the vivid and powerful stories told by people of many different cultures. They have been feeling for answers that will satisfy their questioning spirit, and have used all their artistry to explore the supernatural world.

But what if the supernatural world (whatever it is) could reveal its secrets? What if, instead of people having to grope for the truth about God or the gods, God or the gods were to to draw the veil aside and make themselves known?

This is precisely the claim that the Christian makes about Jesus. For, in the words of one of his disciples, 'No one has ever seen God; but he who is nearest to the Father's heart has made him known.' (John 1:18)

C.S. Lewis had a lifelong interest in mythology, but he came to see it in a completely new light after he became a Christian. In a letter to a friend, he explained that he found the idea of the dying and reviving god very appealing, and was prepared to accept it in pagan mythologies. However, when he met the idea in the story of Christ, it had a different effect on him, because he realized that he was not dealing with human longings expressed in human stories, but with God's reality. The story of Christ is a true story.

The hope of resurrection in the Old Testament wasn't connected with myths about the annual cycle of nature, but with the idea that God was one day going to revive the nation of Israel through a unique series of events.

If we can say that in the story of the life, death and resurrection of Jesus we are dealing with 'true myth', in C.S. Lewis' sense, does it help us to see the shadows of mythology in a new light?

9 'Cross My Heart and Hope to Die'

Omens and superstitions…form the mental instincts that for thousands of years have swayed our reason and no matter how far we advance in science and technology, they still lurk in the corners of our consciousness, often affecting our social behaviour and attitudes to life.

Philippa Waring, The Dictionary of Omens and Superstitions

It is the hardest thing in the world to shake off superstitious prejudices; they are sucked in as it were with our mother's milk…

Gilbert White, The Natural History and Antiquities of Selborne, **1789**

Outwardly the children in the back streets and around the housing estate appear to belong to the twentieth century, but ancient apprehensions, even if only half believed in, continue to infiltrate their minds; warning them that moonlight shining on a person's face when he is asleep will make him go mad, that vinegar stops a person growing no matter how young he is, that a bleeding wart never stops bleeding and the person will bleed to death.

Iona and Peter Opie, The Lore and Language of Schoolchildren

If a man, walking in the fields, finde any foure-leaved grasse, he shall, in a small while after, finde some good thing.

Sir John Melton, Astrologaster, **1620**

What exactly is a superstition? Often people use the word to refer to any kind of belief to which they don't subscribe. And so, to a modern Christian, the beliefs of Romans and Greeks may seem superstitious; to a modern humanist, who has no time for any religion, the Christian is being just as superstitious as the others.

This chapter defines a superstition in the following ways:

A superstition is a belief which can't be defended. No attempt is made to prove whether or not it's true. Someone who believes that black cats are lucky does so without inquiring into whether there are any statistics or research findings which support this idea!

A superstition is a belief which isn't part of a larger system of religion or philosophy. For example, the creation myths of the Babylonians aren't superstitions, because they form part of the whole Babylonian world-view and system of thought. By contrast, the belief that it's unlucky to put up an umbrella in the house is superstitious, because it's an isolated idea which isn't attached to any wider theory or picture of the universe.

A superstition is a belief in which the pay-off matters more than the plausibility. Human beings believe things for two main reasons: first, because they seem to be true; second, because they confirm people's fears or fulfil their wishes. In the first case, it is plausibility that matters; people believe in electricity because when they switch on the light, certain things happen which seem to prove that electricity is real. In the second case, it is the pay-off that matters; people may believe in a certain lucky

To see a black cat is meant to be good luck—unless you live in China.

When the fishing fleet gets back to port, it is good luck to touch the seamen.

WHO SAID IT WAS UNLUCKY TO WALK UNDER A LADDER?

Can you bring yourself to walk under a ladder? This superstition is about something more basic than getting paint on your head.

charm because they are worried about their ability to pass an exam, and having their lucky teddy bear sitting on the desk gives them confidence.

The Function of Superstitions

An investigation of the past suggests that superstitions were ways of responding to certain basic human needs and desires:

The need to feel secure. In a world which can feel difficult, threatening and unpredictable, it's comforting to feel that people know at least some of the basic principles and laws by which it works. French thinker Jacques Ellul says that this is why human beings need some beliefs and habits to be sacred—to make people feel that they belong:

'*To be able to do "anything at all", "whatever comes into my head", is not livable. I can exist only in a certain order, and my freedom exists only if it operates in a certain order. The sacred is the order of the world.*

'*To be specific: thanks to the sacred, man possesses a certain number of points of reference. He knows where he is. It saves his continually having to make exhausting decisions.*'

The need to have rules and conventions for society. People who belong to a community need to agree about how they should behave in particular circumstances. Individuals can't always be free to act in the way they choose. And so following superstitions puts a pattern on their conduct.

The need to have power over the future. Many superstitions are concerned with predictions: do this and bad luck will follow; avoid this, and you will marry within the year. Most people would like some control over their own future, and superstitions offer the chance to believe that they really can influence future events. Perhaps this is why superstitions are especially common among people who do risky jobs.

The Origin of Superstitions

Common sense. Some superstitions have very obvious, down-to-earth explanations. People who walk under ladders may find paint pots descending upon their heads!

Pre-Christian beliefs. Other superstitions go back to pre-Christian times, and make sense as part of a world-view where people felt that they were at the mercy of strange warring powers and conflicting magical forces. Because gods and spirits were thought to live in trees, touching the wood of a tree was probably a way of making sure people didn't provoke their anger when they seemed to be boasting or over-confident about something they were saying.

Christianized superstitions. Some superstitions today are attempts to update older beliefs, or 'Christianize' pagan practices. Saying that 'touch wood' means 'touch the wood of the cross' looks very much like an attempt to find a valid Christian excuse for a pagan custom which was already well established.

Unknown origins. There are other superstitions about which people just do not know how the belief began. Sometimes habits continue for a long time after the reason for them has been lost. There is a village in Sweden where the local inhabitants used always to bow their heads whenever they went past a certain corner of the white-painted church. No one knew why, until the plaster was removed during redecoration—and on the wall was discovered an ancient image which had last been worshipped more than three centuries earlier. Yet the habit had continued unbroken.

Types of Superstition

There are several possible ways in which to categorize superstitions. It has been said that there are three main types:

Religious. These superstitions are connected to beliefs and holy objects. Some people believe that thirteen is unlucky because it was the number of table guests at the Last Supper.

Cultural. These superstitions are connected to ways of behaving in society. Some people believed that walking on the cracks between paving slabs increased a white girl's chances of marrying a black man.

Personal. These superstitions are connected to private rituals that individuals have. Dr Samuel Johnson, the famous eighteenth-century writer, used to trail his stick along the railings when he walked along the street; and if he missed one single rail, he would turn and go back to hit it.

Another way of looking at it would be to say that there are superstitions which deal with good and bad luck; superstitions which deal with omens and signs; and superstitions which deal with major human events, such as birth, marriage and death. The following account expands on these general categories.

Good and Bad Luck

These superstitions are very confusing, because often something which means good luck in one culture means bad luck in another! Black cats, for instance, are popular in England and America—but not in China. White heather is lucky in most places, but not in Scotland, where it is associated with Bonnie Prince Charlie. He was given a sprig of white heather at the start of his attempt to capture the crown in 1745, and the whole enterprise ended in disaster.

Often superstitions about luck involve the making of wishes. If a black cat crosses an individual's path, for instance, that person can make a wish for something they desire. Or, if someone pulls a chicken's wishbone with another person until it breaks, the one who ends up with the longer piece can make a wish. People also believe they can make a wish when they are stirring the ingredients of the Christmas cake—as long as they remember to stir sunwise, for otherwise they will offend the sun god.

Sometimes good and bad luck superstitions are updated versions of older beliefs. Some people believe it is bad luck to see a train pulled by two engines; and this just reflects an earlier belief that it was bad luck to see a cart pulled by two horses.

Many good luck superstitions involve charms and lucky objects. St Christopher charms are supposed to give travellers a safe journey because St Christopher is the patron saint of those who travel; a rabbit's foot is thought to be lucky because rabbits breed quickly, and were once thought to have special creative powers; the three brass monkeys, horse shoes, dice and toadstools are some of the better known items on a long list of lucky objects.

Here are a few superstitions connected with luck:

Acorns. Carrying an acorn in a pocket or handbag brings good luck. The oak tree was sacred to Druids, and was thought to have special powers.

Apples. Eating apples is lucky, and this superstition is probably connected to the saying 'An apple a day keeps the doctor away'. Cutting down an apple tree is bad luck. This probably reflects the idea that spirits lived in trees, and the apple—which came from a tree—bore some of their magical powers.

Candles. Blowing out the candles on a birthday cake in one attempt brings luck. This superstition probably goes back to the Greeks, who saw candles as symbols of life.

Cats. Black cats may be lucky, but white cats are the opposite! And for an actor to kick a cat is extremely bad luck. The play will not go well.

Cuckoos. It is good luck to see a cuckoo and turn over the money in your pocket at the same time. It means you will become wealthy.

Eggs. Knocking a hole through the shell of a hard-boiled egg after eating the egg brings luck.

Fingers. By keeping their fingers crossed, a person can prevent bad luck if they have walked under a ladder, seen an unlucky animal, made an unwise boast, or seen a coffin through glass...and many other things too! Obviously, this comes from the belief that the cross was an extremely powerful symbol, because of its Christian connections.

To meet a grave-digger is often thought to invite one's own death. Does this make grave-digging a lonely occupation?

Friday. Friday is unlucky for births, weddings, starting a new job, or moving house. There are traditions that several disastrous events took place on a Friday: supposedly, Eve ate the forbidden fruit, Cain killed Abel, the Great Flood began, and Jesus was betrayed.

Houses. Walking into each room of a new house carrying bread in one hand and salt in the other will bring luck. This goes back to the idea that any spirits in the room would be pleased with these things, and so would not bother the incomers. Curiously, one new fringe religious group today—the Unification Church—regularly uses 'holy salt' to purify rooms of evil spirits before using them.

Ladders. Walking under a ladder is bad luck. Occultists believe that it is dangerous to break a circle—and walking under a ladder violates the circle formed by the pavement, the ladder and the wall. These three things make a triangle, too, and since a triangle represents the Trinity, walking under a ladder is said to show disrespect to God.

Sailors. Touching a sailor who has just returned from sea is good luck. The thinking is that the sailor has had good luck—returning safely from a risky enterprise—so perhaps the same luck will rub off.

Spiders. Seeing a spider is lucky, and to have one on your clothes means that you will soon make money. But killing a spider is very bad luck.

Omens and Signs

An omen is an event which gives a warning about the future. Sometimes these are slightly unusual, puzzling happenings. For example, when a woman's apron suddenly falls off, the superstition is that she will have a baby within the year. Sometimes they can be very ordinary circumstances indeed. When two people share a towel, the superstition is that they will quarrel before long; when someone drops a spoon, a child will soon come on a visit. And sometimes they will involve specified animals or objects such as cats, pigs, birds, mirrors and salt.

Most omen superstitions are about bad fortune and dramatic events. But there is also a large body of superstitions which tries to predict the weather. Some of them are not so much superstitions as rudimentary common sense:

'Red sky at night, shepherd's delight;
Red sky in the morning, shepherd's warning...'

Here are some omen superstitions:

Birds. If birds fly by when someone is starting on a journey, and they fly to the right, the journey will be successful. But if they fly to the left, the person should stay at home.

Chairs. If a chair is placed against a wall, a visitor will soon come to the house. If a nurse overturns a chair in the ward of a hospital, a new patient will soon be admitted.

Hair. Finding a hair on someone's shoulder means that the finder is about to receive a letter. If the hair is shaped like a letter of the alphabet, this will be the initial of the letter writer.

Peel of apple or orange. If a girl peels an apple or orange in one continuous piece and then throws the peel over her shoulder, it will land in such a shape that it spells out the initial letter of the name of her future husband. If the peel breaks, she will never marry.

Major Human Events

Many superstitions are concerned with the great turning points of life—birth, marriage and death. Since these are the most obvious times of crisis and uncertainty in human affairs, it is not strange that odd beliefs cluster around them.

Birth. Childbirth many years ago was a much more risky enterprise than it is now. A high percentage of children died as babies, and mothers frequently died in giving birth.

Some superstitions were ways of making childbirth easier or more rewarding. Opening doors and locks in a house, and undoing any knots in clothes that a pregnant woman was wearing were supposed to help make the delivery of a baby much more comfortable. If a child had to be delivered by Caesarian section, one consoling superstition said that it would be unnaturally strong, have the gift of seeing spirits, and live to find hidden treasure.

Other superstitions were concerned with protecting the new baby from the powers of evil, or giving it the best start in life. To carry the baby to the top of the house meant that it would be destined to rise in the world. To baptize it quickly after birth meant that fairies or evil spirits could not carry it away. And if it cried at its baptism, that was good; it meant that evil was being driven out.

These superstitions are not really much to do with Christian beliefs about baptism. They go back much further—to the idea that the whole world was inhabited by evil spirits who warred on human life, and that only magic spells and incantations could protect a vulnerable new life from their power.

Marriage. Many superstitions try to satisfy the curiosity of girls about who will marry them, and when. If a man wipes his hands on a woman's apron, says one belief, he is going to fall in love with her. This is because he will have wiped some of her sweat on to his hands, and it will have a magical effect upon him. The girl who catches a bride's bouquet, when it is flung into the crowd after a wedding, will be the next one to be married. But a girl who is a bridesmaid three times will never marry.

Other superstitions try to ward off bad luck from the new marriage: engaged couples shouldn't give one another handkerchiefs; a bride shouldn't make her own wedding dress; a wedding dress shouldn't be worn before the wedding day itself, and the bride should not look at herself in the mirror as she wears it.

The choice of wedding day is important: not the bride's birthday, and preferably not in May (because Maia, after whom the month is named, is the Greek goddess of the elderly). And what a bride wears is important too. Her mother's wedding dress is especially lucky. But she should also wear 'something old, something new; something borrowed, something blue'.

Nearly all of the traditional wedding customs have some superstitious reason behind them. Throwing confetti or birdseed, for instance, is the survival of the custom of throwing corn or rice over a couple—which was supposed to ensure that they would produce lots of children and never go hungry.

Death. There is an almost endless list of superstitions connected with death. It is unlucky to see a hearse or even an ambulance—especially the back of it; to see a coffin through glass; to count the number of cars in a funeral procession; to go past a coffin and a wedding at the same time; to see a hearse followed by a dog, horse or bird; to take a spade indoors. (This is because a spade is the symbol of the grave-digger.)

There are things people can do to ward off bad luck, however. As the hearse passes people could hold their collar, touch wood, cross their fingers or spit.

There are other superstitions about when people are going to die. It is often said that 'people die in threes'. So, for example, if there are two sudden deaths in the same week, the third cannot be far away. A bird perched on the weather vane of a church means a death within the parish before seven days have passed. And the ticking of a death-watch beetle in the house means that somebody will soon die.

It used to be believed that the last person to be buried in a churchyard became the 'churchyard watcher', and had to look after the graveyard—rather than going to their rest—until someone else was buried there, who would then take on the job. Sometimes this meant that when two people were to be buried on the same day, the families would race to get to the churchyard first. Often fights would break out between mourners because both families would be determined that their dead relative should not become the next 'watcher'.

Conclusions

Superstitions remind people of some important truths about human experience. Life can be unpredictable, full of misfortune, risky, and seemingly hostile. Things can happen that seem fantastically lucky—almost as if they have been organized by some secret law of nature. And all people would like to know more about the future than they do.

Superstitions also remind people about the past. They provide a glimpse of a world-view in which the universe is frightening and hostile, but also capable of being manipulated magically for human good. They have been described as 'beliefs which linger on after a religious system has collapsed or been replaced' (Geoffrey Parrinder). And omens have been described as 'a testimony to the almost universal fear with which man has regarded the forces surrounding his life' (T. S. Knowlson). They are a reminder, therefore, that many of our ancestors believed they lived in a very uncertain and unpredictable world.

This world-view is not simply a thing of the past. For many people today—and not just in primitive societies—life really does seem like that. David Martin, in his *Sociology of English Religion*, has said:

'*Far from being secular our culture wobbles between a partially absorbed Christianity, biased towards comfort and the need for confidence, and beliefs in fate, luck and moral governance incongruously joined together.*'

Questions

There are four possible attitudes towards superstitions:

▶ *They're utterly harmless, and people should treat them as a bit of a joke. Although no one seriously believes in them today, there's no reason why they shouldn't hold on to them as part of their culture.*

▶ *They're complete nonsense. No educated person who knows anything about science should perpetuate these ridiculous ideas by passing them on to their children.*

▶ *What if there is something in superstitions? There may be a little grain of truth in them somewhere—and you can't be too careful, can you?*

▶ *Believing in God doesn't leave any room for most, if not all, superstitions. If people believe that there's only one God, and that he is in complete control of all the powers in the universe, he is the only one people need to think about and relate to.*

10 Written in the Stars

Scientists in a variety of fields have become concerned about the increasing acceptance of astrology in many parts of the world. We, the undersigned—astronomers, astrophysicists, and scientists in other fields—wish to caution the public against the unquestioning acceptance of the predictions and advice given privately and publicly by astrologers. Those who believe in astrology should realize that there is no scientific foundation for its tenets.

Statement signed by 186 leading scientists in 1975

After over thirty years as an astrological-consultant, and teacher of astrology to students in about one hundred and fifty countries, I have yet to meet one who, having put astrology to the test, has rejected the subject as nonsense.

Jeff Mayo, leading astrology teacher

People find it hard to resist the temptation to peep into next week's newspaper. And so attempts to foretell the future (called 'divination') have been widespread in just about every human culture in history. The methods have been immensely varied: throwing a handful of dust into the air and tracing the patterns it makes as it lands; staring into a mirror, a crystal ball, or a candle flame, trying to see pictures and images within it; swinging a pendulum and interpreting the directions it takes; studying tea leaves, coffee grounds, bumps on heads or lines on palms.

The Function of Astrology and Divination

The seemingly universal appeal of finding out what the future holds indicates that these varied practices meet some basic human needs.

The need to feel that life can be controlled by regular systems and practices. If there are methods of working out what lies around the corner, people can take more responsibility for their lives.

The need to feel that certain things are pre-ordained. People do not like to think of themselves as the helpless playthings of chance, but that they are living out a pattern which has already been decided somewhere else.

The need to feel prepared to face the risks of the future. Even if what is predicted seems dreadful, people seem to think it is better to know the worst in advance.

This Taiwanese chart shows the zones of a person's palm, which are supposed to mean something in telling the future.

The Origin of Astrology and Divination

The human urge to foretell the future goes back to the very dawn of human civilization. J. Bronowski claims that prehistoric paintings of hunters and animals were probably 'magical' ways of trying to experience the thrill and fear of the life-and-death struggle of hunting in advance. Some of the very first human civilizations studied the stars in an attempt to find clues there to future events.

Methods of divination have not changed much over the centuries. For example, the rules of systems such as astrology, Tarot and I Ching have remained intact for many hundreds of years.

One of the methods which has gone out of fashion, however, is *augury*, using an animal's entrails. This was popular in many ancient cultures, including Babylon and Rome. A specially selected animal was slaughtered, cut open, and inspected closely. Marks on some of its vital organs (such as the liver) would be regarded as signs warning about future events.

Often augury was carried out by specially qualified people, such as members of the priesthood; and in some civilizations there have been gifted individuals who have

been regarded as *clairvoyant*, able to see into the future in sudden flashes of inspiration. In Greek and Roman times, the priestess of the shrine at Delphi was reputed to be able to go into an ecstatic trance and deliver messages—often very cryptic ones—about the future. The same kind of thing has been claimed for American Indian medicine men, voodoo priests in Haiti, and 'second sighted' seers in the Scottish Highlands. Today there are clairvoyants such as Jeane Dixon and Matthew Manning who say that they are frequently given advance warning of coming events in mental pictures.

Perhaps some of these methods came about because human beings were dimly aware of untapped abilities within themselves. There does seem to be some evidence that human beings have a fragmentary ability to see what is coming to them. For example, one researcher who studied the record of an American railroad company over ten years discovered that when there was an accident, there tended to be fewer people than usual on the train; and if only one carriage was affected, there would probably be fewer people than usual in it! And Jeane Dixon has made some spectacularly unlikely predictions which have come true—such as the assassinations of both John and Robert Kennedy. But she has also been wildly wrong.

It seems that the gift is real, but unsafe to rely upon. People who have tried to make a career out of their predictive abilities have often had to resort to cheating and trickery in order to maintain a respectable record.

Divination became suspect when Jewish/Christian ideas began to spread. The early books of the Bible refer to quite a few divining methods. Clearly attempts to read the future were widespread in those days. But as the centuries went by, and the people of Israel learned to depend more and more upon their God, their trust in divining methods waned sharply.

Isaiah, for example, was a *prophet*, which meant that he believed God gave him messages for his people. These messages sometimes concerned the future; but he was scornful of any other kind of do-it-yourself divining:

> 'All the counsel you have received has only worn you out!
> Let your astrologers come forward,
> those stargazers who make predictions month by month,
> Let them save you from what is coming upon you.
> Surely they are like stubble;
> the fire will burn them up...
> Each of them goes on in his error;
> there is not one that can save you.'

And so in the New Testament those who became Christians from pagan backgrounds would often burn the magical books and charts which they had previously used in trying to calculate the future. In the city of Ephesus, for example, it is recorded that 50,000

When a clairvoyant gazes into a crystal ball, what does she really see?

drachmas' worth of scrolls was burned. One drachma was the average worker's daily wage. So this was quite a decisive break!

Understanding Astrology and Divination

There are many methods of divination, but they all tend to rely on the same two things.

System of rules. There are set rules by which certain meanings will be given to certain features. Examples include the patterns in the tea leaves or the position of lines on the hand.

Sensitivity of the reader. No two people are likely to read the same evidence in quite the same way. The pictures one person sees in the bottom of a tea cup may be slightly different from those that appear to another.

For this reason, it has been suggested that the actual methods of divination are quite unimportant. They are just useful props, which help to engage the imagination of the diviner. When someone stares into a crystal ball, the pictures they see are not 'really' there; they are created by the mind. However, as their conscious mind goes blank, they can home in on things which their subconscious already knows in some way, and bring them up to the surface in the form of a picture.

So perhaps divination is not really tapping in to a supernatural library of information but simply making contact with the inner self, which already has insights and images of the future. If there is any truth in this, it suggests a danger for would-be diviners. Not everything in the subconscious is healthy, or deserves to be brought up to the surface. Before Sirhan Sirhan murdered Bobby Kennedy, he is said to have sat for hours staring into a candle flame; and it was through that route that he received the 'instructions' for the killing.

The three most common methods of divination today—the I Ching, Tarot cards, and astrology—demonstrate these points.

I Ching

I Ching, or the *Book of Changes*, is a traditional Chinese method which has risen in popularity since the 1960s. It involves throwing down a handful of coins (traditionally a bundle of yarrow sticks) and reading the meaning of the straight or broken lines which are formed. There are sixty-four possible patterns, or 'hexagrams', and the *Book of Changes* gives explanations for each.

At first sight, this may seem a very limited method. Only sixty-four possible results? But the *Book of Changes* suggests all sorts of different levels of meaning in each symbol used. The combination of one with another can lead to even more meanings. And the commentaries which accompany each reading supply all sorts of other possible extensions too.

Three lines in a certain arrangement mean 'fire'. But fire can stand for warmth, clinging, and dependence, too; it is also associated with the middle daughter, the pheasant, and the eye; and it can also say something about lightning, helmets, weapons, big-bellied men, the tortoise, the hawk and the crab!

So the range of possible meanings is immense. Just as

Astrological charts, signs of the zodiac, popular horoscopes... Do they tell us anything reliable about what is to come?

much depends upon the user's intuition as upon the *Book of Changes* itself. Occult writer Cherry Gilchrist, in her book on divination, makes this comment:

'*The symbol gives rise to speculation, as well as to specific hints as to the meaning of the reading; the hexagram is meant to be an exercise in thoughtful contemplation, and tends to reveal the deeper import of a situation rather than give a single prognostication.*'

Tarot

The Tarot is similar in many ways. It is a set of pictorial cards, each with a different name. Tarot cards were first used in fourteenth-century France, and from there soon spread to other European countries. Nobody quite knows who originated them or why, but the symbols used show some acquaintance with the magical traditions of more than one country. The Tarot was never just a pack of playing cards; from the start, it was designed for supernatural purposes.

As with the I Ching symbols, each Tarot card has a general meaning but many different specific applications. The way to use them is to set them out in one of several prescribed layouts; and, of course, when this is done, the exact position of each card can suggest new meanings, further layers of interpretation. So, once again, everything depends on the mind of the user.

Astrology

Astrology is the attempt to forecast future events through observing the movements of stars and planets. Its origins are obscure. Nicholas Campion, a historian of astrology, claims that in Mesopotamia four thousand years ago 'we find evidence of the emerging combination of astronomy, mathematics and mythology which was to become the basis of astrology'. Not many historians would put the starting point so far back, but it is certain that modern Western astrology came together over a very long period indeed.

The first horoscope to be cast for an individual was probably drawn up in Babylon in 409BC. A few years before, the Greek writer Herodotus commented that the Egyptians were more involved in divination than any other nation, and foretold a person's future by reference to the date of their birth. Two hundred years later, it was slaves from the East who brought astrological ideas to Rome; and the public craze for astrology became so notable that the government became alarmed—and several times had the astrologers expelled from the city.

And so the basic ideas of astrology have been around for a very long time. Remarkably, in two thousand years or so they have shown very little change. Is it because they reflect only an irrational superstition? Or because they have been tried and tested, and proved to work?

It is certainly plausible that human life could be affected by influences from the skies. Certainly, the moon has an effect on the earth's gravitational field, and directly affects sea tides. Sunspot activity creates disturbances in the earth's atmosphere and it seems to be affected by the alignment of the planets. If the different bodies of the solar system react upon one another in this way, isn't it possible that the position of the planets has something to do with human fortunes too?

Michel Gauquelin's interest in this question led him to analyze the birth dates of 576 eminent French doctors.

'*Having (painfully) worked out by hand the position of the planets at the hour of birth of each doctor, I made a statistical compilation of my findings. Suddenly, I was presented with an extraordinary fact. My doctors were not born under the same skies as the common run of humanity. They had chosen to come into the world much more often during roughly the two hours following the rise and culmination of two planets, Mars and Saturn. Moreover, they tended to "avoid" being born following the rise and culmination of the planet Jupiter.*'

Since 1951, when he made this discovery, Gauquelin has continued to work on possible links between the professions human beings follow in later life, their personality traits, and the position of the planets at the moment of their birth. He has been able to demonstrate that there may well be some connections people cannot yet explain.

Gauquelin's ideas have often been attacked, but he is an extremely careful, honest researcher, and so his theories are slowly winning the respect of scientists. Psychologist Hans Eysenck, for example, says that Gauquelin's evidence 'represents what must be the most convincing case that can be made for the basic astrological premise... Perhaps the time has come to state quite unequivocally that a new science is in process of being born.'

Nevertheless, this is not proof that astrology is true. Gauquelin points out that even if he has demonstrated a link between the planets and human careers, there are other parts of his work that undermine some of the other claims of astrology. One chapter of his book *The Truth About Astrology* is headed 'The Horoscope Falls Down'.

The influence of the planets is one thing. The importance of the zodiac—those twelve constellations of stars with names like Taurus, Gemini, Aries, Capricorn—is quite another. In his investigation of claims about the zodiac, he says that 'the results have been consistently disappointing'; and when he has tested astrologers who claim that they can use the zodiac as a guide to human personality, they have failed the test so miserably that some have angrily accused him of rigging the test.

Astronomers point out, too, that the twelve constellations of the zodiac are not really natural groupings of stars. They look as if they are, from earth, but in fact some of them are millions of miles apart, closer to earth than they are to one another! Furthermore, in the same narrow strip of sky in which the zodiac lies, and which includes only a portion of the stars visible from the earth anyway, there is a thirteenth constellation called Ophiucus which was not visible to early astronomers. If the other twelve constellations affect human life, it seems unlikely that the thirteenth could be insignificant!

Conclusions

In assessing the importance of astrology and divination there are several points to consider.

There is a temptation to wishful thinking. The following announcement was placed in the press by a French researcher.

ABSOLUTELY FREE!
Your ultra-personal horoscope
A 10-PAGE DOCUMENT
Benefit from a unique experiment
Send name, address, date and place of birth to:
ASTRAL ELECTRONIC

Many people responded to it, and the first 150 of them were sent a ten-page character analysis. But it wasn't their own: it had been drawn up by a professional astrologer for a celebrated French mass murderer.

Soon enthusiastic letters of acknowledgment began to arrive. Ninety per cent of those who responded felt that the analysis described them very well indeed. Eighty per cent commented that their family and friends agreed!

It is deceptively easy to recognize bits of oneself in a description. Look at this, for example. Does it sound like you?

'*Some of your aspirations tend to be pretty unrealistic. At times, you are extroverted, affable, sociable, while at other times you are introverted, wary and reserved. You have found it unwise to be too frank in revealing yourself to others. You pride yourself on being an independent thinker and do not accept others' opinions without satisfactory proof...*'

This is part of a psychological portrait, created from a news-stand astrology book, which scientist Bertram Forer gave to a group of his students. Each student was told that the portrait had been created uniquely for them, through personality testing; and they were asked to rate its accuracy on a scale from 0 (poor) to 5 (perfect). The average score was 4.26.

It all goes to show that human beings are easily duped. It is all too possible for people who claim special powers to present others with impressive 'information' about themselves, and convince them that they really do have some source of supernatural insight.

Some of the claims of divination do not seem to be founded on very good evidence. Hans Eysenck and D.K.B. Nias end their book on astrology with these crushing words:

'*In this book we have tried to examine the best research done by supporters of astrology and all too often we have been forced to admit that it was amateurish in its conception, faulty in its execution and less than rigorous in its statistical analysis of the data. Even the most quoted studies have weaknesses which rule them out as decisive evidence.*'

The popularity of divination tells us something about human nature. The urge to investigate the future is a natural human impulse. All people want as much warning as they can get of coming calamities; they all need as much information as they can obtain which will help them get the most out of their lives. And so different methods of divination will probably fascinate human beings for centuries to come.

Questions

There are four possible attitudes to take towards this subject:

▶ *The idea that human beings can foretell the future is just a bit of a giggle. It's all utterly harmless, and if people want to consult fairground clairvoyants or read their horoscope, no one should take it too seriously.*

▶ *Divination is complete nonsense. These ideas are antiquated, superstitious, and dangerous. People ought to take responsibility for their own decisions rather than leaving it up to fate.*

▶ *Sometimes these things work. Surely so many people would not build their lives around Tarot cards or astrology if they did no good.*

▶ *If there is a God who is in control of the future, and he can be trusted to tell people everything they need to know, it makes more sense to try to be in contact with him than to attempt to find out the future without him.*

11 The Occult

Occultism is not child's play, and it is very far from being fool-proof; for its pursuit strength is required as well as purity; but all who have touched its deeper issues unite in declaring that it is no will-o'-the-wisp, dancing over a bottomless bog, but a true path to the Light, though narrow as a razor's edge.

Dion Fortune, occultist

The only thing I will say with complete confidence, about that mystic and invisible power, is that it tells lies.

G. K. Chesterton, after experimenting with a ouija board

Magick is a science in which we never know what we're talking about, nor if what we are saying is true.

The Abbey of Thelma, a modern magic order

Superstitions, as described in the chapter on that topic, are rules of thumb that try to explain some of the hidden laws by which the universe works. They don't explain very much (why *should* a black cat be lucky?) and they don't form much of a system. They are simply a jumble of ideas, warnings and guidelines.

But from time immemorial, human beings have also been trying to work out more thoroughgoing theories of the universe's hidden laws, trying to discover methods of gaining secret knowledge and access to unexpected, unusual powers. These attempts include witchcraft, shamanism, magic, alchemy, clairvoyance, medium-ship, divination...and much more besides. This is what is often lumped together under the general heading of 'the occult'.

The word 'occult' comes from a Latin verb which means 'to hide'. The occult is 'the hidden'...anything people don't fully understand yet, anything which seems mysterious and baffles understanding.

The Function of the Occult

There are several reasons why human beings have been so fascinated with the occult. Here are some of the obvious ones:

The urge to understand as much as possible about the way life fits together. Many of the early scientists in Elizabethan days were also amateur occultists; it was all part of the same quest for knowledge.

The need to feel able to combat threatening unseen forces. People with a world-view in which the earth was populated by hostile spirits and evil powers needed some kind of weapon with which to combat the unknown.

The drive to become as powerful as possible. Many occultists have pursued their search because they wanted to gain control of their own lives—and some-times those of others too.

The Origin of the Occult Quest

There is evidence of magical practices and primitive witchcraft in some of the earliest human remains. Occult writer Peter Underwood claims that 'the history of man is the history of magic', and certainly there are few human cultures in which occultism has not been a fact of life.

Magic

Magic in Western civilization started to take its modern shape when the Moors invaded Spain. Most of the

The great double triangle, symbol of Solomon. This symbol appears in the Jewish Qabala represented by the two ancients. It has to do with the very old ideas of the God of Light and the God of Reflections; mercy and vengeance; the White Jehovah and the Black Jehovah.

literature they brought with them was Islamic—and nothing to do with magic—but they also had some more mysterious texts, dating from previous ages. Some of these contained the ideas of the Hermetic tradition and the Jewish Qabala.

These books sparked off enormous interest among Western scholars, and some very important people indeed travelled to Toledo (where the books were being translated) in order to get hold of them.

The Hermetic writings were a group of anonymous documents claiming to be the work of an ancient Egyptian priest, Hermes Trismegistus. They put forward ideas which had been held by heretical groups in the early days of the Christian church, and also some of the teachings of the so-called mystery religions which had been competitors to Christianity in the Roman Empire. More than that, the Hermetic tracts gave obscure promises that this information could become the source of power over all the workings of the universe.

It was an entrancing thought—that people could escape the limitations of mere mortal life and become super-beings:

'*The wise man rules Nature, not Nature the wise man. For the same reason we can accomplish more than the stars. In us, then, should abound so great a wisdom that we thereby shall control all things... The will of man extends over the depth of the sea and the height of the firmament.*'

The Jewish Qabala (which means 'teaching handed down') held out a similar kind of hope. By intricate arrangements of words and numbers, it tried to give an understanding of how the whole physical realm, including human life, was organized. This knowledge could provide supernatural power.

If this was an unchristian notion, not many scholars seemed to see it. Paracelsus wrote that the Qabala was 'beholden to God, in alliance with him, and founded on the words of Christ'.

A very common form of occultism in the sixteenth and seventeenth centuries was alchemy, the attempt to turn base metals into gold. It was not, however, just an early form of science. Modern magician Gareth Knight makes this comment:

'*In its fullness it was a theory of being, or process, embracing all creation. It saw all forms of existence...as rooted in one basic ground of beingness and capable of growth, evolution and transformation.*'

Alchemists were not simply looking for a scientific formula which would enable them to produce vast quantities of gold. They believed that the secret would be discovered only by someone sufficiently sensitive and trained to work it out by intuition. It was for the élite only; it was 'occult'. F. Sherwood Taylor explains this point of view in his book, *The Alchemists*.

'*We constantly hear that the alchemist will use his gold to build bridges or churches, to finance crusades or to relieve the poor; or he may seek to use the stone as an elixir to cure diseases. But he never proposes the public use of such things, the disclosing of his knowledge for the benefit of man. The alchemist himself will apply the gold or heal the few he chooses to heal. Pearls are not to be cast before swine.*'

Witchcraft

Another branch of the occult is witchcraft. Witches generally believe themselves to be followers of an ancient religion, which goes back far beyond Christianity, and which is properly called 'wicca'. There are 'black' and 'white' witches, who work in covens. These are groups which try to produce occult effects, much like the Satanists. Other witches, sometimes called 'green' witches, work alone. They tend to be women who have inherited their beliefs and their craft from their mother and grandmother before them; there is a long family tradition of uncanny powers.

In fact the claims of witches are not very well founded. Wicca is not an ancient religion, but a fanciful reconstruction of something which never really existed.

Earlier this century, an Oxford historian named Margaret Murray began to study the hidden history of witchcraft. She found much of the evidence which interested her in records of the confessions witches made at their trials in the sixteenth and seventeenth centuries. She ignored the fact that these confessions were often extracted by torture and threats, and that they therefore contained exactly what the witchfinders wanted to hear.

And so she came up with the theory that witchcraft had once been an immense, organized system, dominating Europe; but that with the coming of Christianity it had gradually been forced underground and was now furtively practised by only a few. It had never died out, however, and in her books *The Witch-Cult in Western Europe* and *The God of the Witches* she retraced their practices, beliefs and ceremonies. Witches, she said, met joyfully to feast, dance and experience visions, at eight great annual festivals and at smaller meetings in covens of thirteen.

Her theories stirred great interest and were widely accepted. She was asked to write the article on witchcraft for one edition of the *Encyclopedia Britannica*. But she was wrong.

Modern historians have shown that there is no evidence for a widespread, organized religion of witchcraft. Witchcraft was just an example of general occult practices found in many cultures, says writer and academic Mircea Eliade in an article on the topic, not a systematized movement:

'As *a matter of fact, all the features associated with European witches are—with the exception of Satan and the*

Peter Breughel the Elder's 'The Alchemist' depicts a medieval quest with roots much further back in history. Alchemists sought to turn base metals into gold and silver, by the use of a mysterious substance. Shrouded in mysticism and superstition, alchemy was nevertheless the forerunner of chemistry.

A witch and her familiars. Was witchcraft an organized cult in ancient times?

Sabbath—claimed also by Indo-Tibetan yogis and magicians. They too are supposed to fly through the air, render themselves invisible, kill at a distance, master demons and ghosts, and so on… They proudly claim all the crimes and horrible ceremonies cited ad nauseam in the European witch trials.'

Some historians feel that the rumours of witches and their strange powers had a political beginning. Believing in witches and the harm they could do provided a way of bringing out into the open the insecurities many people felt in an age when constant religious wars were making life very unpredictable. Witchcraft provided an enemy to fear and to fight, a scapegoat which could be blamed for all the uncertainties of life.

Perhaps this is true. At any rate, while Murray's theories were still widely accepted, some amateur occultists in Europe and America began meeting in the way she prescribed and trying out for themselves some of the supposedly ancient rituals. From this has come the modern witchcraft revival.

Spiritualism

Another attempt to penetrate the spiritual world was Spiritualism. The modern movement began in 1848 when a family in Hydesville, New York, found they had a poltergeist in their new home. The three daughters of the Fox family tried to communicate with the 'spirit' who was causing the rappings in the walls and the strange noises at night. To their surprise, they found they could; and through a carefully established code the 'spirit' would send them messages.

In many civilizations throughout history, human beings have toyed with the idea that their ancestors could speak to them—through dreams and visions, strange events, apparitions and appearances. But Spiritualism became the first world-wide attempt to build a religious mission out of this idea.

It spread internationally very quickly, and continues to enjoy great influence today. Central to it are 'mediums', sensitive people who can go into trances and produce messages from 'the other side'. Millions of people who are not Spiritualists and have never been to a Spiritualist church have nonetheless sought communication with their dead relatives through such famous mediums as Arthur Ford, Stainton Moses, Ena Twigg and Doris Stokes. Spiritualism has also led to spirit healing, in which some mediums believe they can place their hands on an invalid and cure disease by powers transmitted from 'the other side'—or, in some cases, prescribe medicine through the skill of a long-dead doctor.

Since the rise of Spiritualism, do-it-yourself methods have become increasingly popular. The most famous of these is the ouija board. This is a smooth table around which are placed cards bearing the letters of the alphabet and the words 'Yes' and 'No'. An upturned glass is placed in the centre of the table, and everyone sitting around the table places one finger on the glass. It will then slide around the table, from letter to letter, spelling out messages as it goes. It is very simple...and often frighteningly effective.

These are just some of the most well known varieties of occultism—but actually the list is endless: Chinese *feng shui*, Haitian voodoo, primitive tribal magical practices, Druidism, Indian tantric magic, and many more.

Examples of Occult Phenomena

Manifestations of the occult puzzle many people. Some, indeed, seem to defy a clear explanation. Nevertheless, some facts can be established very clearly.

Explainable Phenomena

It is likely that some things which are presently 'occult' will some day turn out to have quite ordinary, everyday scientific principles behind them; it's just that people don't understand those principles yet.

Take dowsing, for example. This is a method of finding water in the ground. A person simply walks over the field where they think the water may be, holding before them a

Water diviners—or dowsers—have a genuine gift for finding water below ground. No one seems to know how this works.

forked twig (or wire, or plastic, or whalebone—it doesn't seem to matter which). They hold the forked ends with either hand, and as they pass over an underground stream, the end they are not holding will give a sudden, irresistible upward jerk.

No one knows why it works in this way—but it does. Perhaps some day people will discover why. And perhaps people will also discover the real nature of ghosts in the same way. At the moment, the best theory suggests that ghosts are a kind of imprint made on the walls of a room, or the ruins of a building—much like a video being shot of some of the events which took place there—and that occasionally, when the conditions are just right, the recording can unexpectedly be played back.

This would explain why ghosts often pay no attention to their surroundings, or walk through doors which no longer exist. It would explain why people see ghost stagecoaches and animals as well as human beings. It would mean that ghosts have nothing to do with life after death, or the soul living out of the body, any more than making a conventional video has any impact upon the soul or spirit of a living person. They would just be one more bit of the 'hidden' realm which had become open to inspection at last.

Magic

Not everything occult is in the explainable category. Some of it seems to resist exploration. And many of those who have a keen interest in the occult would insist that occult knowledge is only for the few—for a handful of initiates who are prepared to be trained in the secret skills and techniques which bring supernatural power. This, for example, is what magic is all about.

The magic that most people know about is the sort described in fairy tales, in which magicians with pointed hats and curious spells enable the hero and heroine to live happily ever after. But to some people magic is a very real and serious business. Modern magician Dion Fortune says its aim is to 'effect changes in consciousness in conformity with will'. Occultist Peter Underwood says it is 'the means whereby can be discovered unknown forces of nature, and the harnessing and employment of these forces'.

Magic has taken two directions: 'black' and 'white' magic. Black magicians aim to use their powers negatively—often to destroy—and their aim is their own personal growth in power. White magic, according to Gareth Knight who practises it, is 'concerned with what it can contribute to civilization as a whole'.

Dion Fortune believes that magic offers 'a power that is neither good nor evil in itself but only as it is used'. In other words, it is a technique, not a religion. Some Christian writers have pointed out that there is a close parallel between the kind of mental concentration which magicians practise and the meditation techniques of some branches of Christianity. But the aim is different. Christian meditation leads on to prayer and communion with God; occult meditation is an end in itself.

Magicians are not the only occultists. Sometimes confused with black magicians are Satanists, who also aim to use occult forces in a negative way. There are two kinds of Satanists. One very small group genuinely believes that the person called 'Satan' in the Bible is the real God of this universe, who has been displaced by the weak, ineffective Christian God of love. But most Satanists use the idea of Satan merely as a symbol to focus their minds and so give them increased power.

Like magicians, they believe that concentrating the mind can help to harness occult forces. But where magicians tend to work alone—or with only a few other associates, who are soon discarded when their usefulness is over—Satanists work together. Evil actions, they claim, increase power. There are 'lust rituals', in which the whole group may try to work a spell to help one group member seduce someone he or she is attracted to; or 'hate rituals', which project the force of all the group's malevolence towards some enemy whom they are trying to injure or kill.

Does it work? Two things must be said. First, scientists and doctors do not know all that the human mind can achieve. There is some evidence that the mind can influence its environment. For instance, when there is a poltergeist in a house—the kind of strange psychic disturbance which makes furniture shift about in the night, electrical appliances switch themselves on automatically, and objects topple inexplicably from high shelves—it is usually connected to the psychological condition of one of the people living in the house. This person is causing all the upheaval—completely unconsciously. So perhaps it is possible for people to bring about changes around them by fixing their minds with great determination on something they want.

But there is no evidence that this can happen consistently or predictably. Occultists have a high failure rate. They cannot produce effects 'to order', and even in traditional societies medicine men may use a lot of trickery to keep their reputation intact and stay in business.

The second thing that needs to be said is that often those who become involved with Satanism, or magic for that matter, are people who feel strongly inferior and need to imagine that they have some compensating source of power. In the late sixties an American social scientist, Dr Edward Moody, joined an organization known as the Church of Satan to find out why people were attracted to it. He found that a common trait of church members was a strong sense of personal failure.

Signs of desecration in a country churchyard. A black magic ceremony has been held at night, and satanic symbols are left on a cross.

'The cult attracted them because it offered a simple explanation for their inadequacies: they were bewitched or under an unlucky star or not vibrating to the right rhythm.

Whatever the fault, it was not their own. Since the cause of their failure was supernatural, the remedy was supernatural. The rites and medicines of the church promised the success that had so far eluded them.'

Witches

Witches are really just one side of a modern revival of paganism—the following of pre-Christian nature religions, the attempt to return to worshipping ancient Norse, Greek or Celtic gods and goddesses.

The reason for doing so again seems to have something to do with a wish to discover sources of occult power, in this case through developing a sense of oneness with the whole universe. Modern thinker Theodore Roszak defends it in this way:

'Outside our narrow cultural experience, in religious rites both sophisticated and primitive, human beings have been able to achieve a sacramental vision of being… The differences between these traditions—between Eskimo shamanism and medieval alchemy, between Celtic druidism and Buddhist Tantra—are many but an essentially magical worldview is common to them all… This diverse

family of religions and philosophies represents the Old Gnosis—the old way of knowing… I regard it as the essential and supreme impulse of the religious life.'

Spiritualists

Spiritualists believe that mediums can receive messages from 'the other side' and put the living in touch with those who have died. Certainly it is not uncommon for mediums to come up with remarkably convincing messages which contain information they could not normally have known. And so Spiritualists claim, 'We prove survival.' But it has been pointed out that there may be other explanations for the remarkable messages.

Sadly, fraud has played a large part in Spiritualist history. Mediums have carefully researched the lives of their 'sitters' before seeing them, and have then used the facts they have found out to construct plausible messages.

Some mediums are extremely clever at 'fishing' for information and creating the illusion that they have volunteered a piece of information themselves—when in fact they have coaxed it out of the person.

A voodoo stilt dance in Haiti. Is voodoo the same phenomenon as occult practice in Europe and North America?

Even when trickery is not going on, there is some evidence to suggest that mediums in trance can somehow 'feed on' the memories, thoughts and hopes of the 'sitters' themselves, by some sort of telepathy, and translate these ideas into a message. Thus if I remember that my dead wife's favourite chocolates were truffles, the 'spirit' may come across with that piece of information. But the source of it will be my own head!

If the Bible is right in warning that the spirit world contains deceptive, evil, lying forces, there is the possibility that a medium's messages may be interfered with from this kind of source. People simply do not know. As a result, there are no safeguards against it.

Spiritualists as well as Christians, and many other psychic investigators and psychologists, would warn strongly against the use of a ouija board. Quite apart from any 'spiritual' dangers which might be incurred, the ouija board offers one way in which one individual's subconscious mind can send unhealthy wishes to the outside world. That person will end up unconsciously controlling the glass—and making it spell out what he most fears or dreads. Since there are many irrational, destructive and harmful impulses buried deep in the subconscious—normally kept firmly out of the daylight by the censoring process of the conscious mind—it is not a good idea to open up the subconscious too far.

Conclusions

Occultism exists in so many forms and varieties that it is clearly an important human way of looking at the world. It reminds people that there is a lot they still do not know about their lives, and that perhaps orthodox science has limits to how much it can achieve.

It can give a new respect for peoples in traditional societies. These peoples may not be as technologically advanced as some Western societies, but do live closer to nature and have a unique understanding of life. And it can give hope for the future—in the belief that some day people will all learn to discover and use new sources of power within themselves.

It has a doubtful reputation. It cannot be said that occultism is either a true or a safe way of looking at the universe. All kinds of different claims are made by occultists which cannot possibly be true. And dangers exist which need to be taken into account, but which are difficult to assess; it is hard to work out just how much psychological or spiritual harm people can do to themselves by ill-advised occult practices.

The early Christians looked at occultism in pagan religions with a mixture of scorn and horror. 'Turn from these worthless things,' they pleaded with their hearers. And they held that behind the seeming appearances of supernatural power and union with creation, there was actually an evil spiritual reality. Not everything 'spiritual' was good. The apostle Paul described it in this way:

'For our struggle is not against flesh and blood, but against the rulers, against the authorities, against the powers of this dark world and against the spiritual forces of evil in the heavenly realms.'

Questions

There are probably five main attitudes towards the occult:

▶ *It's all a load of nonsense, and talk of spiritual dangers is rubbish. As long as you don't take it too seriously, there's no real harm in it.*

▶ *Occultism works. It is real and powerful. People should not be afraid of it—it offers a doorway to a much more colourful, exciting and satisfying life.*

▶ *Occultism is a pretext for crime. It provides a reason, albeit a false one, for all kinds of wicked abuses of property and of people.*

▶ *Occultism is dangerous rubbish. We live in a scientific age and should have no time for magic, spells, witches, and the rest. We should debunk it at every opportunity.*

▶ *Occultism works—sometimes. This is because it is a mixture of misunderstood science, psychological mind-games and spiritual deception. It can do no good and should be avoided.*

Part Three

The Shadow and the Substance

What Is Popular Religion?
The Substance

12 What Is Popular Religion?

Basic human religious needs and basic religious functions have not changed very notably since the late Ice Age.

Arthur Greeley

The primitive ancient experiences of mankind are everywhere the same, and later men for the most part never transcend them.

Gustav Mensching

'Folk religion'...a general term for the unexpressed, inarticulate, but often deeply felt, religion of ordinary folk who would not usually describe themselves as church-going Christians yet feel themselves to have some sort of Christian allegiance.

John Habgood, Archbishop of York

If there were a simple definition of popular religion it would have come at the beginning rather than at the end of this book! The question has deliberately been left until after the presentation (in Part Two) of the many different forms it can take.

Now it is possible to focus on some characteristics of popular religion, and then put some of its assumptions into words.

Some Characteristics of Popular Religion

Popular religion exists alongside official, formal religion. Whether talking about Christianity, which has been the official religion in the Western world for many centuries, or any of the other major religions or sects which are now represented here, the situation is basically the same. Popular religion differs from official religion in the following ways:

► It is not expressed in any systematic way. It has no formal creed or system of beliefs; its 'subterranean theology' isn't clearly defined and isn't often put into words.

► It deals with what people actually believe and practise, as opposed to what they think (or are told) they ought to believe and practise.

► It has no organization like the church to hold it together.

► It is not as fixed and static as official religions, but changes considerably from one place to another and from one period to another.

► It flourishes outside official religion, but often alongside it, and sometimes even within it.

Popular religion exists in every religion and culture. If, as Arthur Greeley says, 'basic human religious needs and basic religious functions have not changed very notably since the late Ice Age', then one would expect to find evidence of popular religion not only in the primal or traditional religions, but also in the major world religions.

► Hinduism, for example, has been described as 'a vast storehouse of religious experiments', and it incorporates a great deal of popular religion which varies from place to place—even within India itself.

► Buddhism similarly adapted itself as it spread throughout the East and absorbed many beliefs and practices of the primal religions which were there before it came.

► Islam in its purest form has always been opposed to many aspects of popular religion, such as magic and superstition. But some elements of popular religion (such as the rites originally associated with pilgrimage to the Ka'bah in Mecca) were made part of 'official Islam'; and folk Islam as it is practised in many countries today includes many different kinds of popular religion, including visiting the shrine of a saint.

It's hard to find an adequate term to describe it. A large number of different terms have been proposed, and none of them is accepted by everyone. Here are just four of the terms that are used:

▶ *Folk religion*. This is a term that is specially appropriate in Scandinavia and Germany, where the word *Volk* refers to a people in a corporate sense; the expression 'folk religion' therefore suggests the religion of the whole people or at least the vast majority.

▶ *Common religion*. This term suggests the idea that it is the religion of common or ordinary people. The term hasn't been widely accepted, however, because its meaning isn't immediately obvious. One writer, Robert Towler, uses the term to refer to 'those beliefs and practices of an overtly religious nature which are not subject to continued control by the churches and whose significance and importance will not usually be recognized by the churches'.

▶ *Implicit religion*. The implication of this term is that it refers to a form of religion which is beneath the surface. Whereas official religion is explicit, in the sense that it articulates clearly defined beliefs and is expressed in prescribed rituals, popular religion is implicit in the sense that it is implied rather than directly stated.

▶ *Popular religion*. This is the term that has been used in this book, largely because it is the simplest and most easily intelligible expression. The main limitation of the term, however, is that it seems too vague to signify anything other than 'religion that has popular appeal'.

It is often related in some way to 'religious experience'. This book has not asked too many questions about experience, but has concentrated on all the phenomena of popular religion and the human needs and desires that are satisfied by it. At some stage, however, it is necessary to ask what makes an experience a religious experience. The following extract describes such a religious experience.

The relationship between these experiences and popular religion is open to at least three interpretations.

Some would say that this type of experience should be accepted just as it is. Readers should accept the interpretation—or lack of interpretation—that is given by those concerned. It doesn't matter whether the

---

In silence they landed, and pushed through the blossom and scented herbage and undergrowth that led up to the level ground, till they stood on a little lawn of a marvellous green, set round with Nature's own orchard-trees—crab-apple, wild cherry, and sloe.

'This is the place of my song-dream, the place the music played to me,' whispered the Rat, as if in a trance. 'Here, in this holy place, here if anywhere, surely we shall find Him!'

'Then suddenly the Mole felt a great Awe fall upon him, an awe that turned his muscles to water, bowed his head, and rooted his feet to the ground. It was no panic terror—indeed he felt wonderfully at peace and happy—but it was an awe that smote and held him and, without seeing, he knew it could only mean that some august Presence was very, very near. With difficulty he turned to look for his friend, and saw him at his side, cowed, stricken, and trembling violently. And still there was utter silence in the populous bird-haunted branches around them; and still the light grew and grew.

Perhaps he would never have dared to raise his eyes, but that, though the piping was now hushed, the call and the summons seemed still dominant and imperious. He might not refuse, were Death himself waiting to strike him instantly, once he had looked with mortal eye on things rightly kept hidden. Trembling he obeyed, and raised his humble head; and then, in that utter clearness of the imminent dawn, while Nature, flushed with fullness of incredible colour, seemed to hold her breath for the event, he looked in the very eyes of the Friend and Helper; saw the backward sweep of the curved horns, gleaming in the growing daylight; say the stern, hooked nose between the kindly eyes that were looking down on them humorously, while the bearded mouth broke into a half-smile at the corners; saw the rippling muscles on the arm that lay across the broad chest, the long supple hand still holding the pan-pipes only just fallen away from the parted lips; saw the splendid curves of the shaggy limbs disposed in majestic ease on the sward; saw, last of all, nestling between his very hooves, sleeping soundly in entire peace and contentment, the little, round, podgy, childish form of the baby otter. All this he saw, for one moment breathless and intense, vivid on the morning sky; and still, as he looked, he lived, and still, as he lived, he wondered.

'Rat!' he found breath to whisper, shaking. 'Are you afraid?'

'Afraid?' murmured the Rat, his eyes shining with unutterable love. 'Afraid! Of Him. O, never, never! And yet—and yet—O Mole, I am afraid!'

Then the two animals, crouching to the earth, bowed their heads and did worship.

Kenneth Grahame in
The Wind in the Willows

---

person thinks in terms of God or the supernatural or whether they deny the supernatural. People can interpret their experience as they like, whether in terms of popular religion, or atheism or some deep religious faith.

Others would say that there is no supernatural world, and that these experiences prove nothing about its reality. This is Marghanita Laski's conclusion, and she ends her book *Ecstasy* with the words:

'I *should be content and happy to believe that ecstatic experiences are wholly human experiences; that what men have worshipped since ecstatic experiences were known to*

The god Pan, from classical times, is still with us. There are many who move from sensing God in nature to worshipping Nature as a god.

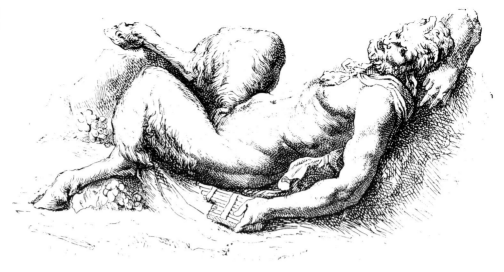

them was their own creative and generalizing capacity...'

A third answer would be that, since all these experiences are tied up with meaning in one way or another, they are all 'religious' experiences of a kind—even if they don't seem at first sight to be 'religious'. They are experiences which can, and often do, lead on to deeper religious faith. The sense of wonder, of mystery, and of questioning finds its fulfilment, for example, through belief in a personal God. In this case it is reasonable to believe that God has put these feelings within us so that people may, in the words of Paul, 'feel after him and find him' (Acts 17:27).

Some Assumptions of Popular Religion

It is not possible to fit the whole of popular religion into a tidy pattern. By its very nature it can't be forced into any neat scheme. However, if the assumptions of popular religion were put into words, these might be some of the main ones. These are assumptions which, in one form or another, seem to underlie most forms of popular religion.

Needs. Religion is primarily concerned with meeting human needs as people perceive them, as individuals and as communities. The basic needs of human beings since the beginning of time can probably be summed up as fertility, physical survival and well-being. Popular religion, therefore, is very people-centred. Instead of saying that humankind's chief end is to 'glorify God and enjoy him for ever', it is mainly interested in God in so far as he is able to meet human needs.
All religion is concerned, to a greater or lesser extent, with meeting human need. But the distinctive thing about

popular religion as opposed to 'official religion' is that this becomes its primary task; and at the end of the day what matters is people's interpretation of what they need.

God. Beliefs about 'God' don't need to be clearly defined. There aren't many people who are totally convinced atheists. The majority of people in the Western world believe in the existence of 'God', but don't have very clear ideas of what he's like. He's generally a personal being, a 'he' rather than an 'it' and he's generally good and benevolent. He has something to do with running the universe, and when people are in difficulties they can ask him to help. But they can't imagine that he's interested in them as individuals, and they don't like the idea of him interfering too much in their lives.
Jomo Kenyatta, the first president of Kenya, wrote these words about African traditional religion. They sum up, however, how many people in Western society tend to think about God:

'So long as people and things go well and prosper, it is taken for granted that God is pleased with the general behaviour of the people and the welfare of the country. In this happy state there is no need for prayers. Indeed they are inadvisable, for Ngai (the High God) must not needlessly be bothered. It is only when humans are in real need that they must approach him without fear of disturbing him and incurring his wrath.'

Grace Davie, a sociologist, uses statistics produced by the European Value System Study Group to draw her conclusions.

'We see that 76% of the sample reported a belief in God; 58% define themselves as ''religious persons''; 50% regularly feel the need for prayer, meditation or contemplation; 46% draw comfort or strength from religion;

and only 4% describe themselves as convinced atheists—on closer inspection these proved a curiously indecisive bunch...

'We live in a country where there are a large number of people who, apparently, continue to believe in God, but who are reluctant to express this belief in churchgoing... We discover that sociologists know very little indeed about the nature of uncommitted religious belief in contemporary Britain apart from the fact that this very wide religious penumbra continues to exist. Indeed it is the most prevalent form of religious life in this country...'

Fate. Although God may be there, he's not in control of everything that happens, because fate is a power that is even stronger than God. Some things in life are clearly already determined and fixed, and there's nothing people can do to change them. Soldiers in the two world wars, for example, used to say, 'If that bullet has got your number on it, your time is up.' A woman who had had a large number of children once said, 'It's fate how many you'll have as far as I'm concerned. It's all planned what

you're going to have. I kid myself I am an atheist, but I'm not.'

Belief in fate is closely bound up with ideas about good and bad luck: if a certain thing happens, it means that something else, good or bad, is going to happen. It's as if parts of life (or even the whole of life) have been programmed.

Ideas about fate are also important in divination and astrology. Reading palms and tea-leaves, and gazing into crystal balls are based on the assumption that the future has already been fixed by fate, and that it is therefore possible to know the future in advance.

When Christianity first came to Britain, people recognized that their traditional belief in fate was being challenged. The difference between the two ways of thinking was summed up by the person in the eighth century who said:

'I hold, as do all Christian men, that it is God's providence that rules and not fate.'

Hippy 'love–ins' in the 60s, with their psychedelia and tribal dances, carried people into some ecstatic experiences. But were these really religious at all? Did they mean anything beyond the experience itself?

In the twentieth century, however, popular religion represents a strange amalgam of pagan and Christian beliefs.

Magic. Certain things in life seem to be beyond human control. But what if there are things people can do to make things turn out well? What if, instead of simply accepting what happens, people do whatever they can to coax nature or God to do their work for them? It is this basic desire to control the fortunes of themselves and others, to 'manipulate enigmatic forces for practical ends' which is summed up by the word 'magic'.

If words like 'magic' and 'manipulation' sound too strong for the kind of things we are familiar with in popular religion, at least they point to the fact that at the heart of much popular religion there is a desire in people to change or at least influence the way things are—in their favour.

While some have argued that magic is at the heart of all religion, others make a clear distinction at this point between popular religion and the teaching of 'official religion'. As Paul Hiebert, an anthropologist, says, 'In contrast to high religions that focus on questions of truth, folk religions seek power to fulfil human desires.'

So, for example, painting animals on the walls of the caves at Lascaux in France may have been a way of ensuring success when hunting them for food. Fertility cults of different kinds in the ancient world promised that the enjoyment of sex in a religious setting would help nature to do its work. Lighting candles and bonfires in winter were originally ways of helping the sun on its way and making sure that it would increase in strength after mid-winter.

Statements like these would be modern examples of the same thinking: 'We always come to church at Christmas and before we fly on holiday.' And after a divorce, 'It would have lasted if they had been married in church.' When baseball players kick up a piece of dirt before batting or taxi drivers put a statue or an icon of a saint on the dashboard of their car, there is an element of magic in what they are doing. And, as the *Encyclopedia of Religion* suggests:

'Most people in the world perform acts by which they intend to bring about events or conditions, whether in nature or among people, that they hold to be the consequence of these acts.'

Merit. There is a basic conviction in popular religion that this is a moral universe, and that there must therefore be some meaning in everything that happens. The only way to make sense of life with all its sadness and suffering is to believe that there must be some reason for what happens, that it can't have happened by chance. Popular religion therefore suggests the simple formula:

good behaviour brings success in life, while sinful behaviour inevitably brings misfortune. You reap what you sow; you get what you deserve.

So, for example, when someone says, 'Why should such a thing happen to him? He never did anyone any harm,' the obvious implication is, 'He didn't deserve to suffer in this way.' Similarly, some people who suffer misfortune try to think of particular sins they have committed for which they are being punished.

Douglas Davies suggests that merit is the 'prime dogma' in folk religion, and explains the idea as 'the

This young Mexican crawled six miles on his knees to reach a church at festival time. One approach to religion tries to build up merit as a way of earning favour with God.

benefit reckoned to accrue to a person as a result of that person's moral endeavours'. He believes that it is only through the idea of merit that people are able to make moral sense of life. If this is true, it explains why people believe that the person who does good will be rewarded, while the person who does wrong is likely to suffer.

Linked with this is the idea that people can merit God's favour; for if people believe that they bring suffering on themselves by doing wrong, the obvious corollary seems to be that if they do right they will win God's approval.

The Christian church has had great problems in its history in knowing how to respond to ideas about merit. The Bible certainly encourages people to obey the laws of God, and talks about 'rewards' in heaven. But it emphasizes very strongly the love and mercy of God. In some parts of the church, however, ideas about merit became very important; it was thought, for example, that people can earn their salvation by living a good life and following God's commandments. And it was this kind of teaching which led in the Middle Ages to the practice of indulgences: people would do particular religious acts or pay money in order to obtain remission of the punishment for their sins. It also encouraged wealthy people to endow chantries in cathedrals, so that after their death masses would be sung or chanted for them, and merit would be transferred to them.

The *Encyclopedia of Religion* quotes the following sentences from a popular Roman Catholic work written in 1881 (F.J. Shadler, *The Beauties of the Catholic Church*), with the comment that 'one could hardly find a clearer statement both of the idea of the transfer of merit and of the transactional manner in which merit is, or can be, understood':

'She [the church] appears before the tribunal of the judge, not only as suppliant, but also as the stewardess of the treasure of the merits of Christ and his saints, and from it offers to him the ransom for the souls in purgatory, with the full confidence that he will accept her offer and release her children from the tortures of the debtor's prison.'

The teaching of Martin Luther and others at the time of the Reformation meant that many of these practices were swept away in Protestant churches. While the Roman Catholic Church has since abandoned many of the older practices and defined its teaching more carefully, it is probably true that, as one theologian has said, 'Roman Catholic theology is inextricably tied up with the concept of merit'.

Perhaps the idea of merit is also linked in some way with the emphasis on morality in some forms of popular religion. There is the feeling that people don't need to be too concerned about worshipping God; there's no need to belong to the church and be an active member in that community or in any other. But they do need to have some moral standards—and morals are the heart of religion.

Richard Hoggart, in his classic *The Uses of Literacy*, saw morality as an essential ingredient in the popular religion of working-class people in the north of England:

'In so far as they think of Christianity, they think of it as a system of ethics; their concern is with morals, not metaphysics.'

This attitude is reflected in the way people describe religion as 'doing good', 'common decency', 'being kind', and 'helping your neighbour'. And he comments:

'After all, doing your best to be an "ordinary decent" person—that is what Christianity means, really...'

13 The Substance

Jesus said: 'Ask and it will be given to you; seek and you will find; knock and the door will be opened to you. For everyone who asks receives; he who seeks finds; and to him who knocks the door will be opened.'

Matthew 7:7–8

We know nothing of religion here: we think only of Christ. We know nothing of speculation. Come and see...

C.S. Lewis, *The Great Divorce*

The final question is the hardest of all. If all the practices and ideas of popular religion that this book has looked at can be seen as shadows, what's the substance? If all these phenomena are evidence of what people believe, are they, are we, any nearer to finding out what the supernatural world is really like?

One possible answer would be to say that these *are* the reality. Celebrating Christmas, wearing a crucifix, attending a church wedding, or reading tarot cards all give us a feeling of security and uplift, and they help to make sense of life. So what more are people looking for? Isn't that all they need from religion?

Another answer would be that there's no substance behind the shadows. That's to say, there's no standard of what religion ought to be like, because religion is whatever the individual makes of it. It's impossible to claim that one kind of religion is better or nearer to the truth than another. The substance of religion simply doesn't exist.

This answer suggests that people can explore 'the truth' in science and in other areas of life but not in religion, because no human being is better placed than any other when it comes to knowing what's really there. People are all working in the dark, and one guess is as good as another.

Another obvious answer would be to suggest that all the world religions claim to offer a version of the substance of religious truth. Each one has its own world-view, its own understanding of what the universe is all about, and some of them are missionary religions which believe they have a message for the whole human race.

Some people raise the question of other religions largely as a way of excusing themselves for not bothering about any religion. But anyone who thinks of the other world religions as serious options for themselves should find out all they can about their beliefs and practices. They also need to ask what's special and unique about their way of looking at the world? What do they regard as 'the real thing'? And on what grounds do they make these claims? What do they offer, and do they offer it to everyone?

At this point many Christians would no doubt want to come in with the answer that Christianity is the substance. One problem with this, however, is that the word 'Christianity' for most people includes everything to do with the Christian religion—which means all the beliefs (including the core of Christian beliefs as well as all the other less important beliefs), all the practices (such as praying and going on pilgrimage), and all the paraphernalia that go with it (such as crosses, cathedrals and prayer books). And if this is what Christianity is, how could anyone claim that all these things together make up 'the substance'? And what if the Christianity that one sees has a fair amount of popular religion mixed up with it?

But what if, instead of trying to claim too much for the Christian religion, we focus our attention on Jesus Christ, the central figure of Christianity? What would it mean to claim that he might be a clue, if not *the* clue to the substance behind the shadows?

A good starting point for this line of enquiry is an incident related in the New Testament in which Jesus comes face to face with an example of popular religion:

'People were bringing little children to Jesus to have him touch them, but the disciples rebuked them. When Jesus saw this, he was indignant. He said to them, ''Let the little children come to me, and do not hinder them, for the kingdom of God belongs to such as these. I tell you the truth, anyone who will not receive the kingdom of God like a little child will never enter it.'' And he took the children in his arms, put his hands on them and blessed them.' (Mark 10:13–16)

In this story some mothers bring their children (including, it seems, some babies) to be blessed by Jesus. No doubt they think of him as a holy man who has supernatural powers. The disciples, however, try to prevent the mothers getting to Jesus, perhaps because they feel the whole business smacks too much of magic, and they suspect that Jesus won't have any sympathy with the superstitions of village women.

But, much to our surprise, Jesus welcomes the mothers and is glad to bless the children. He affirms the instincts of these mothers who want a blessing for their children.

He doesn't stop there, however. While he recognizes the need that they have expressed, he doesn't leave them with their ideas of what they need, because he goes on to speak about the kingdom of God, about living under the kingly rule of God. At this point, therefore, he challenges something in the popular religion of these women.

He speaks about something infinitely greater than the simple blessing that they came for: he offers them an invitation to enter the kingdom of God. If they're willing to live under the rule of God, their deepest needs and longings, for themselves and for their children, will be met as they come to see everything in life from a different perspective.

The following pages shown how this pattern works out in relation to other aspects of popular religion.

Steps in the Right Direction suggests what Jesus Christ *affirms* in popular religion.

Steps in the Wrong Direction suggests what he *challenges* in popular religion.

Steps in Our Direction suggests what he *offers* to popular religion.

We want to find out in general terms what the Bible seems to be saying about popular religion. To do this we look at passages either from the Gospels, from the Old

When mothers brought children to Jesus, the disciples wanted to turn them away. But Jesus thought differently: 'Let the children come to me...'

Testament (which Jesus accepted as 'the word of God') or from the writings of the apostles (who believed that they had been given special authority by Christ himself). Some brief comments on each passage suggest how to make the connection between the world of the Bible and the world of popular religion today.

Steps in the *Right* Direction

Our sense of 'the numinous'. The story of Jacob and his dream at Bethel is a good example of someone who has a strong sense of the supernatural, of what is often called 'the numinous', after a particular experience.

He has fled for his life after having tricked his brother Esau, and stops at Bethel to sleep in the open air. During the night he has a dream and, when he wakes up in the morning, he has the feeling that there's something sacred, holy or even 'spooky' about the place.

His words 'How awesome, how fearful is this place' sum up the feelings that people sometimes have when looking round an old church or a cathedral. They may speak of a mysterious aura that pervades the place. There's a sense of awe, fear and dread; a feeling that one is an insignificant creature in the face of a great mystery or an overwhelming power.

Jacob left Beersheba and set out for Haran. When he reached a certain place, he stopped for the night because the sun had set. Taking one of the stones there, he put it under his head and lay down to sleep. He had a dream in which he saw a stairway resting on the earth, with its top reaching to heaven, and the angels of God were ascending and descending on it. There above it stood the Lord, and he said: 'I am the Lord, the God of your father Abraham and the God of Isaac...'

When Jacob awoke from his sleep, he thought, 'Surely the Lord is in this place, and I was not aware of it.' He was afraid and said, 'How awesome is this place! This is none other than the house of God; this is the gate of heaven.'

Genesis 28:10–13,16–17

Our sense of dependence. We're all concerned about survival—and many millions in the world today have more reason to be concerned than others, because they don't know where their next meal is coming from.

Jesus here makes the bold claim that if we trust God as a loving Father he can look after us, simply because he's in complete control of the natural world.

Our material needs will always be there; but faith and trust in the loving care and the infinite power of God can transform these anxieties which lie so near the heart of much popular religion.

'Therefore I tell you, do not worry about your life, what you will eat or drink, or about your body, what you will wear. Is not life more important than food, and the body more important than clothes? Look at the birds of the air; they do not sow or reap or store away in barns, and yet your heavenly Father feeds them. Are you not much more valuable than they? Who of you by worrying can add a single hour to his life?'

'And why do you worry about clothes? See how the lilies of the field grow. They do not labour or spin. Yet I tell you that not even Solomon in all his splendour was dressed like one of these. If that is how God clothes the grass of the field, which is here today and tomorrow is thrown into the fire, will he not much more clothe you, O you of little faith?'

Matthew 6:25–30

Our sense of 'God'. When Paul comes to Athens, he's shocked to see how popular religion has run riot in a city that is full of idols. But, instead of condemning their beliefs and their rituals, he starts with the inscription under one such idol: 'To an Unknown God'. He recognizes that this expresses an awareness of some supernatural being or beings; but he then goes on to speak of how this so-called 'Unknown God' has made himself known.

Left to ourselves, our idea of God can be vague, confused and blurred. But the Christian claim is that as we look at Jesus of Nazareth, we get a clearer picture of what God is like. When we read the Gospels and begin to take in what he says and how he acts, our picture of God begins to come into focus. The ideas of God which were *implicit* can become *explicit*. We begin to find words for instincts and feelings that are deep within us.

The 'shadows' of popular religion in this case do tell us something about the supernatural. But our only hope of finding the reality behind them is if God takes the initiative and makes himself known.

Paul then stood up in the meeting of the Areopagus and said:

'Men of Athens! I see that in every way you are very religious. For as I walked round and observed your objects of worship, I even found an altar with this inscription: TO AN UNKNOWN GOD. Now what you worship as something unknown I am going to proclaim to you.

'The God who made the world and everything in it is the Lord of heaven and earth and does not live in temples built by hands. And he is not served by human hands as if he needed anything, because he himself gives all men life and breath and everything else...

'God did this so that men would seek him and perhaps reach out for him and find him, though he is not far from each one of us. For in him we live and move and have our being.'

Acts 17:22–25, 27–28

Our hope for a life after death. Jesus says that there are 'many rooms' in his Father's 'house'; and he gives his disciples the assurance that as he returns to his Father in heaven, he is going ahead to prepare a place for them.

'Do not let your hearts be troubled. Trust in God; trust also in me. In my Father's house are many rooms; if it were not so, I would have told you. I am going there to prepare a place for you. And if I go and prepare a place for you, I will come back and take you to be with me that you also may be where I am. You know the way to the place where I am going.'

John 14:1–4

When Jesus is hanging on the cross just a few hours later, one of the criminals being crucified with him insults him. But the other recognizes that there is something different about Jesus; he feels that there must be some truth in the strange claim that he is King of the Jews. So when he says that he wants to be part of that kingdom, Jesus assures him, 'Today you will be with me in paradise.'

If death ends everything, we may well wonder if life has any meaning. But Jesus here confirms the instinct in most people that there must be a life after death, that death can't be the end.

One of the criminals who hung there [on a cross beside Jesus' cross] hurled insults at him: 'Aren't you the Christ? Save yourself and us!'

But the other criminal rebuked him. 'Don't you fear God,' he said, 'since you are under the same sentence? We are punished justly, for we are getting what our deeds deserve. But this man has done nothing wrong.'

Then he said, 'Jesus, remember me when you come into your kingdom.'

Jesus answered him, 'I tell you the truth, today you will be with me in paradise.'

Luke 23:39–43

Our awareness of evil. Anyone with any first-hand experience of the occult doesn't need any persuasion to be convinced of the reality of evil. The apostle Paul recognizes that evil isn't a vague power or an impersonal force. He believes that there are many different kinds of supernatural forces which are evil and are working against us. But whereas the occultist wants to experiment, and in some cases to co-operate with, these powers, Paul believes that he has to struggle against them.

For our struggle is not against flesh and blood, but against the rulers, against the authorities, against the powers of this dark world and against the spiritual forces of evil in the heavenly realms.

Ephesians 6:12

It may be that the language of John's visions in the book of Revelation, with its rich imagery, explains the power of evil better than any straightforward statement. This shouldn't sound too strange to a generation that is familiar with space fiction, horror films and literature about the occult.

Could these be some of those 'stirrings of the soul' of which John Townroe speaks, which 'await recognition, fostering, reflection, interpretation, direction, expression, commitment and fulfilment'?

And there was war in heaven. Michael and his angels fought against the dragon, and the dragon and his angels fought back. But he was not strong enough, and they lost their place in heaven. The great dragon was hurled down—that ancient serpent called the devil or Satan, who leads the whole world astray. He was hurled to the earth, and his angels with him.

Revelation 12:7–9

Steps in the *Wrong* Direction

Needs. If popular religion is largely motivated by our needs—or rather by our ideas of what we need, it's inevitable that it becomes very human-centred.

It's the preoccupation with our needs, and especially our material needs, that Jesus challenges in these words. He tells us that if we accept a different set of priorities and 'seek first his (God's) kingdom', our needs will be met. But we'll also find that our well-being ultimately depends not on meeting our needs, but on being in a right relationship with God.

The different methods of divination which have been used show that we often wish we could know the future—especially when it's likely to be bad. But Jesus teaches his disciples to live in the present, one day at a time. If we will trust God for the present, we can be sure that he has the future under his control.

'So do not worry, saying, ''What shall we eat?'' or ''What shall we drink?'' or ''What shall we wear?'' For the pagans run after all these things, and your heavenly Father knows that you need them. But seek first his kingdom and his righteousness, and all these things will be given to you as well. Therefore do not worry about tomorrow, for tomorrow will worry about itself. Each day has enough trouble of its own.'

Matthew 6:31–34

Our understanding of our personal needs isn't always the same as God's understanding of them. When a paralysed man is brought to Jesus, his needs must seem obvious to the onlookers. Jesus' diagnosis of his condition goes much deeper. He recognizes his immediate need of healing, but offers him also forgiveness from God. In this way he deals fully both with the need which is uppermost in the man's mind and with the deeper need of which he may hardly be aware.

Some men came, bringing to him a paralytic, carried by four of them. Since they could not get him to Jesus because of the crowd, they made an opening in the roof above Jesus and, after digging through it, lowered the mat the paralysed man was lying on. When Jesus saw their faith, he said to the paralytic, 'Son, your sins are forgiven.'

Now some teachers of the law were sitting there, thinking to themselves, 'Why does this fellow talk like that? He's blaspheming! Who can forgive sins but God alone?'

Jesus...said to them, 'Why are you thinking these things? Which is easier; to say to the paralytic, "Your sins are forgiven," or to say, "Get up, take your mat and walk"? But that you may know that the Son of Man has authority on earth to forgive sins...' He said to the paralytic, 'I tell you, get up, take your mat and go home.' He got up, took his mat and walked out in full view of them all.

Mark 2:3–7,8–12

God. Since no one has ever seen God, it's understandable that different people have different ideas of what he's like. But John the apostle here makes the incredible claim that God has taken the initiative to make himself known to us.

No one has ever seen God, but God the only Son, who is at the Father's side, has made him known.

John 1:18

This is the story of a man who hardly thinks of God, because his life is so successful and enjoyable. He probably believes in the existence of God, but doesn't want to trouble him unless he's in real difficulties. He looks forward to being able to 'take life easy, eat, drink and be merry'—when suddenly he dies and finds himself face to face with his Creator.

If God really is the source of our life and of everything that we enjoy, it's understandable that he's not prepared to be kept in the background all the time or to be used only as an insurance policy.

[Jesus] told them this parable: 'The ground of a certain rich man produced a good crop. He thought to himself, "What shall I do? I have no place to store my crops."

Lighting a candle in a dark church—a warm, spiritual reaching out to God who touches our lives from the world beyond. Religious experience is not just in the mind, but includes many kinds of outward acts and rituals.

'Then he said, "This is what I'll do. I will tear down my barns and build bigger ones, and there I will store all my grain and my goods. And I'll say to myself, 'You have plenty of good things laid up for many years. Take life easy; eat, drink and be merry."

'But God said to him, "You fool! This very night your life will be demanded from you. Then who will get what you have prepared for yourself?"'

'This is how it will be with anyone who stores up things for himself but is not rich towards God.'

Luke 12:16–21

Fate.

Fate. The story of creation in the book of Genesis is incredibly simple and straightforward when compared with the Egyptian, Babylonian or Norse creation myths. Everything comes into existence—light, the sky, the land, plants, stars, animals and finally human beings—because God wants them to be there.

In the beginning God created the heavens and the earth. Now the earth was formless and empty, darkness was over the surface of the deep, and the Spirit of God was hovering over the waters.

And God said, 'Let there be light,' and there was light. God saw that the light was good, and he separated the light from the darkness. God called the light 'day' and the darkness he called 'night'. And there was evening, and there was morning—the first day...

Genesis 1:1–5

The sun and moon are simply called 'lights'; they're not there to be worshipped. And the stars are mentioned—no doubt deliberately—almost as an afterthought: 'He also made the stars.' Contrary to the assumptions of astrology, they have no power to control our destiny.

And God said, 'Let there be lights in the expanse of the sky to separate the day from the night, and let them serve as signs to mark seasons and days and years, and let them be lights in the expanse of the sky to give light on the earth.' And it was so. God made two great lights—the greater light to govern the day and the lesser light to govern the night. He also made the stars. God set them in the expanse of the sky to give light on the earth, to govern the day and the night, and to separate light from darkness. And God saw that it was good. And there was evening, and there was morning—the fourth day.

Genesis 1:14–19

Jesus tells his friends that there is only one power we have to respect—and that is God. Nothing, absolutely nothing, in the world can happen without his knowledge or his will. There's no Fate, or Destiny or Luck behind or alongside God which has programmed the whole of life.

He also shocks us by saying that there's something even worse than death. But the delightful paradox in his teaching is that if we know what it means to fear God, we have nothing else to fear.

'I tell you, my friends, do not be afraid of those who kill the body and after that can do no more. But I will show you whom you should fear: Fear him who, after the killing of the body, has power to throw you into hell. Yes, I tell you, fear him. Are not five sparrows sold for two pennies? Yet not one of them is forgotten by God. Indeed, the very hairs of your head are all numbered. Don't be afraid; you are worth more than many sparrows.'

Luke 13:4–7

Magic. The prophet Isaiah has strong words about religious ritual which, however sincere, is divorced from morality. Since we can't manipulate God or even coax him to do what we want, we have to learn to approach him on his terms, not on ours. When we do this we can be sure that he will provide for all our needs; using religion as a kind of simple magic only leads to disaster.

'Stop bringing meaningless offerings!
Your incense is detestable to me.
New Moons, Sabbaths and convocations—
I cannot bear your evil assemblies.
Your New Moon festivals and your appointed feasts my
    soul hates.
They have become a burden to me...
'Stop doing wrong, learn to do right!
Seek justice, encourage the oppressed.
Defend the cause of the fatherless,
plead the case of the widow...'

Isaiah:1:13–14,16–17

One important thing about the disciples of Jesus is that they know they don't have to impress God or other people through their prayers. Another is that they don't have to persuade him to help, because he already knows their needs.

For his disciples, therefore, prayer begins with the worship of God as a loving Father, not with the recital of our needs. If we approach God in this way, there's no place for manipulation of any kind, because we have to say 'your will be done' rather than 'my will be done'. In the context of this relationship we can be sure that the most obvious human needs that we feel will be met ('daily bread'), as well as all the deeper needs which God recognizes (forgiveness, guidance, and deliverance from evil).

'But when you pray, do not be like the hypocrites, for they love to pray standing in the synagogues and on the street corners to be seen by men. I tell you the truth, they have received their reward in full. When you pray, go into your room, close the door and pray to your Father, who is unseen. Then your Father, who sees what is done in secret, will reward you. And when you pray, do not keep on babbling like pagans, for they think they will be heard because of their many words. Do not be like them, for your Father knows what you need before you ask him.

'This is how you should pray:

"Our Father in heaven,
hallowed be your name,
your kingdom come,
your will be done
on earth as it is in heaven.
Give us today our daily bread.
Forgive us our debts,
as we also have forgiven our debtors.
And lead us not into temptation,
but deliver us from the evil one.'''

Matthew 6:5-13

Merit. The Pharisee in this parable of Jesus is confident that he has accumulated a great deal of merit through his decent life and his religious observance. The tax collector, on the other hand, has abandoned this whole way of thinking—perhaps because he recognizes that it leads either to pride or to despair. Instead he throws himself on to the mercy of God.

So when Jesus ends the parable by saying that it's the tax collector and not the Pharisee who goes home in a right relationship with God, he's turning upside down the assumptions of much popular religion.

To some who were confident of their own righteousness and looked down on everybody else, Jesus told this parable:

'Two men went up to the temple to pray, one a Pharisee and the other a tax collector. The Pharisee stood up and prayed about himself: "God, I thank you that I am not like all other men— robbers, evildoers, adulterers—or even like this tax collector. I fast twice a week and give a tenth of all I get."

'But the tax collector stood at a distance. He would not even look up to heaven, but beat his breast and said, "God, have mercy on me, a sinner."

'I tell you that this man, rather than the other, went home justified before God. For everyone who exalts himself will be humbled, and he who humbles himself will be exalted.'

Luke 18:9–14

When we speak of people being 'dead to the world', we mean that they're unable to respond to any stimulus. According to the apostle Paul, this is a fair description of the human condition: we're all as good as dead as far as God is concerned, because we're unable to respond to him.

Popular religion suggests that strenuous religious effort and/or gradual moral improvement will accumulate merit. But Paul challenges this assumption, when he says that our situation is so bad that it needs God to bring us to life. He has to take the initiative to bring about a drastic change in our condition. Our part in the process is to change our minds, and to believe what Jesus has done for us.

Forgiveness comes to us not as a reward, but as a gift. When this kind of radical change has taken place in us, we certainly will devote ourselves to 'good works'—not as a way of winning God's favour, but as a way of expressing our gratitude to him.

As for you, you were dead in your transgressions and sins, in which you used to live when you followed the ways of this world and of the ruler of the kingdom of the air, the spirit who is now at work in those who are disobedient...

But because of his great love for us, God, who is rich in mercy, made us alive with Christ even when we were dead in transgressions—it is by grace you have been saved. And God raised us up with Christ and seated us with him in the heavenly realms in Christ Jesus, in order that in the coming ages he might show the incomparable riches of his grace expressed in his kindness to us in Christ Jesus. For it is by grace you have been saved, through faith—and this not from yourselves, it is the gift of God—not by works, so that no one can boast. For we are God's workmanship, created in Christ Jesus to do good works, which God prepared in advance for us to do.

Ephesians 2:1–2,4–10

If these are some of the ways in which popular religion is moving *in the wrong direction*, we now see some of the ways in which Jesus moves *in our direction*, offering new ways of thinking which meet our deepest needs and take the place of those assumptions that we're willing to abandon and put on one side.

Steps in *Our* Direction

Direct access to God. Popular religion sometimes suggests that we can't hope to communicate directly with God, but that we can (and should) approach him through intermediaries such as saints. If God is too great and too holy to listen to us, they can sympathize with us in our problems, and are closer to God and holier than we are. They are therefore in a better position than we could ever be to get through to God and to persuade him to do something for us.

Paul, however, insists that there is only one possible intermediary between ourselves and God—the man Jesus.

...God our Saviour...wants all men to be saved and to come to a knowledge of the truth. For there is one God and one mediator between God and men, the man Christ Jesus, who gave himself as a ransom for all men...

1 Timothy 2:3–6

Why go through an intermediary when you can get straight through to the person at the top?

The unknown writer of the letter to the Hebrews assures us that there can't be anyone in heaven who is more human than Jesus himself. If he went through such intense temptation and suffering while he was on earth, we can come direct to him when we find the going hard.

...we do not have a high priest who is unable to sympathise with our weaknesses, but we have one who has been tempted in every way, just as we are—yet was without sin. Let us then approach the throne of grace with confidence, so that we may receive mercy and find grace to help us in our time of need.

Hebrews 4:15–16

A sense of identity. We've seen that a great deal in popular religion is concerned with identity: who are we? Paul believes that Jesus offers his disciples the security of a relationship with God in which we can call him 'Father'. When we know who we are, we can face the future without fear.

...you did not receive a spirit that makes you a slave again to fear, but you received the Spirit of sonship. And by him we cry, 'Abba, Father.' The Spirit himself testifies with our spirit that we are God's children.

Romans 8:15–16

We're all part of a family; and being members of a tribe, a race or a nation with its own particular culture enables us to know where we belong.

Being a disciple of Jesus means that, in addition to all these groups, there is a wider community to which we belong—'the people of God'—a community in which barriers of language, race and culture can all be overcome. There's no place here for 'believing without belonging', since being committed to the head of this new community, Christ himself, means that we are also committed to the other members of the community.

...you are no longer foreigners and aliens, but fellow-citizens with God's people and members of God's household, built on the foundation of the apostles and prophets, with Christ Jesus himself as the chief cornerstone. In him the whole building is joined together and rises to become a holy temple in the Lord. And in him you too are being built together to become a dwelling in which God lives by his Spirit.

Ephesians 2:19–22

A radical change for human nature. Popular religion tells us that we're basically all right as we are, and that we need to do the best that we can in life and turn to God for help whenever necessary.

Jesus tells a distinguished religious teacher, however, that we need something much more radical: we need nothing less than a spiritual 'rebirth'. Instead of trying to put ourselves right with God's help, we need a complete change of heart.

Now there was a man of the Pharisees named Nicodemus, a member of the Jewish ruling council. He came to Jesus at night and said, 'Rabbi, we know you are a teacher who has come from God. For no one could perform the miraculous signs you are doing if God were not with him.'

In reply Jesus declared, 'I tell you the truth, unless a man is born again, he cannot see the kingdom of God.'

'How can a man be born when he is old?' Nicodemus asked. 'Surely he cannot enter a second time into his mother's womb to be born!'

Jesus answered, 'I tell you the truth, unless a man is born of water and the Spirit, he cannot enter the kingdom of God. Flesh gives birth to flesh, but the Spirit gives birth to spirit. You should not be surprised at my saying, "You must be born again." The wind blows wherever it pleases. You hear its sound, but you cannot tell where it comes from or where it is going. So it is with everyone born of the Spirit.'

John 3:1–8

A seed has to give up its existence completely as a seed in order for a new plant to grow. In a sense, it 'dies'. In the same way, a person must give up their old existence in order to have eternal life. The natural world provides an analogy of the spiritual world. So it makes sense after all for Christians to celebrate the resurrection of Jesus in the spring. As the traditions of the church year were developed in the northern hemisphere, it is the northern spring that has become the season in which Easter is celebrated. Perhaps also the events of Good Friday and Easter can be seen as the fulfilment of all those different ideas about death and resurrection which are found in other religions.

'Unless an ear of wheat falls to the ground and dies, it remains only a single seed. But if it dies, it produces many seeds. The man who loves his life will lose it, while the man who hates his life in this world will keep it for eternal life. Whoever serves me must follow me; and where I am, my servant also will be. My Father will honour the one who serves me.'

John 12:24–26

An assurance of victory over evil. We've seen that myths—both ancient and modern—are full of the conflict between good and evil.

For Paul, however, victory over evil is no longer a pious hope or wishful thinking, because Jesus defeated all the powers of evil through his death on the cross. This message isn't a myth like the myths of the ancient world, however, because it is rooted in history.

God made you alive with Christ. He forgave us all our sins, having cancelled the written code, with its regulations, that was against us and that stood opposed to us; he took it away, nailing it to the cross. And having disarmed the powers and the authorities, he made a public spectacle of them, triumphing over them by the cross.

Colossians 2:13–15

In the world as it is there's nothing to make us believe that the situation will gradually improve or that good will ultimately triumph over evil.

According to the apostle John, however, God sent Jesus into the world to deal with the root of the problem. Behind our sinful nature is the source of all evil—the devil. John believes that Jesus came to destroy, to undo, all the works of the devil. The crucial conflict has been fought and won, and the final outcome is certain. It's hardly surprising, therefore, that the cross has been such a powerful symbol for Christians, and that it has played such an important part in Christian art. And with this conviction about victory over evil, there's something to sing about!

How great is the love the Father has lavished on us, that we should be called children of God! And that is what we are! The reason the world does not know us is that it did not know him. Dear friends, now we are children of God, and what we will be has not yet been made known. But we know that when he appears, we shall be like him, for we shall see him as he is. Everyone who has this hope in him purifies himself, just as he is pure...

He who does what is sinful is of the devil, because the devil has been sinning from the beginning. The reason the Son of God appeared was to destroy the devil's work.

1 John 3:1–3,8

Hope for the future. The myths of the ancient world have their own vision of the end of the world: at times they're little more than doom and gloom, while at other times there is hope for a better world. But now that we have nuclear weapons, not many of the scenarios in space fiction are very optimistic.

In contrast to this, the second letter of Peter speaks of a catastrophic end to the universe as we know it; but beyond that there's something infinitely better to look forward to—'a new heaven and a new earth, the home of righteousness'.

You ought to live holy and godly lives as you look forward to the day of God and speed its coming. That day will bring about the destruction of the heavens by fire, and the elements will melt in the

Easter lilies are a symbol of life, of beauty, of something new breaking through. For Christians spring and Easter speak of Jesus who brings new life.

heat. But in keeping with his promise we are looking forward to a new heaven and a new earth, the home of righteousness.

2 Peter 3:11–13

We have to have funeral ceremonies of some kind—either with or without God. Is there anything we can say as we bid farewell at the graveside or in the crematorium? Or do we just remind ourselves what a wonderful person he or she was?

John's vision of a new heaven and new earth, which is often read at funeral services, expresses the confidence that there is a world where 'there will be no more death or mourning or crying or pain...'

Then I saw a new heaven and a new earth, for the first heaven and the first earth had passed away, and there was no longer any sea. I saw the Holy City, the new Jerusalem coming down out of heaven from God, prepared as a bride beautifully dressed for her husband. And I heard a loud voice from the throne saying, 'Now the dwelling of God is with men, and he will live with them. They will be his people, and God himself will be with them and be their God. He will wipe every tear from their eyes. There will be no more death or mourning or crying or pain, for the old order of things has passed away.'

Revelation 21:1–4

We end our exploration with a well-known passage which brings together many of the concerns of popular religion:

▶ our need for security, protection and guidance

▶ our longing for identity, meaning and comfort

▶ our desire to celebrate and enjoy all the good things in life

▶ our fear of the future, of death and of evil

All these needs are expressed in this psalm, and the writer believes that ultimately it is God, 'the Lord', who meets them.

> *The Lord is my shepherd, I shall lack nothing.*
> *He makes me lie down in green pastures,*
> *he leads me beside quiet waters, he restores my soul.*
> *He guides me in paths of righteousness for his name's sake*
> *Even though I walk through the valley of the shadow of*
>   *death,*
> *I will fear no evil, for you are with me;*
> *your rod and your staff, they comfort me.*
>
> *You prepare a table before me in the presence of my enemies.*
> *You anoint my head with oil; my cup overflows.*
> *Surely goodness and love will follow me all the days of my*
>   *life,*
> *and I will dwell in the house of the Lord for ever.*

Psalm 23

For the Christian, however, the psalm points not only to God, but also to Jesus. When he made the incredibly bold claim, 'I am the good shepherd,' he was saying, 'Believe in God, believe also in me... It's good that you believe in God; but believe also in me, because I am the one who shows you what God is like and what the supernatural world is all about. I am the one through whom God has come to meet you. I am the one who can meet the needs that you are aware of as well as the needs that you're not aware of...'

Can we therefore go one step further than our popular religion—and find that it's not just a distant and unknown God who is 'my shepherd', but God as he has shown himself to us in Jesus?

Could he, then, be the final clue to the substance beyond the shadows?

For Further Reading

These books were used and quoted in preparing the text:

Walter M. Abbot, *Documents of Vatican II*, Chapman, 1967
Edward Bailey ed, *A Workbook in Popular Religion*, Partners Publications, Dorchester, 1986
John Betjeman, *Collected Poems*, J. Murray, 1979
Janet and Colin Bord, *The Secret Country, More Mysterious Britain*, Paladin, 1985
Gyles Brandreth, *The Book of Superstitions*, Carousel, 1985
Paul and Tessa Clowney, *Exploring Churches*, Lion, 1986
Owen Cole, *Six Religions in the Twentieth Century*, Hulton, 1984
Tom Corfe, *St Patrick and Irish Christianity*, Cambridge, 1982
Arthur Cotterell, *A Dictionary of World Mythology*, Oxford, 1986
F. L. Cross ed, *The Oxford Dictionary of the Christian Church*, Oxford, 1974
Kevin Crossley-Holland, *The Norse Myths: a Retelling*, Andre Deutsch, 1980
Oscar Cullmann, *The Early Church*, SCM, 1956
Tony Cummings, *Desperately Seeking Mary* in Buzz magazine, December 1985
H. R. E. Davidson, *Gods and Myths of Northern Europe*, Penguin, 1984
Grace Davie, *Religion in Development*, in *Modern Sociology, An Annual Review*, vol 5, ed M. Haralambos, Causeway Press, 1989
Mary Douglas, *Purity and Danger: an Analysis of the Concepts of Pollution and Taboo*, Routledge and Kegan Paul, 1966
Roderic Dunkerley, *Beyond the Gospels*, Penguin, 1937
David L. Edwards, *Christian England, vol 1, Its Story to the Reformation*, Collins, 1982
Mircea Eliade ed, *Encyclopedia of Religion*, Macmillan, 1987
Mircea Eliade, *Occultism, Witchcraft and Cultural Fashions*, University of Chicago Press, 1976
T. S. Eliot, *Collected Poems*, Macmillan, 1988
Jacques Ellul, *The New Demons*, Mowbray, 1975
John Exard, *The Long Climb Back to Glory* in The Guardian Weekly, 15 January 1989
H. J. Eysenck and D. K. B. Nias, *Astrology: Science or Superstition?* Penguin, 1984
D. H. Farmer, *The Oxford Dictionary of Saints*, Oxford, 1987
Cherry Gilchrist, *Divination: the Search for Meaning*, Dryad Press, 1987
Robert Graves ed, *The New Larouse Encyclopedia of Mythology*, Hamlyn, 1986
Victor J. Green, *Festivals and Saints Days*, Blandford, 1979
W. H. Griffiths Thomas, *The Catholic Faith*, Church Book Room Press, 1952
Thomas Hardy, *Complete Poems*, Macmillan, 1988
Richard Hoggart, *The Uses of Literacy*, Penguin, 1957
Christina Hole, *British Folk Customs*, Hutchinson, 1976
J. C. Holt, *Robin Hood*, Thames and Hudson, 1989
Walter Hooper, *They Stand Together: the Letters of C. S. Lewis to Arthur Greeves (1914-63)*, Collins, 1979
James Jones, *Finding God: a Guide to Christian Basics*, Darton, Longman and Todd, 1987
Philip Larkin, *Collected Poems*, Faber, 1988
Marghanita Laski, *Ecstasy: A Study of Some Secular and Religious Experiences*, Cresset
C. S. Lewis, *The Allegory of Love: a Study in Medieval Tradition*, Oxford, 1979
C. S. Lewis, *Surprised by Joy*, Collins, 1958
Lion Handbook: The World's Religions, Lion, 1982
The Living Festivals Series, Religious and Moral Education Press
    Fay Sampson, *May Day*, 1985
    Antony Ewens, *Christmas*, 1982; *Hallowe'en, All Souls' and All Saints'*, 1983
    Norma Fairbairn and Jack Priestley, *Easter*, 1982; *Holy Week*, 1984
    Margaret Davidson, *Shrove Tuesday: Ash Wednesday and Mardi Gras*, 1984
    Jack Priestley and Harry Smith, *Harvest and Thanksgiving*, 1985
David Martin, *A Sociology of English Religion*, SCM, 1967
J. C. J. Metford, *Dictionary of Christian Lore and Legend*, Thames and Hudson, 1983
Edward J. Moody, *Urban Witches in Conformity and Conflict*, ed J. P. Spradley and D. W. McCurdy, Little, Brown and Co, 1971
Barry Norman, *Roll 'Em! The Western Rides Again*, in Radio Times, 1-7 July 1989
James Obelkevich, *Music and Religion in Disciplines of Faith*, ed J. Obelkevich, L. Roper and R. Samuel, London, 1987
Iona and Peter Opie, *The Lore and Language of Schoolchildren*, Oxford
W. Ellwood Post, *Saints, Signs and Symbols, A Concise Dictionary*, SPCK 1989
Theodore Roszak, *Where the Wasteland Ends: Politics and Transcendence in Postindustrial Society*, Anchor Books, 1973
Brian Shuel, *The National Trust Guide to Traditional Customs of Britain*, Webb and Bower, 1985
Brian Sibley, *Shadowlands: the Story of C. S. Lewis and Joy Davidman*, Hodder, 1985
John Cyril Sladdon, *Boniface of Devon, Apostle of Germany*, Paternoster, 1980
Thomas J. Talley, *The Origins of the Liturgical Year*, Pueblo, 1986
F. Sherwood Taylor, *The Alchemists*, Heineman, 1952
Robert Towler, *Homo Religiosus: Sociological Problems in the Study of Religion*, Constable, 1974
R. F. Treharne, *The Glastonbury Legends: the Quest for King Arthur and the Holy Grail*, Sphere, 1971
W. A. Visser 't Hooft, *Evangelism Among Europe's Neo-Pagans*, International Review of Mission, 1977
Benedicta Ward, *A New Dictionary of Christian Theology*, SCM, 1983
Timothy Ware, *The Orthodox Church*, Penguin, 1963
Philippa Waring, *The Dictionary of Omens and Superstitions*, Treasure Press, 1984
Marina Warner, *Alone of All Her Sex: the Myth and the Cult of the Virgin Mary*, Picador, 1985
Gilbert White, *The Natural History and Antiquities of Selborne*, 1789
Ralph Whitlock, *A Calendar of Country Customs*, Batsford
R. McL. Wilson, *The New Testament Apocrypha, vol 1, Gospels and Related Writings*, Lutterworth, 1963

Index of Subjects

Acknowledgments

Ancient Art and Architecture/Ronald Sheridan, pages 78, 79, 108, 149; Barnaby's Picture Library, pages 111, 129, 138 /Brian L. Arundale, page 53 / Andrew Besley, page 54 /Tony Boxall, page 152 /Ferry Photographs, page 50 / A.J. Fox, page 139 /R.A. Hall, page 100 /George Hindmarch, page 52 / Laenderpress, page 74 /Bill Meadows, page 82 /Gustav Reitz, page 66 /Mavis Ronson, page 85 /David Simson, page 146; Janet and Colin Bord, pages 15, 88, 114-15 /Paul Broadhurst, page 67; Bridgeman Art Library/© ADAGP, Paris, & DACS, London, 1990, page 90 /Louvre, Paris, page 86 /Private Collection, page 80 /Science Museum, page 20; British Museum, page 95; Camera Press/Alfred Gregory, page 12 /Dave Repp, page 145 /Antonio Serafini, page 122 (above) / William Vandivert, page 11; Cephas Picture Library/Chris Gander, page 30 /M.J. Kielty, page 34 /Mick Rock, page 103; Keith Ellis ARPS, pages 27, 33, 37; Tony Ellis, pages 36, 51; Mary Evans, pages 16, 117, 122 (centre), 124, 144; Fritz Fankhauser, page 99; Fortean Picture Library/Paul Broadhurst, page 137; Sonia Halliday Photographs, page 107 /Jane Taylor, page 40; Robert Harding Picture Library/British Museum, page 136 /George Rainbird Ltd, pages 44, 77, 134, 135 /Geoff Renner, page 21 /Trevor Wood, page 28; Hutchison Photo Library/P. Edward Parker, page 46; Mansell Collection, pages 61, 63, 65, 101, 119, 130, 156; Photoresources/C.M. Dixon, page 14; Popperfoto, pages 38-39; Peter Stiles, page 122 (below); Sefton Photo Library/Brian Jackson, page 72; Tate Gallery, page 87; Zefa (UK) Ltd, page 42 /Bob Croxford, page 128 /Kurt Goebel, page 71 / Zentrale Farbild, page 70

Chapter heading graphics by Tony de Saulles